Border

C000077559

One dog's _

Tamsin Morris

All profits from the sale of this publication
will be donated to Dogs Trust

Supporting
DogsTrust
100%

see www.borderlesscollie.com for more details

First published as an e-book in 2014.
This imprint published in 2016 by
Borderless Collie, Tarves, Aberdeenshire.

ISBN: 978-1-5262-0159-1

Typesetting and cover design: Chris York
Printing and binding: Ingram Spark

To purchase a copy of the publication in ebook format (ePUB or Kindle) please visit:
www.borderlesscollie.com/buy

About the Author

Tamsin was born amongst the fields of Northamptonshire, but on a passing whim moved to the frozen depths of Aberdeenshire to study ecology at university. Subsequent trips to far flung destinations followed, but somehow the stark beauty of empty beaches with a backdrop of glistening mountains always enticed her home to Scotland's east coast.

To my boys,
the best travelling companions a girl could ever have.

Chapter 1

Latvian liabilities

After the briefest flash of eye contact, the mechanic leant against our campervan and gazed at the ground.

'So. How's it doing?' Chris asked.

'Your engine is bad. Very bad. It burn oil. All time. I check ... how called ... turbo and it OK, so is engine. You need to make again engine.' This broken English reply was directed at a point six inches to the left of my foot. I felt the first wave of panic wash over me.

'And how much would that cost?'

'Probably 700 Lats.' Roughly £700.

'OK,' I said doubtfully, 'and how long would it take?'

'Two weeks. Maybe more.' The idea of two weeks staying in a backpackers hostel whilst shelling out three weeks worth of our travelling budget wasn't appealing.

'And if we don't get it done? Will it last for a bit anyway? We're actually heading for Spain.' The mechanic's gaze flickered up to Chris' hopeful face, before darting back to the floor.

'Spain!' he exclaimed, 'Spain? I not try even for beach. It will not drive 200 kilometres.' And with that he pushed himself upright, shrugged and walked away.

Deep depression settled. We were lot more than 200 kilometres from Spain, but we were also a hell of a lot more than 200 kilometres from home. We were stuck in deepest Latvia, complete with a large chunk of our worldly possessions and a dog that we'd fought tooth and nail to bring with us. With a bouncy collie in tow we couldn't afford to abandon the van and carry on with just our backpacks. Somehow we had to keep the campervan on the road, even if it only took us straight back to Scotland.

Suddenly the future didn't look so bright. We'd thrown in jobs, rented out our house and vaccinated Oscar against pretty much every disease known to man in order to do this. We were footloose and fancy free and I, quite frankly, was loving every minute of it. In my mind I was a successful thirty-something career girl who was enjoying a bit of 'travelling' and showing the world that a grown-up gap year could be done. Even in the company of a dog. Now in the course of a single conversation I'd been transformed into an unemployed, slightly grungy failure, who was about to have to hitchhike from Latvia to Aberdeen, accompanied by the increasing liability of a distinctly smelly dog.

~

Twenty-eight months earlier, it had all seemed very different. I'd been sitting on a picnic blanket, knocking back a few too many glasses of champagne. Celebrating a first wedding anniversary is the kind of thing proper grown-up people do, so I'd decided to ruin the effect by drinking sufficient wine to reach the expansive, loving stage.

'What about,' I slurred, 'buying that van, making it into a camper and all that stuff, then driving round Europe. You know, like a gap year but for grown up people. Mountains and things in the north and then speak Spanish in the south. Drink wine, eat olives, do no work.'

Regrettably for our finances, Chris had made an equally valiant effort with the champagne and was in no fit state to provide a voice of reason.

'Sounds like a plan to me. I'm up for it if you are. I might be thirty something, but,' Chris paused whilst I sniggered unkindly, relishing my position as the younger half of the relationship. 'But I can still have an adventure. Even if I am a sad old fart.'

'OK, so it's a deal. We might be sensible and grown-up and married and shit, but we can still hit the road. We don't have to have to get a proper pension and start spending our weekends in Ikea.

We can have a road trip instead. Get a boat to Norway or some-thing, then drive east, see the iron curtain and all that stuff.'

'Yeah, just imagine. Poland, Latvia...' Chris' face lit up as he dragged countries from the inner recesses of his addled brain. 'Plus we can talk loads of Spanish. In Spain, obviously, not Latvia. Practice the stuff from evening classes and get completely, you know, fluid.'

'You mean fluent. True. And if we have this campervan, we won't spend much money and... Oh.' Suddenly my brain recon-nected. This was all well and good, but we had Oscar. A beautiful grey and white collie that I adored. How had I managed to forget our dog, even in my alcohol fuelled state?

'What?' Chris slapped at a midge on his arm. 'What's wrong?'

'Oscar.'

'Oh bugger. I'd forgotten about him. Could we leave him behind?'

'I don't think so. I'd cry. And he'd miss me. Well, OK, I'd miss him'. Suddenly it looked like we were back to being sensible and married. Maybe I'd get the Ikea catalogue out when I got over the hangover.

And then, a flash of inspiration.

'But, hang on,' I said, scowling as I dredged through my memo-ry, 'can't dogs get passports too? I think they can go to Europe if they get a passport. I'm sure people take dogs to France on holiday.'

'Now that would be good. Because...' Chris paused and frowned too, 'do you think that would mean Eastern Europe as well? Now they're in the EU and stuff, would Oscar be able to go there too?'

'Bloody hell. Do you think so? Now that *is* a plan. A European adventure, complete with dog.'

~

Earlier that day, we'd decided to celebrate matrimonial success by the purchase of a new DVD player. Or at least, a new to us DVD player. Advertised in the local paper, and not obviously

3

stolen, it had seemed a bargain for £30. And as we'd been chatting politely to the owner, Chris had developed a fixed stare that I should have known meant trouble.

'Is that your VW then?' he asked, peering into an adjacent barn.

And at that point, I should have run. I should've got out of that house as fast as I could. And then I would never have been contemplating hitching from Latvia to Aberdeen. And my life would have been simple, structured and substantially wealthier. But I didn't. I too peered into the barn and saw the light in Chris' blue eyes and remembered how he'd been 'owned' by a VW campervan during his psychedelic student days. And I just smiled and chatted to the owner. As if it made not a jot of difference to my life.

A long story followed about how the owner usually worked on the snowploughs in Afghanistan and had bought the van for a hobby whilst he was in the UK, with the so-far-unrealised plan of converting it into a campervan. The idea that someone who spent his working life pushing snow around an inhospitable country might then want to spend his holidays camping in the damp British countryside is, on later reflection, not that convincing. In fact I don't know if they even have that many snowploughs in Afghanistan. But conveniently, now that we were looking, he thought he'd mention that he was thinking of selling it. If we happened to be interested?

Enter stage left, bottle of wine, fruit of the vine. Or, more to the point, bottles and fruits. Of course, it shouldn't have taken the subsequent £10,000 and 13,000 miles for me to learn that life changing decisions are best taken when sober. But by the bottom of the bottle, the die was well and truly cast, and a significant chunk of my life had changed forever. And somewhere in the depths of Eastern Europe, a Latvian mechanic rubbed his hands in glee.

Rash as it seems now, after only a few hours let loose with fizzy alcohol, we were convinced we wanted to spend a full two grand on a clapped out electrician's van that would alter the course of our lives. Especially on one that sounded like a tractor and only

4

travelled marginally faster than your average Massey Ferguson.

And so, a few days later, we purchased the van, took it home (a whole six miles and we didn't break down – surely a good sign?) and christened it Bagpuss. Because it was a sort of pink and white thing, and although it was a saggy old, baggy old thing, we were sure we would come to love it.

We established the vaguest of routes that involved as many countries as possible, starting with Norway and ending up, in theory, in Spain. We thought we should try to avoid too much summer heat – Oscar was born in the far north-east of Scotland, so whilst he can eat bucket loads of porridge and drink more whisky than me, he isn't good in the heat. Although, in true Scottish style, that doesn't stop him going out anyway and taking part in the annual burn and peel routine. A quick session with a route finder on the web told us we were looking at a route of about 13,000 miles, in a van that could barely make it to the shop. But where there's a will, there's a mechanic standing ready and waiting to suck his breath through his teeth, shake his head and take your cash.

~

And so we began the planning. We started saving every penny we could and began the dog on the long, long route to a passport. By the end of the year, our bank account was looking healthier and the plans were a little clearer in our own minds, even if they weren't too clear to the wider world. We'd made some limited progress with converting the van into high class accommodation, although it was still a bit rough around the edges. Before we finally threw caution to the winds and told our respective bosses just where to stick their jobs, it seemed a short tester session was in order. The time had come, we decided, for a dry run. We would head for the open road in Bagpuss, throwing in a practice ferry ride for good measure and we'd spend a couple of weeks touring, all three of us, plus a pack of cards and some good books. We'd see a few tourist sights, have a few glasses of the local brew and really get into the swing of things by even using Euros as well.

In short, we were off to Ireland for two weeks. Whilst November isn't exactly the peak Irish tourist season we figured it would be the ultimate test – long dark wet winter evenings huddled together in the van would soon tell us if we were fit for the larger scale continental version.

Cunningly, Chris had arranged to work in Bristol the week before our planned sailing for the Emerald Isle. So it was agreed that Oscar and I would drive the van from Aberdeen to Carlisle (me driving, Oscar map reading), meet up with Chris, then we'd all head across to the ferry and be sinking our first pint of Guinness before sunset. Well, before the ten o'clock news anyway.

And so, early one Saturday, I piled all our stuff into the still unfinished van, installed Oscar on his specially made dog seat with the A-Z, set doors to automatic and cross-checked. Oscar looked at me in confusion, then huffed loudly as he realised Something Was Going On.

In fact, Oscar is one of the most capable dogs I have ever encountered when it comes to making his feelings known. He's a slightly scruffy cross-breed dog, with a posh blue merle collie Mum, who had a passionate but unplanned liaison with a passing Labrador. The subsequent puppies came out a hotchpotch of grey, black and white, making Oscar one of the most distinctive dogs in town. He has typically Labrador floppy ears, hanging around the sides of an unquestionably collie-like face. And, just to ensure he is never involved in a case of mistaken identity, he has one brown eye and one half brown, half blue eye – like David Bowie, but much cooler. We've had him since he was nine weeks old, so all his foibles, failings and general screw-ups can be laid squarely at our door.

Within a few months of arriving in the house, he'd made it abundantly clear who was the boss and in the years since, nothing much has changed. Rather than being a loving affectionate dog that dotes on our every word, he is a stand-offish character, always ensuring we know he is merely tolerating us for the time being, pending an offer from someone or something better. But for all that, he's universally loved by us, our families and most of the lady-dogs he's ever met.

So as I installed him in the navigator's seat, I was under no illusions that he'd be tolerant of my driving and conversational deficiencies. As we rolled out of the drive and onto the road south he heaved another sigh, twitched his ears, and then flopped onto the seat, his back firmly turned in my direction.

'This', his expression had clearly said 'should not happen to a dog.'

His lack of enthusiasm was compounded by my inability to master the vagaries of the van's gearbox. Or, more specifically, the vagaries of changing from first to second gear. Other gears were fine, so on downhill sections I could just cruise off in second – but for every downhill junction, there seemed to be at least five uphill ones. Each one followed the same pattern: I'd lurch onto the junction, flooring the accelerator and hearing the engine rise to screaming pitch, at which point Oscar would head for cover. I'd then struggle desperately with the gear stick, flailing it around as if stirring lumpy porridge, followed by a hideous crunching sound and an inevitable exclamation:

'Fuckit!'

Then more scrunching and the van would grind to a halt in the middle of the junction, cars would pile up behind, and the whole process would start again. Of course, by then the expletives were coming thick and fast and I was questioning the parentage of the van, Chris, the previous owner, his Afghan snowploughs and anyone else who might have spent more than 15 minutes in my company. Generally once I'd got a few hundred metres up the road I would either finally locate the missing gear, or I'd find a downhill stretch and slam it into third, then wait 10 minutes to reach walking pace.

By the time I approached Glasgow my nerves were shot to pieces and the dog hadn't opened his eyes for over a hundred miles. But at least Carlisle was starting to appear on the signposts – the destination where I knew I could pass over the van, which in my own mind was no longer the cute and cuddly Bagpuss, but had been rechristened the 'Fuckit Bucket'.

But the Fuckit Bucket fun was only just beginning.

About ten miles north of Glasgow, a red warning light began to glow on the dashboard. Taking the responsible approach, I ignored it for as long as possible. But within a few minutes the temperature gauge had soared off the scale and I had pull onto the hard shoulder. I rang the breakdown company and had one of those conversations that fuel Scottish nationalism, as the call centre, clearly based in south-east-England, struggled to assimilate the concept of north of Glasgow.

In the meantime the police had decided to pitch up and join the party and were sitting behind the van with all their lights flashing. This seemed to have potential for more harm than good, with multiple pile-ups only narrowly avoided as people gawped in amazement that something as clapped-out as the van had been stopped for speeding. As I sat in the pouring rain, waiting for the arrival of the tow truck, that anniversary bottle of wine and the warm slushy feeling of the world being my oyster all seemed a very, very long way away.

But the cheery breakdown men arrived, spoke to me in broad Glaswegian, towed the van off the motorway and spent some time sucking their teeth in dismay.

'Aye….tricky,' they announced, helpfully. If I had a pound for every time I've since heard that, the Fuckit Bucket would long ago have gone to the big scrapyard in the sky and I'd be driving round in a brand new Winnebago.

'Can you fix it though?' I asked, trying, and failing, to keep the irritation out of my voice.

'Weel, ane o thir hoses is leakin.' Assuming he was still talking about the van and not some personal problem, I smiled encouragingly.

'And, so that means....'

'We've nae spares fae a van as aud as this ane. But, ah kin nick oot leaky bit.' I wasn't convinced this was a great idea, but I was pretty low on options. 'Dae ye hae a knife?'

That's not necessarily a sentence you want to hear when you're in one of the more dubious suburbs of Glasgow, but I leapt into the van and returned only a few seconds later with a cheese knife, inwardly praising the practicality of travelling with your own kitchen.

'No Cheddar though, sorry,' I joked. The mechanic looked at me in confusion. 'Never, mind, doesn't matter.'

A few moments and swearwords later, the offending section of hose had been removed and the engine was ticking over nicely, with the temperature gauge gradually subsiding.

The mechanics escorted me back to the motorway with evident relief and headed off to the delights of Glasgow on a Saturday night. Unfortunately for Oscar, Glasgow on this particular Saturday night seemed noisier than usual and it dawned on me that I was travelling on Bonfire night. The cacophony of fireworks going off all around might have looked pretty, but they were rapidly resulting in the dog becoming a nervous wreck, and in urgent need of some doggy Valium. But we headed on our way – me and the now neurotic dog. I'd been given instructions by the mechanic to stop after 20 miles and check the hose wasn't leaking, so I duly pulled into a service station near Hamilton. I poked various bits of engine in an attempt to look like I knew what I was doing, rang Chris on his northbound train to update him and then prepared to head off again. Jumping into the van with a new found enthusiasm in my step, I turned the key.

Absolute silence.

Trying to stem the rising panic, I got out, poked a few more bits and turned the key again. Still nothing. Not even a single clue as to what might be wrong. I ambled around the service station, looking for a lorry driver who might be able to help, but was met with blank looks. It did give me an opportunity to admire some more of Glasgow's fireworks though, which reminded me: I needed to rush back and hold the dog's paw before he went into full scale panic attack. Sitting back in the van, I rang the breakdown company, again, and went through the whole rigmarole for a second time. With a degree of suspicion, they agreed to send another mechanic and this time, having got wise to the wait, I got into the back of the van, stuck the kettle on and settled down with tea and a book. There are some advantages to travelling snail style with your house on your back.

A new breakdown guy arrived, obviously annoyed at having his Saturday night interrupted. He spent some time poking around in the van – to be honest not looking much more knowledgeable than me.

'Yer alternator's fucked, hen,' he suddenly announced. Not needing a bit of attention, or slightly dodgy, but totally and unquestionably fucked. 'Ye need anither ane, but ye'll nae git ane in Glesgae nou, it's aw shut, hen.' Ignoring the strange local reference to chickens, I asked if I could get a replacement another day.

'Weel, thare's nae place open in the morn aither, so ye'll hae tae wait till Monday. Ye'll need tae gae tae Paisley than, hen.'

'Clucking great!' I thought.

By this time, my options seemed to have been reduced to sleeping in the van at the slightly dodgy service station, or finding a hotel nearby and waiting for the garages to open again on Monday. After further discussion and a few panicked phone calls, I persuaded the mechanic to tow the van to the nearest hotel that had agreed to take the dog.

Which returned me to the problem of the dog. Whilst the guy had been poking around in the engine, he'd made a succession of loud clanking noises, which had combined with the fireworks to result in dog meltdown. The final straw came when the van was loaded onto the tow truck at the same moment as Oscar decided it was his only safe refuge and he had to be forcibly removed from the door – looking like some activist being dragged away by the police. As I wrestled him to the ground he began a full demonstration of all the symptoms of a doggy panic attack, lying on the floor, shaking all over and whimpering. Try as I might to explain this to the breakdown guy, he wasn't all that understanding of this mad woman and her neurotic dog who were seriously interrupting his Saturday night.

In the end my only solution was to gather up Oscar in a 25 kilo armful, get into the front of the tow truck and carry him on my lap all the way to the hotel. Which meant I got to arrive at the hotel not only tired, pissed off and confused, but covered in dog hair and dribble as well. To the credit of the hotel receptionist, she didn't bat an eyelid, but checked us in and let the breakdown guy drop the van in the car park like a giant suitcase.

By this time Chris' delayed train had made it only as far as Lancaster, so he found a bed for the night there and was subjected to a telephone torrent of abuse from me concerning the Fuckit Bucket and all that was wrong with both him and it. After unleashing my cloud of fury I emptied the carefully packed wine and chocolate from the van, curled up on the bed with the still neurotic and shaking dog, and waited to see if it would look better in the morning.

Which it didn't. The hotel was in one of the less salubrious parts of Glasgow, none of the motor supply shops were open until Monday and the van looked very sad in an abandoned heap in the car park. But later in the day Chris arrived, survived my punches and verbal abuse and then set to assisting with dog rehabilitation therapy. And on the positive side, I'd significantly expanded my Mechanics of the World knowledge. Which, it turned out, was going to come in handy.

A Monday morning ring round the local garages finally turned up a replacement alternator in a back street of Paisley and by some electrical trickery Chris managed to get the van to start. This was a one-off stunt and couldn't be repeated, so he revved the engine all the way to the garage, terrified of stalling or having to ask for directions in his best English accent. But he made it, the van was fixed, the painful hotel bill paid and we were once more on the road to Stranraer, albeit heading for a slightly later ferry than originally planned. Calming the dog took longer, but he was eventually persuaded to re-enter the chamber of horrors that we called the van, and, huffing loudly he settled down again onto his dog seat, located between the two front seats.

And all went well until we arrived at Stranraer, when the fan belt snapped and we watched in horror as the temperature gauge went off the scale again. Fortunately we had a spare fan belt, but the relevant bits of old, oily machinery couldn't be persuaded to move. A third call to the breakdown company followed.

'I'm sorry, Ms Morris, but it does appear there's some long-term problem with your vehicle,' (as if I didn't already know that). 'Was it in good condition when you left home?'

'Well, I think it was' I lied, unconvincingly. 'Anyway, this is a different problem, so it can't be the van, it's just bad luck.' It seemed best not to explain that this van seemed to have more problems than they had break-down trucks.

'I'll see if I can get someone out, but we can't keep doing this. Will you be heading home soon?'

I tried not to think how I'd answer that question if we had a repeat of this fiasco once we'd headed into Europe. After some further pleading a local mechanic was found, who appeared with the ideal solution to all mechanical problems – a bigger hammer. With a carefully placed 'thwack' the offending bolt was released and he had us back on the road for the third time.

The nearest campsite then refused to have anything to do with either us or the dog, leaving us to spend a noisy night in a nearby lay-by with an assortment of lorries waiting for the morning ferry. And so began my education into just how long you need to spend revving a lorry engine before you can finally drive it away with all lights blazing.

This wasn't exactly the practice run we'd had in mind. Although to be fair, once we finally got to Ireland all went well – it was frequently damp, dark and cold, but we had enough chocolate, beer, clothes and card games to get through and we got to see some beautiful scenery in the brief hours of daylight. We successfully crossed both the Irish Sea and the border between Northern Ireland and Eire. Most of the locals clearly thought we were barking mad to be trying to do the tourist thing in November, but once they'd decided we weren't actually dangerous they were friendly and helpful. Our return journey was somewhat less chaotic, and we worked out a suitably edited version to relate to other people – including my parents.

The journey out had been an unmitigated disaster, but we were both comforted by the fact that we had managed to survive – even Oscar, who gradually got over his panic attack and returned to a normal dog existence (albeit with an increased dislike of fireworks and breakdown trucks). The idea that we could survive three breakdowns in the dark and cold was both depressing and encouraging – depressing that the van was so unreliable, but encouraging that we'd managed to keep going and hadn't killed each other. And most hopeful of all was the fact that we'd quite enjoyed the holiday bit in Ireland – even with the damp and cold. Neither of us had flipped out and been unable to co-exist in a space the size of an en-suite bathroom and we hadn't even had too many rows. So whilst it could hardly be described as a successful dress rehearsal, it did give us the courage to think we might just manage the continental version.

Sitting back in the comfort of our house, we congratulated each other, with the predictable use of fermented grape juice. Oscar was back to 'normal', or the closest semblance he has to normal and we were all still together – even the van was back in its usual space on the drive.

'Well, Mr Oscar Dog.' I said, as two back paws tried to ease me off my own settee. 'You are a travelling dog extraordinaire. We can't call you a border collie, not with your dubious parentage. But just think, by the end of this trip we'll definitely be able to call you a border-less collie!'

But Oscar just huffed loudly. It really shouldn't happen to a dog.

Chapter 2

Raising roofs and g-string beds

Our Ireland misadventure clearly demonstrated that we hadn't spent enough time getting the van ready for a continental tour. Not only was the engine in a questionable state, but the innards still needed to be made into an all-singing, all-dancing home for three. Prior to our multi-breakdown fiasco, we'd made a few improvements to the inside of the van, removing some of the surplus rubbish and putting in makeshift cupboards and a temporary bed. But it was clear that before we could reasonably expect to live in the van, we needed to complete its 'Road to Damascus' conversion to fully fledged campervan.

During the first anniversary bottles of wine we'd discussed this conversion.

'So,' I'd asked, 'how exactly does the van become a campervan?'

'It's not difficult really, I've converted a van before.' Chris said, full of the confidence that comes with alcohol. This supposed 'conversion' was in his student days and although that was some time ago, he was confident he'd get this van done in a few months.

'But it's a lot of work; do you really want to do something like that?'

'Yeah, I enjoy that sort of stuff, and it won't take that long.'

When I first met Chris he was working on the west coast of Scotland as a countryside ranger. He had long, sun-bleached hair and the look of a wild Bohemian. Then, the day before his thirtieth birthday, he'd developed a sudden fear of having long grey hair and had gone from flowing locks to a convict cut in the space of an hour. Now he gave the outward impression of being a nice, sensible chap, the kind of guy you could introduce to your mother. What I maybe hadn't realised was that unlike Samson, cutting off

Chris' hair hadn't changed his underlying characteristics. There was still a part of him that wanted to be wild, free and reckless. So buying the van and setting sail for Europe was all part of the inner dream. As too was the idea that he could quickly and easily convert a van into a camper. And one year of marriage isn't enough to be able to spot the tell-tale signs of someone being ridiculously over optimistic. So I nodded enthusiastically, whilst making rash promises that I would 'do' the curtains. Quite what I was going to do to the curtains wasn't clear, but I was sure I ought to have some useful skill to bring to the party.

And so began an endless trawl though the second-hand ads in the paper as we looked for suitably priced parts. Before the Ireland trip, we'd pieced together some bits quite quickly. These included an ancient gas-powered fridge carrying more rust than a super tanker, some kind of electrical connection box (which I've yet to understand) and various bits of cupboards and seats. As we continued, post-Ireland, at a more frenetic speed, we began to hang around the most dubious corners of Aberdeen scrapyards, like a pair of slightly shifty magpies. And I learnt that some scrapyards are tidy and clean with parts neatly labelled and women can go in, buy something and only cause every member of staff to stop working and stare as if she has a Wellington boot on her head. Other scrappies are different. These are the ones where things aren't tidy and clean, where nothing is labelled and a woman entering sets off the burglar alarm. There is one particular site in Aberdeen which is the low point of all scrapyards. Even outside the yard the ground is so covered in oil, diesel and other unnamed fluids that the dog won't walk on it. And that's the dog that will happily roll in a fresh pile of horse muck.

But we braved this yard on regular occasions (although always leaving clear directions with a responsible person, just in case we never returned). Our first mission was the search for a raising roof which could be clipped down whilst we zipped up and down autobahns, but pushed up in the wink of an eye to allow us ample headroom for cooking our gourmet meals and entertaining house guests. Or something like that. And just such a roof finally turned up in 'dodgy-scrappers-r-us'. Which would've been fine, except for the minor inconvenience that it was already attached to a van.

But undeterred by such trivialities, Chris took a giant tin opener to the scrapyard, and divided the scrapped van into two. Then we forced assorted friends and relations to help us take the roof home, undertake minor repairs to fix the leaks, then lift it onto our van for test fittings and so on. By the final stage of Project Roof, all our friends were suddenly busy (how strange) and the heavy lifting had to be undertaken by the local aerobics class, who seemed remarkably happy to pump iron (well, fibreglass) on our drive.

As more and more friends got drafted in to help us with the van refit, we had to reveal some of the details of our plans for a grown-up gap year. With dog. Responses ranged from 'you mean you're dropping out' to out and out laughter (although to be fair that usually came at the point where we mentioned the van). Some friends understood entirely but most people struggled to understand why we were having a gap-year now.

I wouldn't like to give the impression that either of us is old, exactly, but we were a little above the average age for a gap year. We'd decided we would hit the road in June 2005, when Chris would be 36 and I would be 31. Most of our friends seemed to be settling down with mortgages and children; only moving house when they needed more space for their new sports car and that sort of thing. Not voluntarily moving out of a house and into a van that, by rights, would only ever be fit to go to a sporting event to sell burgers and ice-cream.

It seems to be perfectly acceptable for 19 year-olds to head off on their travels, but not for anyone the wrong side of 30. At least, not until you are very much the wrong side of 30 and preferably the wrong side of 65. Then, strangely, it becomes OK again – once you've paid the mortgage, packed the kids off and are finally free once more. In between was our generation. The 25 to 50 year olds who have big mortgages, expensive children and no choice but to focus on maximising their earning power to pay off debts at every opportunity. And there was no doubt that taking a gap year would make a significant dent in our financial status. Not only would we use up all our savings, but we'd also reduce our earnings to nothing. It wasn't just the money we'd spend, it would also cost us in money that we wouldn't earn. It was easy to see why so few people from our generation were taking a grown up gap year. They were all tied up in their everyday struggle to meet the financial commitments they'd made. In terms of travel, they'd become the 'missing generation'.

There seemed to be a lot of pressure on us to settle down, earn a decent wage and start a pension, then wait until retirement before we thought of anything more outrageous than a few weeks in the sun. But we are also of the generation that has seen how many years of saving into a pension fund can mean nothing if the stock market has an off day, or the boss turns out to be spending it all on a boat refit. And who've seen the job for life turn into a job for ten minutes at the whim of a passing politician. So whilst we weren't about to throw caution to the wind and set out on the yellow brick road with only a guitar to our names, neither were we prepared to work continuously for the next thirty-something years. And hence the grown up gap year.

We've both travelled a bit before, and have had periods of time when we were 'between jobs', but we've also had long periods of proper jobs, with pensions, payslips and in-trays all of our own. But Chris had witnessed his parents work hard – relentlessly hard – for 50 years, planning to do all their travelling and general living once they retired. Then he'd seen his father be struck ill within weeks of retiring, and their plans had crumbled around them into a pile of beta blockers and pacemakers.

Our so-called careers were in the environment sector, which is often billed as uplifting and rewarding work. And whilst it does often live up to that, it also has its moments of tedious bureaucracy and irritating colleagues. Both of us are originally from the English Midlands, but many years ago we'd made separate, but like minded decisions to get away from the hustle and bustle of England and move to the peace and tranquillity of northern Scotland. We'd then met in Scotland and the rest of our history is a series of attempts to be in the same part of the country with two fulfilling jobs

But despite the fact that we both loved Scotland, including our quiet little village in northern Aberdeenshire, we also knew there was a whole world out there, waiting to be explored. I'd been working for four years on a European-funded project to involve local people in restoring the nearby river and estuary. In between the inevitable form-filling, this had been a rewarding few years, but it was also a fairly demanding job – dealing with curious locals, grumpy farmers and frustrated fishermen as well as government bureaucrats. The deal from Brussels had always been for a fixed period of time, so I knew my contract would be ending in the summer of 2005.

Chris, meanwhile, had moved away from his early working life, spent in the romantic idyll of countryside rangering, and was desk-bound working for a research institute in Aberdeen. In theory he was there to act as the communication bridge between the wider public and the brilliant, but socially challenged scientists. But in reality he seemed to spend most of his time peering at a gaping chasm rather than acting as a bridge and it was fast becoming clear that he wouldn't last much longer. Chris has a tendency towards an over-active conscience and he felt frustrated and guilty at his inability to achieve what he was supposed to be doing. From this perspective, the decision to pack it all in for a while and head off into the sunset wasn't that difficult.

Financially things weren't impossible either. We had a small but perfectly presentable house which could be rented out, we had two salaries coming in and had adapted to a near monastic social life, so the savings account was steadily growing. And the dog now had his very own passport. It seemed there was nothing stopping us. But the constant surprise of those around us nagged at me incessantly during those months of preparation. Try as I might, I could find no way to silence the doubters. It felt like the best thing we could do was throw ourselves into the conversion of the van and hope that, as it became more obviously a campervan, people would begin to see our point of view.

And as the van began to spread its wings as a fully fledged campervan, our plans began to crystallise. Our route would begin with a ferry crossing from Aberdeen to the Shetland Islands and then onto Norway. We'd head north through Scandinavia, then journey back south through Finland and into Eastern Europe. From there it all became more sketchy, but we planned to finish up in Spain, where we'd search for gainful employment. We expected to be away for about ten months in total and we hoped to spend no more than £1000 per month. Of course, the Latvian mechanic knew it wasn't going to work out quite like that, but at the planning stage, we still had the Fuckit Bucket faith.

And why Europe? Why not the Trans-Siberian or something even more exotic? Partly because beneath all our desire to be ageing hippies there was just a slight hint of realism that told us that any more than one continent in a campervan might be pushing our luck. And I suppose in many ways, Europe doesn't seem a particularly adventurous destination. But now that the European Union had grown so dramatically, I wanted to see if this continent really did hang together as a place. I'd like to pretend that's because I'm a politically savvy, critical thinking kind of girl. When in reality, my curiosity was primarily driven by self-interest. Not that long after we'd bought the van, the river restoration project I worked on had received a visit from our European Commission funders. They spent the best part of a day pulling my work to shreds and telling me how backwards we were, compared to the rest of Europe. At 6 o'clock, unable to take any more, I'd come home and burst into floods of tears. Then I launched into a full scale rant at Chris the second his foot hit the doormat.

'What's the point?' I'd asked, angrily. 'Why am I bothering to jump through all their frigging hoops. It's not even worth it for the amount of money they're giving us. The whole European Commission's just one giant bureaucratic nightmare. All they're interested in is have you ticked this box, have you filled in that form, why's there a difference of half a Euro here? They've got no ability to see the bigger bloody picture.'

Chris did his best with tea and sympathy, but being a man, and therefore from Mars, he'd also tried to be pragmatic.

'I guess it's their way of checking that everything's being done above board. They've got to try and make some kind of level playing field across the whole of Europe. So they have to check up on everyone. It's not you personally they're having a go at. Maybe they're just trying to be even handed.'

'I don't care. What's the point of having a Union if it all just descends into this pointless farce. It's not a useful concept as far as I can see. It's just an excuse for a bunch of grey suits to get a power trip every so often by telling us our bananas are the wrong shape. Or our forms aren't filled in right.'

'I'm not sure that's strictly true. I think it's a lofty ideal and all, it's maybe just a bit screwed up by people. Anyway, try and think about our trip instead. That'll be your chance to see the reality on the ground. You can see if we have got anything in common with the other countries and if it really is worth having a Union and a Commission to police it all. By the time we've visited all those countries, you'll have a better idea about the state of Europe than most people.'

Chris' attempt to look on the positive side didn't cheer me up at the time, but over the months that followed I mused on some of his ideas. I'd begun to feel pretty jaded with the whole concept of a single European entity but maybe this trip would be an opportunity to see if the bureaucracy was worthwhile. Was I a Europhile or a Europhobe? And how does Scotland fit in to all this? As a small country nestled on the very edge of the continent, I was interested to see if it measured up to the rest of the Union. Were our hyper-critical Commission monitors right – is it the slow man of Europe or does it have more to offer than they'd realised?

There were other pluses to a trip in Europe rather than choosing some far flung destination for our grown-up gap year. Not only did it mean Oscar could come with us, but a winter in Spain was an appealing prospect. By travelling through the north and east of Europe in the summer we could arrive in Spain at the beginning of winter and stay for a few months. Many years earlier, Chris and I had taken a trip to Argentina. We'd both loved the country and been fascinated by the people, but our pidgin Spanish left us frustratingly unable to communicate. Keen to learn more about the people of this and other South American countries, we'd enrolled in Spanish evening classes and had been studying the language ever since. Then Oscar had arrived on the scene and our chances for a few months in South America had been significantly curtailed. But the language lessons had continued and now we both had a desire to see if we could make a final break-through on the communication front and live in the Spanish speaking world.

It all seemed to make perfect sense to us, but that's not to say there weren't many moments of doubt between the first-anniversary bottles of wine and our final departure. In order to make it sound slightly more socially acceptable, Chris would point out that he'd been doing a part time MSc for the last couple of years, so the travelling time could also be spent writing up his dissertation. Whilst this made him look less of a drop-out, it didn't do much for me. As we came closer to departure, part of me began to wonder if we'd got it all horribly wrong. Maybe it wasn't the right thing to be doing?

Ironically, I was probably helped by becoming ill with a failing thyroid gland at this point. The thyroid gland seems to be one of those things, like loo roll or your mother tidying up behind you, that you just don't miss until it's not there anymore. And then you wonder how you ever got along without it. My hair fell out by the handful (not on my legs obviously, that would have been too much to hope for), I felt shattered all the time and I cried constantly for no reason.

Fortunately the symptoms were caught fairly early on and I was put on the correct replacement medication within a matter of months. Yet just a few months of feeling truly lousy was enough to make me reassess the importance of the things around me. I realised that, whilst I enjoyed my job (or at least the concept of it), I didn't want to spend my whole life working.

Nobody knows why some thyroid glands give up the ghost and it had come as a bolt from the blue, with no family history or early warning signs. If that was lurking out there, what else might be? What if I was struck by cancer or some other terrible disease? What if I never made it to retirement, or even to 40? What became obvious was that I didn't know either way. Given the uncertainty, I was going to take the chance, ignore the doubters and do something whilst I still had the stamina for it.

But if people were shocked at our decision to take a grown up gap year, mentioning the dog brought on an extra dimension of disapproval. Even those who were supportive of the gap year concept seemed shocked at the idea that we were taking Oscar with us. Some of them needed convincing that what we were proposing was even legal. Because the pet passport scheme was new, most people had never heard of it, and assumed Oscar would need to spend six expensive and unpleasant months in quarantine when we got back. If he even got back. I lost count of the number of people who gave a sharp intake of breath when they heard the 'Oscar plan'.

'What!' they'd exclaim. 'He's going with you? But what about all the nasty diseases he'll catch over there? And think about the heat. He'll never cope. He won't have any routine. Dogs need routine you know.'

Somewhat to my surprise, the only note of optimism amongst these naysayers came from an unexpected source. When I tentatively explained our plans to the vet, with lots of emphasis on my now extensive knowledge of the passport regulations, she simply shrugged.

'Sounds OK to me. You've obviously thought about it and Oscar'll probably love it. He's such a friendly dog, he'll be delighted with all the new people.'

Inwardly I began to heave a sigh of relief.

'Really? You think it's OK? You don't think we're evil dog owners who should be reported to the RSPCA? And what about the lack of routine? Will he be alright with that do you think? Even if we take him to Eastern Europe?' I gabbled, as if Eastern Europe was some far off, uncharted destination that might still have dragons. Which I suppose, in Oscar's terms, it probably was.

'It'll be fine, I'm sure,' Heather laughed. 'Maybe don't take him for long walks by their nuclear power stations though. Routine or no routine, it'd be a shame for him to come back glowing in the dark.'

~

As the day of our departure grew closer, the van slowly became more refined. And if we were going to live in the van for ten months, we needed some essential home comforts – including a bed. Not just any bed, but a cunning machine that would turn from divan to comfortable seat in an operation that we'd eventually get down to milliseconds. Again the legally-questionable Aberdeen scrapyard provided the solution when another distinctly scummy van arrived, complete with the right style of bed and a full set of questionable stains on the upholstery.

As the one who'd promised that the conversion was a simple job, it seemed only reasonable that Chris should tackle the removal of the dodgy bed. So early one morning, he headed into the scrapyard alone and set to work amongst the rotting scrap. It's never pleasant going under anyone's bed – heck, its not even pleasant going under your own bed – but when the bed in question is in an old rotting campervan of dubious pedigree, it requires a full white suit and detox procedure. Chris suited up and headed in, and found, to his horror, a clearly worn (albeit not recently) black thong hiding under the bed. Trying desperately to keep his imagination under control he threw the offending item to the front of the van and continued his work. Realising that he was missing a vital tool for setting the bed free, he headed back to the car to fetch a bigger spanner. When he returned to the van, his own toolbox had disappeared and he was forced to wander the site, questioning large, muscular men.

'I wondered if you might have accidentally picked up my toolbox from that van over there. Only accidentally of course, I'm not accusing you of anything, clearly, just wondering if you might have, erm, been passing?'

After being threatened with grievous bodily harm by two or three people, he finally found the culprit – a large Aberdonian man who didn't look like he'd seen a shower in a long time. He hastily returned the box and began emptying tools from various unpleasant looking pockets, whilst loudly proclaiming his innocence.

'Fit aboot tha box? Ah thought it wis wi' van. S' shite onyway.'

Thanking him politely, Chris shuffled back to the van and braced himself to begin again. Looking down into the van, it was only then that he realised it wasn't just the toolbox that had been taken for a walk by the tattooed Aberdonian. The black thong was also nowhere to be seen.

Chapter 3

Cutting loose

In May 2005, we purchased an expensive series of ferry tickets and ceased to be gainfully employed. Freedom beckoned, but first the focus had to shift from the interior of the van back to its dubious engine and the MOT it needed to pass to give us 10 legal months on the road. The MOT was due four weeks before we planned to leave, and, of course, the van failed comprehensively. In fact, it failed more completely than any vehicle I have ever known. But not until after we'd both quit our jobs and paid for the ferry tickets, leaving us with few options for delaying the trip whilst we sought replacement parts, vehicles or lives.

So all we could do was leave the garage with a blank cheque and stomach the horror of a £1,500 bill on its final return. Given that our entire budget for the trip was £10,000, this disaster potentially wiped six weeks of travelling off the agenda. Combined with the Ireland fiasco, it also planted some serious seeds of doubt about the van's ability to manage this trip. We knew it wasn't in fantastic shape, but I'd somehow assumed it would limp round. Now I was beginning to wonder. And, of course, those seeds of doubt were to become a full-grown forest as I pondered our future on the Latvian garage forecourt.

But the van was finally dragged kicking and screaming through its MOT a week before we were due to sail. Neither of us got much sleep for the remaining few days. Every hour of every day was spent finishing off the van conversion, packing away bits of our house and wondering what we would forget.

Our friend Rich had agreed to rent the house, and much to our luck was furniture-less himself, so we only had to pack away small amounts of junk, but even that seemed time consuming. And the trade-off we'd made for being able to leave all our stuff in situ during his lease was that Rich could move in before we left, so not only did we have boxes of our own rubbish everywhere, we also ended up tripping over half of Rich's stuff as well. No matter how tidy someone is, we discovered there's just not enough room in our house for three adults, supplies for a campervan and a dog.

Whereas I had a clear system of one pile for the van and another pile for the charity shop, Chris seemed incapable of grasping such a difficult concept. Every so often I'd find something vital in the pile for the junk shop, or some old magazines and a washed out T-shirt in the pile of essentials for the van. And I'd sigh deeply. Again.

I've always found that the day before a holiday is spent rushing round madly, wishing you'd never agreed to go away in the first place. And if it's one day of mayhem for a fortnight's holiday, it would appear that it multiplies up for ten months of travelling. So you spend several weeks in chaos, snapping at everyone and seriously asking the dog why he can't pack his own stuff. To which, I'd like to note, I never got a decent answer. We spent more time with Heather, triple-checking all the border control requirements and building up a dog first-aid kit which was substantially larger than ours. Naively, I asked if she could give me a lesson in how to take a dog pulse so I could recognise if all was not well in Oscar land. I wasn't entirely prepared for the reply:

'Sure. In fact, why don't you come into the surgery and I'll show you how to do pulse, respiration and temperature.'

'But don't you take temperature…..from the….ummm…..' I stuttered.

'Yep.'

Gulp. 'Great, yes, of course, that's fine. Can't wait. Shall we do it tomorrow?' I asked, a little too brightly.

An entertaining half hour was spent in the vet's surgery the following day, as I crawled round the floor behind Oscar, trying to shove a thermometer where the sun most definitely does not shine.

Chris, of course, had volunteered to take the head end within seconds of hearing the plan. Eventually mission was accomplished, but I could tell Oscar would probably prefer to be left to die in peace rather than succumb to the horror a second time. And I crossed vet off the list of potential new careers I could consider on our return.

As our final few days in Scotland drew near, we had a leaving barbeque for friends, work colleagues and, it transpired, for Oscar's friends. Within the first hour the front drive had been barricaded off and turned into some sort of dog crèche – a motley collection of dogs bounding round, chasing tennis balls, Frisbees and burgers. The rest of us sheltered under a neighbour's gazebo we'd borrowed for the occasion, avoiding the showers and the midges in true Scottish barbeque style.

Finally the last day dawned. We were booked on an overnight ferry from Aberdeen to the Shetland Islands, which would take about 12 hours, followed by a ferry from Shetland to Bergen in Norway a couple of days later. We'd had to spend some time arguing with the ferry company to convince them that a dog could even cross from Shetland to Norway. This crossing had yet to be conquered by the canine race and I'd had several confused conversations with their head office, conveniently located in the Faroe Islands.

By contrast the Aberdeen to Shetland leg seemed well prepared for dogs, and Oscar already had a premium kennel booked. He'd had pretty good sea legs on the tester trip to Ireland, but he has been known to eat his dinner, run around madly and then throw up all over the bedroom floor, so I had a nagging fear that I'd be spending the majority of this voyage holding a doggie sick bag. As I'd already had to hold one in the past for Chris, I had visions of being stuck with a sick bag in each hand, not sure whose back to rub first. And after 12 hours of a puking dog and husband there was every chance I'd be chucking myself over the side as well.

But before we could even get as far as checking out the quality of the sick bags, we had to get to the damned boat in the first place. We needed to leave the house by 4.30 pm in order to make the boat. So at 2.30pm, when there still appeared to be several days more work, Chris succumbed to the inevitable.

'How about ringing the ferry company, in case we can change the booking for tomorrow?' he asked, desperately trying to sound nonchalant.

'OK, I'll see what they can do.'

After a few minutes on hold I got through to a very cheery sounding woman and explained our predicament:

'So you see we've still got days of packing to do and we'll never be ready and it's all hopeless and I'm about to kill someone. So, I wondered, can we get on Sunday's ferry instead?'

Presumably the woman at the ferry office was pressing the big red button marked 'Panic', but she managed to sound calm and professional and duly looked up the Sunday ferry.

'Well, yes you can, there's just one cabin left, so you could swap your tickets.'

I felt a warm rush of relief spread over me, before suddenly remembering to ask:

'And is there room for the van on that boat too?'

'A van, oh no, I don't think so, there's only room for the two of you, so you'd have to leave the vehicle behind.'

Whilst that was unquestionably a tempting option, I had to bear in mind that we were supposed to be sleeping in this particular vehicle for the next 10 months. With regret, I put the phone down and headed back to the kitchen with the bad news.

For the following two hours all hell broke lose in the house as we ran around like the proverbial coloured flies. It finally reached a head at ten past four, when I discovered Chris had decided this would be a good moment to try some additional welding on the table. Resisting the temptation to put the welding rods somewhere where he'd never get the right mix, I contented myself with hissing at Rich through my teeth,

'Tell me he's NOT still welding at ten-past four.'

To Rich's credit, whilst I must have looked like someone about to commit murder, he stayed calm, made me a cup of tea and provided a sound track of soothing platitudes.

By 4.40pm we were all piled into the van, bits of table still poking out the window.

'Where did you say the garage key was again?' Rich asked, in a resigned voice.

'Where's the axe?' I barked, in a voice that was anything but resigned.

And then, at last, we were off, turning out of the drive for the final time in 10 months and heading down the road to Aberdeen. It still surprises me how quickly you can change your life. In less than an hour we were on the ferry, with the van parked up and both of us crawling around Oscar's kennel, arranging blankets, bowls, toys and room service. And a few minutes later somebody somewhere released a rope (do they still do it like that?) and off we floated, into the big blue yonder. As simply as we'd both commuted to work in the previous few years. Yet this time we sailed past the offices and out into the North Sea. And Rich presumably passed that hour removing the remaining evidence of the landlords and settling into his new abode. And there we all were, lives completely altered, in the blink of an eye.

~

The Aberdeen to Shetland ferry sails north every night, arriving in Lerwick at 7am, where the well-rested travellers leap off the boat and face the excitements of the Northern Isles. Or at least, that's the theory. Being grown up gappers, and not your average 19-year old, we'd gone for the luxurious option of a cabin, rather than seats, for the overnight crossing. Disappointingly, dogs aren't allowed in the cabins (possibly for fear of the sick bag scenario), so Oscar was installed in his canine cabin equivalent whilst we settled into our grown up cabin upstairs.

I ate half the restaurant so my stomach couldn't move with the boat, and then headed off for what I hoped would be my first full night of sleep in three weeks. We were away from the tools, the packing, the last minute things to finish at work, Chris' MSc and the final phone calls. But when I crawled onto my small bunk, I found it hard to fall asleep. Presumably I was suffering from a combination of the adrenaline that had been flowing for the last few days and the nagging nervousness of waiting to see who would be sick first. The slight queasiness that seemed to be building was probably not from the boat, but from the idea of being let loose on a continent, with no ties, no deadlines, just an open road and a full tank of fuel. Or at least, I like to think it was such poetic concerns, but in reality it may well have been due to worrying about Oscar – alone in his little kennel on the car deck.

By 1am I had, of course, convinced myself that he was lying on the floor, whimpering and crying, being violently sick and generally wondering why we'd abandoned him to such a cruel fate. Predictably, by then the boat was starting to list alarmingly and I was being flicked across my bunk. I knew from past experience that I can keep sea sickness at bay if I lie absolutely still, but to stand up and wander around is fatal. And to go down to the car deck, with the diesel fumes and the deafening engine noise, has only one outcome – and it isn't a pretty one. I decided desperate times called for desperate measures.

'Chris… are you awake?' I asked in a stage whisper, designed to sound quiet and concerned, whilst being just loud enough to wake him.

'Feuwhewofwat?' came from the other bunk.

'Oh, you are awake, that's good.' Chris dragged himself from a deep sleep. 'I was hoping you might go down and check on Oscar.'

Silence.

'I'd go myself, but I'm too stiff and sore to move after doing all that packing and tidying that you didn't get round to doing. Don't worry if it's too much trouble, it's just… well, carrying all those heavy boxes while you were still finishing off those essays, it hasn't done my back any good at all.'

I'd like to say I felt guilty at such emotional blackmail but, technically, I'd be lying. Faced with the prospect of clearing up dog sick whilst barfing myself, there was no depth to which I was not prepared to sink.

To his eternal credit, and somewhat to my surprise, Chris dutifully got up and lurched downstairs. A few minutes later he returned, looking a little pale.

'Oscar's fine, but I need to open the window and stare at the horizon for a while.'

I tried to look concerned and sound genuinely taken aback that he felt sick.

'Is the boat moving dear, I hadn't noticed? Never mind, take plenty of deep breaths. Oh, and the windows don't open.'

As Chris collapsed in a green tinged heap, I finally managed a few hours sleep before being woken at 6.30am by the tannoy announcing our impending arrival in Lerwick. We hastily dressed and rushed down to the car deck – Chris to check on the van and me on Oscar. Both seemed unscathed by their night of lurching and listing and Oscar leapt back into Bagpuss like the old travelling hand he wasn't.

Our arrival in Lerwick was followed by two days of gale-force winds, whipping the sea into a swell ready for our 15 hour voyage to Norway. Battling against the wind we hiked to the ferry office to confirm our check-in arrangements. But instead we were told, in no uncertain terms, that there was no way a dog could travel on the ferry and that we should never have been issued with tickets in the first place. Feeling the bottom fall out of our world, and quickly totting up the miles and pounds it would take us to get back to Aberdeen and down to a port in the south, we both tried not to panic. And failed. Rather than remaining cool, calm and collected, we gibbered in stereo at the woman in the office, demanding to know why our little darling couldn't come with us.

Sometimes I wonder if a dog is any different from a child. Perhaps more inclined to leave hair around the house, and marginally less likely to demand an expensive education. But at times it's hard to spot the difference between us and parents wanting to take their small child into a chic wine bar. It was a full nerve-wracking ten minutes before we managed to find the magic words. Not 'please' as I was always taught, or even 'here's a tenner, love' as Chris suggested. But the simple phrase 'we're not coming back'. And at once, all was clear, problem solved. Because the customs at Shetland aren't equipped to receive animals, we could go to Norway, but we couldn't come back.

Once they'd realised we were so completely barking we were not only planning to take our dog on a 15 hour ferry, we were also planning to drive a few thousand miles through Europe with him, in order to come back via England, everything became so much simpler. They confirmed our one way tickets, admired the photo in Oscar's passport, and sent him off to prepare for being their first Shetland to Norway dog passenger.

Left with one day to pass in Shetland before the arrival of the Norway boat, we meandered across the island to Scalloway, a small town clustered on the western coast of the Shetland mainland. As we sauntered down the main street, our struggles with the Norwegian crossing were put sharply in perspective by the discovery of a memorial to the World War Two 'Shetland Bus'. In an effort to help the Norwegian resistance in their fight against Nazi occupation, small fishing boats spent the war years making regular clandestine trips from Norway to Shetland, often in the worst of the winter seas. A mix of weapons, undercover agents and radio equipment was smuggled into Norway, whilst Norwegian refugees at risk of arrest from the Gestapo were ferried to safety in Shetland. The trips took 24 hours and were always fraught with danger, at risk from both the weather and attack by German planes and boats. Despite tragedies, an impressive 350 refugees were safely evacuated and the bond between Shetland and Norway was cemented in local minds.

Seeing this grim reminder of past voyages made me realise that our exploits were not as dare-devil as I liked to kid myself. We are lucky to live in an age and location where our greatest concern was shipping a dog between countries.

But part of me still hoped for crowds of waving well-wishers to appear the following day and witness Oscar's step into a brave new world of dog travel. So I was disappointed to discover that the only witness for his embarkation would be the customs guy. Disappointment turned to panic as I watched him searching the campervan in front, pulling up seats, opening cupboards and peering suspiciously into the engine compartment.

The regulations as to what you can take into Norway are surprisingly strict – because it's not part of the EU, alcohol limits are a measly one bottle of wine and one of spirits each. Given that we knew alcohol was pricey in Norway we'd been a little bit reckless on our limits, interpreting the each as including the dog and the van. Even more surprisingly, there is also a limit on the amount of food you can take in. Presumably this is so that cheapskate campers like us don't arrive in the country with all the food they need, but instead have to purchase astronomically expensive Norwegian food, to bolster the local economy.

As we were planning to spend about six weeks in Norway, we didn't want to blow our entire travelling budget on two bags of Norwegian pasta, so we'd filled every nook and cranny of the van with food. You couldn't open a cupboard without being struck on the head by a falling bag of rice, or put your shoes on without first emptying out the muesli bars stashed inside. I was conscious of being significantly over the food limit as well as the alcohol allowance, and the prospect of watching it all disappear into a customs bag wasn't appealing.

As the driver of the van in front began sticking his van back together, we drew level with the customs man and greeted him with what we hoped were charming, friendly, open, but clearly 'not-guilty-your-honour' smiles. He looked back with an unquestionably dour face.

'Tickets!'

Unfortunately, this was enough to wake a sleeping dog. But, rather than leap up and bark and growl at the open window as he usually would, Oscar miraculously just sat up, looked out at the customs man, wagged his tail and then laid his head on Chris' shoulder in a never-before-seen impression of loving dog.

And even the heart of a customs official can be moved by such a display. He spent some time patting Oscar, who responded with small licks and a wagging tail, then gave the rest of the van a cursory glance, and sent us on our way.

'Now you take care of that dog,' he called after us.

'Don't worry officer, we will. Give the nice man a goodbye wave, Oscar.'

Finally, a successful result for the dog-hampered traveller – you may not be able to go into restaurants, enter certain parks or even take your pampered pooch into all the museums, but you may just get through customs in two shakes of a dog's tail.

Chapter 4

Continental dog

The Norway boat provided a new class of travel for Oscar's cabin – this time he had a penthouse suite on the top deck, with a view out to sea. We could even sit with him for most of the journey, avoiding a repeat of the midnight emotional blackmail scene. It also turned out to be where the crew came out for a cigarette break, so we were soon a fount of knowledge on all the boat gossip. By taking turns to do the night watch – Chris checked Oscar at four then slept late, and I got up at six to hold his paw and mop his fevered brow – we both got a reasonable night's sleep and could then watch the boat's passage through a myriad of islands into the port of Bergen.

Having survived countless hours at sea to get this far, our next hurdle was to get Oscar through customs. When we collected our tickets in Shetland, we had been given a red sticker for the van, which loudly proclaimed in big black writing, 'Something to Declare'. With this ominous warning slapped on the van we had no choice but to drive off the boat and into the red channel – the one I've always thought of as reserved for alcoholics and drug dealers. Whilst we were slightly guilty on the alcohol front, we hadn't exactly packed the van full of crack cocaine – but here we were in the queue that had rubber gloves and full body searches written all over it.

Nervously approaching the front, I smiled politely at the official and asked the ubiquitous question of the Brit abroad:

'Do you speak English?'

He shook his head and shrugged. Fair enough, but our 'Scandinavian for Beginners' phrasebook (printed circa 1974 and 10p from the local charity shop) seemed to lack the crucial phrase:

'Here is my dog, this is his passport and his micro chip is located by his left scapula'.

Had I been looking to ask whether or not the room included a trouser press and linen service I'd have been fine, but canine travellers weren't covered. I resisted the temptation to speak more loudly and instead waved the passport at him hopefully. Picking up on my gist, he disappeared into the adjacent hut before returning with a scanner to check Oscar's microchip. One of the requirements of the pet passport system is for all pets that travel to be fitted with a microchip, so they can be scanned and matched up to the passport. I assume this is because one Labrador can look a lot like another, and if they aren't chipped we might get all sorts of illegal immigrant Labs coming in, obviously intent on taking our women and Bonios.

The chips are injected under an animal's skin and our vet had spent some time scanning Oscar's chip to check it was working, before writing some technical vet words in his passport. It seems that just writing 'somewhere on his back' as a location would not be enough to justify so many years of education. So instead some frighteningly large words had been employed to describe what we all know as 'the bit of the dog that you usually pat'. But I'd never tried to scan Oscar, so I was slightly thrown when the customs man passed me the scanner, opened the passport to the ID number, folded his arms and looked at me expectantly.

Feeling under pressure I took a confident hold of Oscar and starting wiping the scanner round his back in a similar manner to the way they scan baked beans at the supermarket. For a disturbingly long time this only resulted in silence from the scanner and a deeply aggrieved look from Oscar. Eventually I heard a hopeful sounding beep, and, assuming it wasn't coming from a nearby supermarket, I glanced at the scanner screen. Seeing a long number, I passed the scanner over to the customs man, only to discover the screen now said 'Low Bat'. The man looked at the passport, looked at the screen and shook his head. Fighting off rising panic, I went back to Oscar, repeated the procedure and rushed back. Again 'Low Bat' and this time the man shook his head and looked up at the boat, which I knew was returning to Shetland in only a few hours time. The pet passport rules were pretty clear – no microchip equals go home. Do not pass go, do not collect £200. But of course I knew we wouldn't be allowed to go home, because we couldn't get back through customs at Lerwick. I had a horrid vision of all three of us condemned to spend the rest of our lives sailing across the North Sea, never being allowed off the boat at either end and returned to my scanning work like a whirling dervish. When I got the low battery message for a third time, I thumbed through the phrase book for 'Excuse me but I believe the battery is flat'. All I found was 'May I order breakfast for 7am'. At last I succumbed to my ancestry and began explaining in slow, loud English:

'I THINK THE BATTERY IS FLAT, THE NUMBER IS ONLY SHOWING FOR A SECOND' whilst waving my arms around in an attempt to demonstrate what I meant.

After he'd looked at me for a while as if I was mad, I persuaded the customs man to leaf through the passport and find Oscar's picture. Pictures aren't obligatory in dog passports, but being a bit of a softie on my dog, I'd found a charming shot of him sitting with his head at a rakish angle, and had included it anyway. The customs guy seemed quite delighted with it and spent some time looking at Oscar from all angles to check he really was the dog in the picture. Then he clapped me on the back and sent us on our way. Hearts pounding, we drove into the Bergen traffic and never looked back at the boat that had so nearly become our home.

~

In our hurry to escape from the port we'd forgotten to check exactly where we might be heading, and soon realised that a desti-nation of 'err…Norway' wasn't going to get us far in the Bergen traffic. Even worse, they were all driving on a different side of the road (if I've learnt nothing else from 10 months in Europe, I've learnt not to call it the wrong side of the road).

After driving around in a helpless panic for half an hour, we found a small lay-by and pulled over to regroup and deal with the dog's desperate need for a pit stop after 15 hours on a boat without a dog bin in sight. As I crawled around behind Oscar with a standard issue Aberdeenshire Council poo bag in hand, I wondered if the Council's tourism department would be grateful to us for our plans to leave small bags advertising Aberdeenshire across an entire continent. Come to think of it, we could have asked them for sponsorship – but maybe a bag of gently sweating faeces isn't how they'd choose to market the area… 'Come to Aberdeenshire, better than a steaming turd any day'.

Once the ablutions were finished, we had another problem to tackle – how to find our way out of Bergen. Necessity quickly became the mother of invention and Chris, the closest we'd got to a gadget geek in the family, picked up our brand new, never-out-of-the-packet satellite navigation system and began tapping buttons hopefully.

When I left gainful employment, my colleagues had racked their brains long and hard for a useful leaving present. Because I worked in a male dominated group, they were filled with horror at the idea of me driving all the way round Europe. Not out of concern for my safety, or even for the environment, but for the potential for getting lost and having to face every man's greatest horror: asking for directions. To avoid this nightmare, they'd clubbed together and bought a brand new satnav as my leaving present – because where would you be without a gadget? At the time, expecting bunches of flowers and gentle sobbing at my leaving, I'd been a bit disappointed, but as the calm voice in the box led us through the Bergen traffic, I had to concede that maybe they knew what they were doing.

Pulling up at the first campsite, we braced ourselves for Norwegian prices. But it was still difficult not to react when the receptionist quoted a price I'd expect to pay for a small house in rural

Scotland. I did wonder if we were actually buying the entire plot of land, rather than just camping on it for a night. And even then it was still an extra £1 for each four minutes of shower. As I am now acutely aware, 4 minutes isn't quite long enough to wash and rinse your hair, but it is just long enough to get it all covered with shampoo.

After arranging a small mortgage in exchange for a night's camping, we headed off to explore the Norwegian wilds. Finding a small hill nearby, we set off enthusiastically – only to discover the Norse weather gods wanted to test my recent repairs to my water-proof trousers. Which failed.

Dripping wet we returned to the campsite to find a full scale row going on between our German camping neighbours and the Germans who had since tried to sneak into our parking space as a way to get better TV reception. Not having a TV we'd been blissfully unaware of parking in the middle of the airwaves – instead our Scottish camping training had led us to park on the highest ground in case of sudden flooding. Given the recent downpour I wasn't keen to lose our Noah's ark, even if you could get Sky Sports there. Our first lesson in continental camping – stay away from high spots unless you've got a big TV aerial and are prepared to spread out your towel over an entire parking spot.

We passed a couple of days in Bergen, admiring the colourful wooden buildings in the harbour of Bryggen, Norway's financial powerhouse during the days when being big in dried fish and shipping gave you economic dominance. The city itself has a colourful past, seeing battles between the English and the Dutch as well as almost instant German occupation during the Second World War. Tragically, in 1944, an accidental explosion on a munitions ship awaiting repair caused major damage to the area around the harbour and significant loss of life. Amongst the continent-wide horror of World War Two this terrible event is usually recorded as little more than a footnote, despite the devastation it caused. Since then, the area has been carefully restored and the decline in fishing activity has been off-set by the arrival of the oil industry, bringing with it much of Norway's current wealth.

Norway is now one of the richest nations on earth and it frequently tops polls for quality of life. Sauntering around Bergen, the people did indeed seem almost smugly content with their lot. We jumped on buses around town and marvelled at the way the dog was allowed entry, although I was slightly less enamoured with the cost of a dog bus ticket. Oscar rose to the occasion though, and spent most of the bus journey entertaining passengers with his version of 'I'm-such-a-cute-dog-and-they're-dragging-me-round-the-country-when-all-I-want-to-do-is-rest-my-head-on-your-knee'. And the naïve Norwegian bus passengers soon believed he was a loving, affectionate dog. They'd stroke his head, then pat him, then open up in conversation and start telling us the stories of their quite contented lives. Of course, those of us who know Oscar well are aware that he has an attention span shorter than a goldfish and will be deeply in love with you one second and then have forgotten your name a few moments later. Which just goes to show, you can snip off his balls, but some element of masculinity will always remain. But it did give us our first indication that Oscar might be going to make a real difference to this trip. In the space of a couple of bus rides we chatted to more people than we'd met on week long holidays. People had quickly opened up and told us of their lives, their loves and their losses – or at least, their dog related ones, anyway.

When Oscar had charmed most of Bergen, and we'd recovered our land-legs, we headed off inland, keen to experience some of Norway's famous countryside. A 45-minute fjord crossing seemed remarkably brief after the recent ferry trips and we quickly found ourselves in a magical campsite above Loftus, looking out across a fjord to the snow covered mountains opposite. Every so often there would be a dramatic rumbling like thunder and I'd glance across the valley to see a plume of snow falling off the hillside and plummeting down towards the water. Our plan was to spend a few days exploring the mountains and fjords around us, admiring the dramatic landscape left by thousands of years of scouring glaciers.

Excited at the prospect of investigating the area, I woke early the next morning to discover the snow slides were no longer visible – along with the mountains, the fjord and even the tree next to the van. All I could make out were the rivulets of water running down the windscreen as a dense cloud of drizzle settled over us.

The rain looked set in for the day, so we resigned ourselves to our first serious test of how we would survive with the three of us cooped up in the van with condensation soaking into every pore. Chris decided it would be a chance to get on with some MSc work, so he pulled his laptop from the safe and settled down with a boring book and an earnest look on his face.

I'd found it harder to think of something 'improving' I could do in the long damp hours in the van. Before we left, my parents had dedicated themselves to the challenge of finding a variety of 'good' books for us to read. I'd given them a list of various books that looked as though they might have a good word-for-weight ratio (font size 10 on toilet paper being my preferred option for maximum entertainment versus minimum space) and they'd scoured the bookshops of the UK. Of course, nowadays you can take a Kindle. But then what do you do if you run out of toilet paper?

They'd also bought me a harmonica. Although my closest experience to harmonica playing was listening to a Bob Dylan CD, my theory was that I could learn a musical instrument and it would take up less space than my toothpaste tube. For someone who grew up playing double bass in local orchestras the idea that a musical instrument could be carried without a requirement for a hernia was still quite a novelty. But I could see that Chris's concentration might not benefit from me struggling through 'Harmonica, Lesson 1'. So instead I rustled round in the 'book bag' and pulled out 'War and Peace'. I dropped it on to the nearest worktop and listened to the satisfyingly loud thump.

I entertained myself with the sound of an intellectual tome

bouncing off the cupboard, but a glance from Chris suggested he was less impressed with my demonstration of academic weightiness. Nothing for it then. With the rain still bucketing down outside, I settled down to 'War and Peace', page 1. As they say, the longest journey starts with a single step.

Chapter 5

Scott of the Hardangervidda

To my surprise 'War and Peace' quickly drew me in and I realised that the Peace sections at least were a kind of Russian 'Pride and Prejudice'. It certainly proved to be value for money – £1 in Oxfam keeping me entertained for several weeks. But after a few hours of the niceties of Russian high society, Oscar made it clear that he wasn't so interested in who Count Whatsit married and that, rain or no rain, it was time for a walk.

After an unsuccessful attempt to force Chris to go, I donned leaking waterproof trousers and a currently not leaking (but give it time) jacket and Oscar and I set off at a slow trudge. The village gradually appeared out of the mist and I headed into the tourist office to assess our options for walking in the Hardangervidda National Park. The response wasn't good.

'The summer bridges haven't been put up in Hardangervidda yet. I'm afraid you must walk either across snow bridges or stop at the first river.'

'Which means what exactly?' I asked, nervously.

'The summer bridges are only put up in the summer.' It was becoming clear they thought I was rather dim, but I persevered.

'But what about the snow bridges, how deep are they?'

'Snow bridges are fine in the middle of winter because the snow is really thick and will take your weight. But now, in late spring, they're not so reliable. Because the snow is starting to melt you can't tell what's solid and what's not and the bridge might give way beneath you and you'll fall into the melt water below.'

'But if it's June now, when does summer start? Do the bridges go in soon?' I asked, trying not to sound accusatory.

'They only go in once most of the snow has melted and the river levels drop back down. It might be a few weeks before they're put up round here'.

So far I felt I wasn't making a whole lot of progress with the Norwegian tourist scene, so I moved on to my search for a Norwegian vet. In order to comply with pet passport regulations that are specific to Norway, Oscar had to be wormed within seven days of arriving in the country and the worming had to be witnessed by a vet. Quite how they were planning to check we'd done this wasn't clear. Would the immigration authorities start chasing us after seven days and force feed him worm tablets, or would we, and any worms Oscar might have, be deported on the worm refugee boat?

It wasn't something I planned to check. After all the hassle to get Oscar here, I had no intentions of being shipped home for the lack of two small tablets. The polite young man in the tourist office, already convinced I was fairly stupid, found me a vet and booked us in for an afternoon appointment.

Oscar and I trudged back in the continuing rain and informed Chris of the impending visit. A few hours later we all headed off in the slightly lighter rain and searched for the vet's house – supposedly an un-missable red building. On our third trip along the road we finally spotted it and a few minutes later the vet arrived, looking appropriately Scandinavian (you know, big, tall, blond, muscular – yeah, it was tough) and complete with a 4 wheel drive that had spent considerably more time off road than your average Chelsea tractor.

We chatted briefly, then ceremoniously handed Oscar his worming tablets (hidden inside large blocks of Cheddar) whilst the vet stamped and initialled the passport, agreeing with our lack of enthusiasm for this whole procedure.

'It is all pointless filling of forms. But I prefer the forms to working with the owners of animals. They are much more difficult.'

Are we really that bad? Would Heather, our vet, agree with him? Am I just like a parent at the school open evening, demanding that my little darling be given full attention, and preferably top marks.

46

Deciding it was best not to check, I moved onto the less controversial topic of the weather and the lack of summer bridges.

'It's the oldest spring anyone can remember and the sheep can't travel to their summer food because there's still too many snow to be cleared,' he explained, somewhat despondently.

'When do you think the snow will clear?' Chris asked.

'Who knows? Maybe middle July?'

This wasn't looking great, but my annoyance at the refusal of the Norwegian weather to play ball was being replaced by a growing sense of fear as I faced our next dilemma – how much does a Norwegian vet cost? I considered the need for a bank loan when we visit the vet in Scotland, multiplied by the inflated prices that go with the pet passport scheme and the fact that we could barely afford a bus ticket for the dog in Norway. Sweat began to collect on my palms.

When we could string out the weather conversation no longer Chris finally asked, in a slightly high pitched voice:

' So. How much do we….owe…..you?'

The vet looked at us and smiled.

'You have signalised to me that you do not bring much money and it was your own cheese, so there is no charge.'

And with smiles all round we headed off, rejoicing in the discovery that even though you have to pay for toilets, showers and dogs on buses in Norway, there are still a few things left that are free.

By the time we got back to the campsite the weather had changed completely and the sky was an eye-wateringly bright blue with not a cloud in sight. But by then it was 6 o'clock in the evening and I assumed our hill walking plans would have to wait for the morning. Then, just as we settled down for another night of pasta and tomato sauce, Chris was hit by a brainwave.

'It won't get dark, so why don't we walk up now?'

'But what if we get lost?'

'Well, does it matter? We can wander round all night if necessary – it won't get that cold and there'll be enough light to see the paths.'

Somehow part of me found it hard to get away from the British walking mentality of 'always be down by nightfall'. But maybe the rules change when there's no nightfall. Looking at the guidebook there was a walk up to the nearest mountain top which would only take a few hours and would give us a height gain of about 800 metres. The sky was clear, we'd get fantastic views and we could take a camping meal and the stove and have supper on the summit. Even if we didn't make it back down till three in the morning it would still be light and we could, due to being drop-outs, lie in for the morning because we had no jobs.

In a flash we grabbed packs and dehydrated food and hit the road. As we marched out with walking poles and rucksacks the campsite owner looked at us in surprise. But when I explained our theory, he nodded thoughtfully.

'Yes, you're right. It will be light all night. In Norway, when the weather is like this, we say we will sleep in winter. Enjoy your walk.'

And a few hours later we were rewarded by fantastic clear views across fjords and mountains. The air seemed to have been washed clean by the heavy rain and the patches of snow around us sparkled like jewels. We settled down to a plate of luke-warm chilli, which, in the way of all camping foods, would have tasted disgusting in the house, but in the great outdoors, with the sweat drying on my back, couldn't have tasted better.

What was even better was the feeling that it didn't matter how long we stayed up there. We could sit there all night if we wanted (although I'd probably have needed more chilli for that) and watch the dusk turn to dawn with nothing in-between. And then we could sleep all the next day without having to worry about going to work, or doing all the stuff that has to be done at weekends so you can survive the next week's work. I was beginning to get a sneaking suspicion that the life of a drop-out might suit me rather well.

~

Filled with enthusiasm from our first foray into the Norwegian wilderness, we headed further east into Hardangervidda national park. Described in the guidebooks as Northern Europe's largest mountain plateau we were expecting an empty flat top of rock and shrubs, perhaps looking a bit like the Cairngorm Mountains of our home. What we got looked closer to the South Pole in winter.

The summer bridge versus snow bridge debate was still worrying me, so we checked with other tourist offices as we travelled along the road to Hardangervidda. The general view seemed to be that the summer bridges, which get washed away every winter, wouldn't be put back in place until July by which time we hoped to be much further north. Some of the streams could probably still be crossed by snow bridges, but each crossing would be a risk as the snow continued to melt.

Based on this depressing prognosis we figured we could head into the park with a tent, camp near the edge and manage a few short day walks, even though we wouldn't be able to get close to the centre. So, with fully laden packs, we headed into the Hardangervidda. Even Oscar took his fair share with his own small doggy rucsac filled with several days of food and folding dog bowls. He spent the first few minutes having a tantrum about the mundanity of this (after all, why have a pet human and then carry stuff yourself?) but eventually the excitement of the surrounding patches of snow got the better of him and he headed off to be manic in snow drifts.

The access route to the park was on a small rocky ledge on the side of the reservoir and wasn't overly exciting – in fact after several hours of trudging we had to resort to playing 'I went to Norway and I didn't buy....', running through the alphabet reminding ourselves of all those small luxuries we could no longer afford. But after lollipops, mangoes and nut and fruit chocolate, we arrived at our first Norway mountain hut just inside the park boundary.

The Norwegian hiking organisation, Den Norske Turistforening or the DNT, run a network of huts in the wilderness areas of

Norway. Facilities vary between the huts but in general they have a sleeping area, cooking area and some form of pit toilet. There is also a supply of food in most huts, which is left for hikers and can be used on an honesty basis, with visitors putting money in a box for the value of the pasta, rice, hot chocolate or whatever they've taken. Once you become a member of the DNT you get a key to all the huts and you then pay for your night's accommodation at the hut – leaving your money in the same box.

Campers can camp outside the huts and use the toilets for a reduced fee, helping to lower the potential human pollution load on otherwise pristine wilderness areas. As we'd yet to join the DNT, we couldn't get into the main hut, but we went for the toilet only option and pitched our tent nearby. The smaller hut was open and we went in for a quick nose around – discovering that not only did you pay for your accommodation by honesty box, you could even leave your credit card number in the box to be billed later.

The only downside of the Norwegian huts is that dogs can't go in, so Oscar was left on the porch whilst we explored. In some of the bigger huts they have a 'hund' room where dogs can be left, but I could see a full scale Oscar tantrum coming on if we tried that, almost certainly resulting in us being run out of the hut. Instead we'd decided that whilst in Norway we'd take the tent for us all to sleep in, but use hut toilets and kitchens wherever possible. Our backpacking tent is so small we have to sleep head to toe and then Oscar curls up in the porch. By the morning he has usually pushed the inner tent door back as far as possible so he is lying in comfort and Chris and I are squashed up against the back wall. It's a dog's life you know.

After a pleasant night camped by the hut I awoke in our usual squished huddle and heard that all too depressing sound of rain on the tent roof. Looking out all I could see was white – cloud and rain swirling round the tent in equal measure. After procrastinating for as long as possible the decision was made that we'd bite the bullet and head off anyway.

I soon began to feel like an extra in Scott of the Antarctic. The lumpy ground of the plateau was completely covered in snow, which was joining up with the white of the swirling cloud to make one giant morass of white. I was startlingly disorientated by the removal of all points of visual reference. For several minutes, I stood still, slightly dazed as I blinked continually. Were my eyes open or shut? I wasn't sure I could tell any more. When my eyes were open there were no edges or solid shapes to prove that I was still looking out. There was just wall to wall white, as if my eyes were closed. Occasionally I could just make out Chris' figure ahead of me, looking for all the world as if he might at any moment tell me he was going out for a walk and could be some time…

With the polar conditions it was a strange and brutal experience and we slowly fought our way towards the central area of the park. At times the cloud would lift and I'd get brief views of lakes and small hummocks around us, all softened by the covering of snow. We probably crossed several snow bridges, but the snow was so deep there was no way to know what was beneath us. Nothing seemed to be giving way, so we continued until we reached a lake and a couple of old buildings, half buried by snow. As I slumped to the ground in the small lee of a doorway, Chris pulled out our chocolate supplies. Nibbling on the half frozen bar I gazed around me at the harsh landscape.

'According to the stuff at the tourist office, some of the Norwegian resistance people had to survive up here during the war. Can you imagine? It's tough enough in full waterproofs with bucket loads of chocolate. I don't think I could cope up here for weeks on end.'

Chris' hood nodded. 'It's bizarre though isn't it? Somewhere as remote and rugged as this. I mean, you don't expect it to have been involved in a human war. It feels like it should be above it all, somehow. You wonder if there's anywhere left that's untouched.'

'I guess that's Europe for you though. So many people, so many wars, not that much space. It's a wonder we haven't all killed each

51

other off by now.'

And it did seem amazing that somewhere so remote and wild could have been involved in a world war. German forces had used a site near Hardangarvidda for the creation of 'heavy water', one of the steps along the road to the construction of an atom bomb. Allied Forces and the Norwegian resistance had skied from the snow covered centre of the plateau to the plant, where they'd undertaken a daring sabotage raid and set back Hitler's nuclear dreams.

After only a few days away from home I was becoming more aware of the complexity of Europe's history, which seemed like it touched every inch of the continent. It was also making me re-consider some of my views on the European Union, perhaps ironically in one of the few countries that refuses to join. Many of my frustrations at work had come from the arrogance and intransigence of the European Commission. I'd frequently wondered if there were any positives to this archaic organisation. But already, both here and in Scalloway and Bergen, I'd seen the tragic human impact of war between European countries. No matter what our differences were and no matter how difficult a system it was to manage, surely a set-up that brought unity between countries had to be better than the potentially catastrophic alternative.

After a brief respite for lunch and my Europhile musings, we consulted the map and realised we'd covered only 5 kilometres, despite walking for several hours. The floundering in the snow was slowing us down so much that we were unlikely to reach any more landmarks in the afternoon, so we accepted defeat graciously and floundered back to the tent. Altitude-wise, the tent was only a couple of hundred metres lower, but returning was like entering a different country as the snow gave way again to green grass and the wind and swirling cloud calmed down to a gentle fog. We collapsed by the tent for a while and then headed to the nearby river to fill up on water.

But filling bottles and cups with water is a tricky business if you're next to a raging Norwegian torrent. Leaning out from the bank, I temporarily lost concentration and inadvertently sent a plastic mug down the river. In the two seconds it took me to realise what I'd done and try and rescue it, it was too late and the mug was soon being swept down the river and out towards the North Sea, never to be seen again.

Chris rolled his eyes.

'Looks like we'll be sharing a cup of tea in the morning then.'

Chapter 6

The Trollheimen trauma

Before we'd left home, people were constantly asking if I was worried about our step into the unknown. Was I scared about the van breaking down, or, possibly just as likely, our marriage breaking down? But in truth most of these things only caused a minor blip on my radar of worry – somewhat naively, as it turned out. But what really frightened me before we left home was the idea that Oscar would contract some terrible illness, or be beaten up by a big rabid dog or go into terminal decline due to lack of routine. He'd not been given a choice in this whole venture, but had instead been dragged along because it was what we wanted to do.

Oscar was the grand old age of 3 when we set off on our voyage and the idea that our selfish plans might result in him failing to reach the senior dog food stage filled me with panic. This wasn't helped by all the doom and gloom when we explained that he was travelling too. After the first few days in Norway I realised that the country wasn't brimming over with rabid dogs waiting to attack and that Oscar was fine. And, of course, as soon as I began to relax we hit the first of our serious dog disasters – and broke his wag.

It started harmlessly enough. An old school friend, Eli, had decided to join us for a couple of weeks in Norway. Blond and sporty, she could blend in easily with the toughest of the locals, so we headed to the Trollheimen national park, where we were reliably informed there would be less snow and more hiking. Trollheimen is full of large mountains – including some over 5000 feet – but being slightly further north, seemed to get less of a pounding from the damp stuff. On arrival, we picked out a three day walking route through the park, with a hard first day, a marginally easier second day and a cushy third day of only six miles.

Setting off, we soon found the first day to be as hard as we'd expected – 16 miles across several significant hills, with deep snow much of the way and the odd crevasse to jump just to keep us on our toes. We perfected a style of walking whereby Eli and I followed Chris as much as possible so we could use his footsteps to help get through the deep snow – hoping he wouldn't notice that we were suddenly interested in being just behind him. Oscar loved the entire day's walk – he spent the whole time dancing around, rolling back and forth and jumping into snowdrifts. Every time we hit a serious downhill bit he would either roll his way down or take a flying leap, land on his belly and see how far he could slide, toboggan style. Whereas I teetered down clutching my walking poles, whimpering gently. I blamed my fear on my knowledge of just how much the subsequent physiotherapy might cost after a short tumble, whilst Oscar danced around in happy ignorance of the potential cost of doggy physio.

We arrived at the first night's hut desperate for food and rest. Cruelly I could just see the hut, but the bridge over the adjacent river had been washed out, forcing us to search for a crossing point and eventually jump from rock to rock in an ever more desperate attempt to reach a cup of tea and half a pound of chocolate. By the time we finally arrived at the hut, I felt like a washed out, dishevelled heap. But rather than being met by the muscular, check-shirted warden of my expectations, a grey haired, fully skirted matron from The Sound of Music tottered out towards us.

'Blimey,' Eli muttered under her breath, 'we're a bit under-dressed for this place.'

'Good evening. How may we help you?' trilled the Mother Abbess.

'She needs a bed in the hut and we need somewhere to pitch our tent. If possible, please,' I added as the Mother Abbess stared me down.

'That's not possible I'm afraid. You haven't booked. You will have to leave.' So far this wasn't looking hopeful for a late evening sing-song. Which was a shame, because my Edelweiss is hard to beat.

'Umm.. are you sure?' Chris asked. 'We've come quite a long way today.'

'Absolutely not. There is room only for...' But just as she began to tell us to sing for our supper, Oscar slunk out from behind the pile of backpacks. He gazed up at the Mother Abbess, then lay down beside her, flopping onto his side with a look of exhaustion. And the Mother Abbess became putty in his paws.

'Well, maybe, we can squeeze you in. But you can't camp near the hut. You must use the second site, on the island in the river. Come in now and I'll show you a bed for Miss.....'

'Williams,' Eli filled in quickly, glancing back at me in surprise as we all trooped in, leaving Oscar crashed out on the porch.

Slowly the Mother Abbess warmed up, until we'd just about got her to the stage where I was brave enough to mention the blisters that were appearing on my heels. And in no time at all she'd raided the hut shop, found some expensive blister plasters, charged us a special 'discount' price for them and then thrown in two free packets of Chocolate Hob-Nobs as well. In Norwegian price terms, and given that those biscuits had been helicoptered into the hut, it was probably the equivalent of someone laying on a full three course meal in a flash restaurant. Maybe she actually was a nun. By the time I'd wolfed down the first packet of biscuits, I was wondering if we could get her deified.

After cooking our dehydrated supper in the hut (our budget wouldn't stretch to Mother Abbess' wholesome menu), Chris and I moved out to our island campsite. Eli came with us and once we reached the tent, she collected up our boots and took them back to the hut so they could be left in the drying room overnight. After a few minutes in the tent, Chris suddenly looked out.

'Where's Oscar?' he asked, sharply. 'Have you seen him recently?'

'No, not since we got back here. He was behind us when we crossed onto the island. Oscar, Oscar!' The usual whistles and shouts followed, but drew no response and, with a fast flowing river on either side of us, genuine panic began to set in.

'Shit, where is he? Do you think he's gone in the river? Why weren't you keeping an eye on him?' I snapped at Chris.

'Why weren't *you* keeping an eye on him? I'll go down the other end, see if he's there.'

'Ouch!' I exclaimed, as another stick stabbed into my foot. Left with no shoes we were scampering around in socks, swearing as every pebble and stick cut the soles of our feet in the desperate search for Oscar.

After what seemed like endless terrible minutes, I suddenly heard shouts in the distance.

'Tamsin, Tamsin, it's OK, he's here.' Eli yelled, and a few moments later, she appeared on the far bank of the river, complete with Oscar. 'He turned up at the hut, just as I was going in. I figured you'd be panicking, what with the river and everything. Here you go.'

Oscar was duly passed across by the scruff of his neck, and I launched into a tirade of parental bollocking, threatening the removal of all Bonio privileges. Oscar stood stock still in front of me, tail dangling between his legs as he gazed back at me. Then, as I paused to draw breath, he let out a deep, echoing belch. Chris looked at me and shrugged.

'Next time, we may as well bring kids instead. We've already got a teenager.'

I nodded. 'You're right. I think that was the doggy version of 'Whatever'.

The following morning Saint Mother Abbess told us of the year of the high flood, when campers had to be taken off the island by helicopter. But by then I'd had a good night's sleep, untroubled by the thought of floods and wash outs. It did make me look at the river with renewed respect, but as the map for our second day's walk seemed to have no significant watercourses marked on it, I quickly forgot about the risks of the Norwegian torrent.

Sitting by the hut, happily munching my breakfast, I watched as the various residents prepared for the day ahead. After a few minutes I was joined by a forty-something woman and her two teenage daughters. We chatted politely about the weather forecast, whilst she whipped out a complicated petrol furnace thing, set it up in a matter of seconds and began to make porridge. With the other hand, as a cloud of flies gathered around us, she pulled together a heap of damp twigs and lit a smouldering fire with a single click of her lighter. And in between, she supervised the strapping of the younger daughter's ankle and the packing of all three rucksacks. I was beginning to be seriously impressed and asked where they were heading.

'Well,' explained super woman, 'we're spending three weeks walking in the park, covering all the main mountains. We've just been camping wild for the last seven days, but the girls were keen for a shower, so I thought we'd stay in the hut for one night. I prefer to stay out on the mountains, but I don't want to put them off by making it too hard for them, so I agreed we'd come here. We'll probably camp for the rest of the trip.'

Now I was impressed. Seven days of food for three people was a lot to carry, and a long time to survive as a family in the wilds without having a row. My sister and I can barely manage ten minutes in a town centre before we descend into bickering.

'Don't you argue? I mean, just the three of you, without seeing other people?' I blurted out. The woman thought for a moment.

'No, not really. We have all that we need with us and if we get bored then we just talk or play games or sing together.'

So here were the Von Trapp family, to complete the Sound of Music line-up. What did that make me? Maria? Hardly. I felt seriously out classed by this incredibly competent woman with her smiling, happy children. All I'd managed so far was some blisters and a dog with teenage angst.

To add to my feelings of inadequacy, within a few minutes of leaving the hut I discovered that the map had lied. The second day's walk was more like a paddle, with hundreds of melt water streams to cross. Some of these I managed to jump, but not always successfully, so by lunchtime I had one bootful of water to demonstrate my abject failure to jump quite far enough. By mid afternoon the streams got too wide to jump and we'd reached the stage of wading across. The first few steps would seem fine, then gradually the cold would start to bite and eventually the intense pain would be all consuming and I'd hop and jump around on the other side cursing and whimpering, emptying the ice-cold water from my boots as quickly as possible. I gave yet another offering to the river gods by losing concentration again and letting my walking pole be whipped away on the torrent – presumably to join the plastic mug. Somewhere on the Norwegian coast there must be an assortment of washed away camping gear – probably enough to start a slightly damp outdoor shop.

To my relief, the next hut wasn't full of the cast of any stage musicals, but was completely empty. We occupied it in solitary splendour, spreading damp clothes and boots from wall to wall. The following day, quite convinced we had just six flat easy miles left to cover, we loitered by the hut, generally taking it easy. We knew that a ferry service came along the lake once a day, so we planned to be away just before the boat docked and disgorged a load of tourists. Shortly before lunchtime we left our picture-postcard hut and headed on our way, our minds cheered by the appearance of boardwalk placed across the damp bits of track. Excited that this might mean a day without wet boots we skipped along the boardwalk, chatting merrily.

The first indication that all might not be quite as idyllic as we first thought came when the board walk suddenly stopped. We were unexpectedly plunged into wet bog and our pace slowed dramatically once we were off the dry boards and into boot sucking, squelching mud. A few minutes later we came to a stream – not huge, but certainly big enough to warrant a bridge on most footpaths, even in Scotland. The total absence of a bridge brought to mind those summer bridge conversations, and the volume of water implied that, as the vet had suggested, the snow on the higher ground was just getting going with its spring melt.

By balancing and hopping carefully from rock to rock we managed to cross the stream, but our two hour stroll was starting to look slightly harder than we'd expected. Just a few moments later we rounded a corner to meet an almighty torrent of water, rushing down the hillside and plunging noisily into the lake. Trying not to make eye contact with each other, we searched up and down the river for a bridge.

'Well if someone's gone to the bother of putting in boardwalks earlier, they'll certainly have added in a bridge for this lot. It'll be round here somewhere,' I said, more confidently than I felt.

After a few minutes of fruitless searching we moved out of the denial stage and into the anger stage.

'Come on, there's got to be a way of crossing somewhere!' Chris exclaimed.

'We could walk back to the hut and maybe catch the ferry out instead?' I suggested.

'We'd never get back there in time. The ferry went past ages ago. It's supposed to leave again in ten minutes and it's taken us the best part of 40 minutes to get here.' Reality was starting to bite. 'And if we try and make it and miss it, we'll have to walk all the way back here and do this crossing all over again.'

Faced with such a dire emergency we acted like the mature adults we were and sat down to make a significant impact on our remaining packet of Sound of Music biscuits – hoping that the extra calories would fill us with inspiration.

Chris, as the tallest and most well balanced (I mean that purely in the physical sense), eventually decided to attempt a tester crossing. After wading part way out the water was soon starting to gurgle around the bottom of his shorts. If he wanted to get any further he was either going to have to do the rest of the walk in drenched shorts, or strip off and go for an underwear only crossing. It's one thing to strip down to your slightly sweaty pants in front of your wife, but it's quite another to have to do it in front of her best friend. A moment of panic flashed across Chris's face.

'Bollocks' he suddenly blurted out, 'I would have to be wearing my grey trolleys!'.

His description wasn't far from the truth, and it certainly wasn't the kind of underwear that would be causing Calvin Klein any worries. Eli and I laughed unkindly for a while, before realising that if he needed to strip, we would as well. Not so bad for me, but not great for Eli, who is quite a private person at the best of times. Having been the bridesmaid at our wedding I could see she was thinking of the kind of headlines normally generated by a husband, wife and bridesmaid all running round the countryside in their underwear.

After stripping off ready for a crossing, the next test was to see if Chris could actually make it across. The water was flowing so fast it was hard to stand up against its force, so he used a combination of poles and extendible dog lead to get across. When he finally made it to the other side the air was full of our cheers and his swearing as he waited for the agonising cold pain to ease off. He then tied the dog lead to a tree on the other side, to give us the equivalent of a rope to hold as we struggled across.

'OK, that's me across,' Chris chirped, smugly. 'Now you two just have to get over.'

'Whoa, whoa, not so fast, saggy knicker boy,' I yelled. 'Aren't you forgetting something – what about the rucksacks?' A reproachful silence followed. 'I don't think there's any way I can manage to balance across with a pack on my back and still have any hope of standing up. The water's too strong.' I was beginning to despair. 'What about you, Eli?'

'I'm not sure. I'll have a go. What is it you're supposed to do?'

'Only put the pack on one shoulder, then if you get swept away you can get your arm out and you won't be dragged under by its weight,' I parroted the Lonely Planet's 'Walking in Norway' section.

'Great' Eli said, hoisting her rather large rucksack on to her shoulder, 'thanks for that cheering thought. OK. Here goes. Pull the lead as tight as you can.'

'Ow, ow, ow, fuck, fuck, fuck, it's cold,' she spluttered as her feet touched the water. A few seconds later she was floundering around and beginning to lose her balance.

'Come back here if you're slipping,' I yelled, leaning over the edge of the water as far as I could to drag her back to shore. As she danced around on the bank, waiting for her feet to regain some colour, Chris and I looked at each other across the raging torrent.

'OK, if you hold the lead taut, I'll come back and take the packs across,' Chris announced, swallowing hard. I opened my mouth to ask if he was sure, but decided against it – if he wasn't sure, we didn't have a whole lot of other options. Bravely, and perhaps surprisingly given our underwear jokes, Chris ploughed back to our side of the torrent, heaved a pack onto one shoulder and floundered back to the far side. A few minutes later, he returned and started across with the second pack, whilst Eli and I hauled on the dog lead to give him a hand hold. I glanced at Eli, and once Chris was safely on the far side, muttered to her:

'We're being a bit girly about this, you know. I mean, making the guy do all the carrying across and stuff.'

'Yeah, we are.' Eli looked me straight in the eyes. 'But you know, I'm OK with that. I know you were impressed with the super woman yesterday, but frankly, you couldn't manage to even get on the gymnastics beam at school, let alone balance on it. You'll just have to accept that your talents lie in other areas and that your balance is, well, shit. And I'll just have to accept that I'm not quite the tough I-can-do-it-all-myself single woman I thought I was. It's not very girl power, but there's not much we can do about it right now.'

And to be honest, she had a point – we were in a place where discretion and valour could go and have a bun fight for all I cared.

With the packs safely portered across by our knight in not very shining underwear, I was next to face the music and take the plunge. Stepping in was by far the worst bit, as the freezing cold water sloshed around my inner thighs. Once I started stumbling across, the fear of being swept away took over and I forgot about the numbness in my legs. As I hauled myself out the other side, the agonizing cold aches took over, but by then I was just glad to be on dry land. I had a brief moment of believing we might make it back to the van in one piece. But the moment was short-lived, as I looked across and saw Oscar, still standing on the far bank. We hadn't considered how we would get him over – although he can swim, the water was far too strong for him and he would soon be swept away. None of us had the balance to be able to get across without holding onto something, and it's not possible to carry 25 kilos of dog with only one hand.

Eli was first with a bright idea.

'Why don't we empty out a rucksack and carry him across that way?'

'Oh great, so I get to carry a bag back across, fill it with a squirming dog and then try and balance back, while he kicks me off my feet. Sounds fun. Any other ideas?' Chris asked.

'Are we sure he can't swim across?' I suggested, hopefully.

'No way, he won't cope with the pull of the water in the middle and he'll hit the rocks.'

'And there's no way you can carry him?' I asked.

'I don't think so. I might be able to get him to swim half way and then drag him across the fast bit by his harness?' Fortunately Oscar's always worn a harness rather than just a collar – I hate walking dogs that are pulling and choking on their collars, so the harness lets us stop him pulling without choking him to death. And, as it turned out, gave us something to hold without strangling him whilst he swam against the flow.

It all sounded fine in theory, but Oscar was yet to be convinced. Chris spent some time paddling on the edge, trying to persuade Oscar it was just a quick swim and he'd hardly notice it, but he

64

simply wasn't up for it and kept retreating to the bank. After we'd all hung around in our knickers for far too long, Chris lost patience, picked Oscar up, carried him as far as he could and then plonked him in the water, grabbed his harness and yanked him across. Poor Oscar's face will stay in my memory for a long time – the look of incredulity that the humans whom he thought he had so firmly under control would dare to drop him into the middle of a raging torrent. Once he realised that we really were rebelling this badly and that he was going to have to swim he started kicking like mad, but only made very slow progress across the torrent. There were a few terrible moments when I thought he was going to be swept away, before the pair of them finally made it to the other side. Oscar leapt out in an indignant huff and proceeded to shake very, very cold water over me. Then he went and sat in a sulk on a nearby rock, and refused to speak, or look, at anyone. I don't think we'd ever been so deeply in disgrace, and that includes the times we'd stopped him in mid hump of an attractive looking lady-dog.

The final one to cross was Eli – who was persuaded to plough in more quickly than expected when some other walkers turned up and joined the crossing queue. Eli had been standing around in her knickers for quite long enough by then, and the thought of trying to chat to some complete strangers whilst she worried about how recently she'd done her bikini line was clearly too much. She'd ploughed in, floundered and come out the other side before the surprised walkers had an opportunity to figure out what was going on. Once they realised that everything we were doing, they would have to repeat, they became noticeably less chirpy.

When we were all safely on the other side we re-grouped with some extra chocolate rations, re-dressed and started off again, hoping there were no more hidden rivers. It was only then that we noticed something different about Oscar. He normally walks with his tail in the air, wagging it gently as he investigates new smells. But now he was walking with his tail firmly between his legs and without a hint of a wag. Thinking he was still in a grump about our appalling behaviour we spent a while patting him and feeding him the remains of our food. But no matter what we did, he couldn't be persuaded to wag his tail. Some careful investigations showed that it could still be moved, so probably wasn't broken, but there was no way he was wagging for love, money or even that nice looking Labrador bitch down the road. Our best guess was that he'd hit it on a rock during the crossing and it was badly bruised. I felt terrible that we'd managed to break his wag – and after only a few weeks away. What other horrors would this madcap journey involve if Norway, supposedly the safest and easiest country we would be visiting, had managed to remove his wag? This really shouldn't happen to a dog.

It was a somewhat subdued party that made its slow, still slightly damp way back to the van. I had enormous blisters on my heels from walking with wet socks, Chris had strangely mottled feet from all the cold water and Oscar had no wag. Only Eli seemed to have survived the journey relatively unscathed. And even she was starting to refer to the whole escapade as the 'Trollheimen trauma'.

Once we'd recovered slightly, we drove the van to the nearest town and found a pizza shop where Eli got out her Visa card and asked, in a clearly not-to-be-messed with tone:

'What's the biggest one you do? Give me three.'

After gorging ourselves on finest pepperoni and mushroom, we spent the rest of the evening trying to cheer up Oscar, and were eventually rewarded with a tiny little mini wag. But it was to be a full week before his wag returned to normal and it will probably be a lifetime before he forgives us for dragging him through the Trollheimen trauma.

Chapter 7

Are there toilets in Hell?

Our recovery from the Trollheimen trauma was helped by the fact that we needed to spend a couple of days on the road, eating up miles so that Eli could catch her return flight from Narvik, about half way up Norway. In order to keep our sanity whilst we plodded northwards, we stopped for a couple of tacky tourist sights. One of these was never designed to be a tourist sight, but provided entertainment to speakers of the English language – a town named Hell. There wasn't a whole lot in Hell as it turned out, but we amused ourselves with pictures beneath the railway station sign – extra pictures for Oscar who is often referred to as H from H – Hound from Hell. Showing a surprising sense of irony, beneath the main sign for Hell the railway company had also painted the words Gods Expedition. As it turned out, this wasn't an oblique religious reference but just the old Norwegian word for cargo handling, although it still kept us entertained. Of course, it would've been more fun if it had been frozen over, but you can't have everything. As we prepared to hit the road again, I glanced around us.

'Is anyone else finding this morning's coffee is starting to press? Are there toilets in Hell do you think?'

'I'm not sure, Tamsin. Maybe not. Maybe it's deliberately set up to be like that. You know, no toilets anywhere in the town so heathens get an idea of what they might be facing,' Eli suggested, not altogether helpfully. 'Or maybe there are some, but they can only be used by those who are going to heaven. In which case, you are, unquestionably, stuffed.'

'Ha, ha. Very funny. So it's divine intervention – wandering round with an uncomfortably full bladder is supposed to be some sort of a terrible warning to me that I should mend my ways or face purgatory without a pee.'

As it turned out, Hell wasn't blessed with toilets so I spent the remainder of that day wondering if this really was God's way of telling me to drink less. Weak bladders, be warned.

Our other significant tourist stop was at the Arctic Circle. Whilst this was a particularly tacky stop, with lots of large American tourists and overpriced postcards and not a whole lot else to see, it was a significant milestone for the Fuckit Bucket. This was the van that couldn't even make it to Stranraer, and yet had managed to drag itself as far as the 66 degrees mark. That's a long way for a heap of crap! Despite the postcard prices, we felt obliged to send cards to the various doubting Thomases who had been expecting to see us broken down on the road to Aberdeen harbour. That's not to say all was exactly well with the van. It seemed to be putting out black smoke at regular intervals – particularly when the engine first started – sometimes enough to stop you seeing the car behind. It also seemed to be developing significant oil leaks and we had to be more careful where we parked it – setting it up for a quick exit before the locals noticed the oil spill that had just been deposited in their town. For two people who used to work in the environment sector it was hardly ideal, but we also knew that a Norwegian garage would wipe out our savings. So for the time being, we tried to ignore it and naively hoped it might miraculously fix itself, rather than die completely in an inconvenient location. Like Latvia.

Another of the van's recurring problems was having the internal heating permanently stuck in the on position. This meant that whatever the outside temperature, hot air was always being blown into the cab whilst we were driving. This hadn't been a problem in Scotland, for obvious reasons, but as the Norwegian summer temperatures began to rise, and with three of us in the van, plus un-wagging dog, it began to get a little sticky. Cue Chris spending a morning under the van, trying to change the heater valve – he'd bought a spare one before leaving the UK, but hadn't had time to install it. A kindly Norwegian garage let him park the van on the forecourt and use their tools, without charging us, and, although there was a lot of swearing whilst the actual changeover was going on, the difference in comfort levels was immense. Suddenly we didn't have to drive with all the windows wide open and the dog hanging his head out, desperately panting.

But the van was at least getting us places and we slowly wove up the skinny bit of Norway, until we got to Bodo where we could take a boat across to the Lofoten Islands. By this time the temperature had risen dramatically, and despite our location inside the Arctic Circle, Norway was in the grip of a heat wave with daily temperatures in the high 20s. This was to be the start of our exceptional weather luck, and as the sun blazed down on us, Northern Norway couldn't have looked more scenic.

The Lofoten Islands are quite staggeringly beautiful – steep-sided, dramatic peaks poking up from the water, with beautiful small villages nestling on the shores, all stunningly reflected in the smooth water of the inlets and bays. We wandered around the islands, admiring the mountains, trying to avoid the sheds full of drying cod (which smelt remarkably similar to dog's breath to me) and stayed up every night to watch the midnight sun. Each night we would go to bed in the full sunlight, closing the van curtains against the bright light, and realising that our bodyclocks were getting gradually more confused. Wandering round in the evening I would think it was about seven o'clock, only to look at my watch and discover it was closer to midnight. When I began to think about going to bed, expecting it to be about eleven, it was usually closer to three in the morning, and the following day I wouldn't wake until nearly noon. It was like being a student all over again, although we hadn't packed enough baked beans to really relive the whole university experience.

Whether it was the fine weather affecting them or whether they are always like that, I don't know, but the Norwegians we met were all kind and friendly, in a very under-stated way. There was no rush of enthusiasm when you first spoke with them, nor would they come up and offer help in an in-your-face kind of way. But once asked they would do everything they could to assist you, without making you feel uncomfortable or obliged. By the time we'd spent a few weeks there, I was beginning to wonder if I could take Norwegian classes when we got back, and live out the rest of my days in a small village somewhere by a glistening fjord. But I suppose the price of alcohol, and the need for it in the dark days of winter, might be more of a problem than it seemed when watching the midnight sun with a glass of smuggled wine.

The only cloud in our Norwegian sky was the depressing news from back home – after our initial whole van cheer for the success of the London Olympic bid, we were soon brought back to earth with a bump by the London bombings. Reception on World Service wasn't great, so we struggled to find out what was going on, but would occasionally manage to read the online news in an internet cafe, or see the front covers of British newspapers in more touristy places. The subsection of newspapers available was reasonably right-wing and the views expressed seemed to move closer and closer to outright racism. With each depressing headline I felt further removed from the UK, and buried my head deeper in the Norwegian sand.

After a few weeks on the islands, and after sending Eli back to the depressing reality of the UK, we decided we really had to move on. We were in danger of spending all our money and time in Norway and never making it as far as Finland, let alone the rest of Europe. So we headed back to the Norwegian mainland and into the northern city of Tromso.

For me Tromso displayed all the attributes that make Norwegian towns such nice places. The campsite was on the edge of town but with reasonable public transport links into the centre. On the opposite side of the campsite were the cross country ski trails for the town. Some of these were floodlit so you could ski in the winter evenings, but in the summer they made a fantastic network of trails for walking and running. When we'd arrived at the campsite, I'd run through my usual list of questions about the important things in life:

'Is there somewhere nearby where I can take my dog for a run?'

'Yes of course,' replied the dazzlingly blonde receptionist, 'you can take him on the ski trail by the campsite. Just cross the little bridge by the laundry room.'

'I was planning to take him for quite a long run though, 50 minutes or so. How long is the path?' I asked, based on my experience with British campsites, where they often think a dog walk means 200 yards from the van. The receptionist looked at me blankly.

'You can go for as long as you want.'

'Yes, but how long is the actual path?' I tried to clarify.

'It's as long as you want. Don't worry, your dog will be tired.'

I put this enigmatic answer down to linguistic confusion, but shortly after leaving the campsite I came across a map of the trails, showing something close to 30 miles of routes laid out all around the valley. Even Oscar was going to be tired after running round that lot.

Tromso also has its very own Arctic cathedral, built in a modern style with dramatic triangle sections and narrow slats of windows snaking down each side of the triangles. On summer nights they have a midnight sun concert and so at 11pm I headed out from the campsite and walked down to the cathedral through a nearby residential area. It looked like midday in any suburban district – full daylight illuminating the people who were out watering their gardens, washing their cars and generally pottering as if it was a Sunday afternoon. When I reached the cathedral there were only about 50 people there, but the music was utterly spellbinding. A single saxophone played for much of the time and the smooth, chocolatey music melded perfectly with the sun streaming in through the windows and casting a golden glow over the proceed-ings. I defy anyone to sit through that and not have every hair on the back of their neck standing to attention.

I would have been happy to settle in Tromso and never leave, but the price of the campsite meant that sooner or later we had to move on and look for cheaper towns. But we still weren't quite ready to face up to leaving Norway, so we took in a brief sojourn to the Lyngen alps, aiming for a two day walk across the mountains and then hitching back to the van. But this time, we'd learnt at least something from the Trollheimen trauma. I wasn't the super woman who could hike for days, complete with picture perfect children. But I did manage to remember to take hiking sandals and when we hit another river crossing, I ripped off my boots, put on my sandals and strode powerfully through, balanced on two tough sticks carefully strapped to my wrists. Maybe I was getting the hang of this Norwegian wilderness woman thing.

We emerged at the other side of the mountains unscathed, and despite being two smelly people with large rucksacks and an equally smelly dog, we were soon picked up by a driver. He turned out to be one of the few Norwegians who spoke no English, but we all smiled at each other enthusiastically and after a silent drive, he dropped us back by the van, politely ignoring the dog hair left in the back of his car. And this seemed to sum up the Norwegians – quiet and maybe even a little dour to begin with, but always happy to help if asked (even if only asked with a thumb).

Chapter 8

MAMBA

After nearly seven weeks in Norway, the time had come to drag ourselves onwards and so, one fine sunny morning, we packed up and headed to the Finnish border. I fully expected another all-body-cavity-search experience with Oscar at Customs and began to tense up at the first border signpost and hut. About a mile further on I realised it wasn't the first signpost and hut – it was the *only* one. We were already into the land of Father Christmas and birch twig beatings (albeit not usually together). So much for a dramatic entry into the European Union with its carefully controlled borders.

After about 10 minutes of Finnish driving the rain started to patter on the windscreen, gathering pace until it had turned into a full-on raging storm. This probably wasn't the best introduction to a country and it wasn't helped by our first visit to a campsite, which turned out to be substantially more expensive than Norway. Loath to pay the price of a small hotel for a campsite, we headed on to the village and discovered a convenient lay-by with public toilets and a scenic lakeside view. As the rain settled into a constant drumming on the roof, so we settled into our lakeside lay-by for the night, with another few pages of 'War and Peace' knocked off during the inclement weather. As the evening wore on it became clear we weren't the only people who'd thought the campsite prices were steep, as campervan after campervan rolled into the lay-by. By 9pm there were 11 vans corralled into the small concrete area. If we'd been able to afford the local beer it could've turned into a party.

Knowing that my American-residing sister was visiting my parents in the UK, it seemed a good opportunity to make just one phone call and speak to all the family at once. I set off down the road to the nearest town in search of a payphone, only to find a

73

broken one outside the shop. After some further investigation, I found a reasonable looking hotel which seemed a likely candidate for a public phone. As I entered the bar, the pool balls stopped rolling and a group of drunk men turned around to stare at the newcomer. Had I been slightly quicker on the uptake, I could probably have escaped in the seconds it took them to focus and realise I was an unaccompanied female of the species. Regrettably, I wasn't quite sharp enough and by the time I'd realised I needed to make a quick exit I was surrounded by a gaggle (is there a collective noun for them?) of Finnish fishermen all keen to tell me why I should pop upstairs and admire their collection of newly-tied flies. Smiling politely whilst eyeing up the exit strategies, I listened to their slurred outpourings with a mixture of entertainment and mild concern. One particularly persistent character, who wasn't falling for the 'I'm-sorry-I-speak-no-Finnish' line, quickly switched into surprisingly good English:

'And where do you come from, beautiful lady?' Resisting the temptation to suggest the lay-by up the road, I owned up to setting sail from Scotland. After some discussion amongst the others as to the exact location of Scotland, my keenest admirer chipped in with a remarkably reasonable point:

'Why are you travelling to Finland then? It looks the same as Scotland and the weather is just as bad.'

There wasn't a lot to say to that, so I smiled in what I hoped was a non-committal manner and continued to back towards the door.

'Ahh, but I bet us Finnish fishermen are much more attractive than Scottish ones. Is that why you've come here?' I'd never been asked before to make a comparison of the aesthetic values of Scottish versus Finnish fishermen, but based on my now extensive experience of both, it would undoubtedly be a hard fought battle for the Mr Beautiful Fisherman title. Everything's relative, I suppose.

After promising him that Finnish fishermen were clearly far more attractive than Scottish ones, I managed to extricate myself as far as the door and make a break for freedom. I soon decided the phone call would have to wait for another day and I hightailed it back to the security of the van. However, I could at least chalk it up as one point to the European Union – some things were the same across Europe, and drunken men and their belief that after five pints they are indisputable sex gods would appear to be one of them.

The previously un-researched similarities between Finnish and Scottish fishermen also set me wondering as to the other shared characteristics we might find across Europe. The continuing presence of World War Two's trail of destruction had convinced me that a Union might be a good idea. But I still wasn't sure what, if anything, we all had in common. Now that we were about to travel from the very north to the very south of Europe, I was interested to see just what the similarities were. And the differences. Could we all learn from each other? Was there a perfect European country lurking out there somewhere? Would one of the new Eastern countries prove to be the European Utopia, or did everywhere have its negatives? So far the scenery of Norway had looked pretty Utopian to me, but the killer prices and dark winters maybe struck it off the short list for a European heaven on earth. Finland was certainly a contender for European forest of the year, but did that make it the best of the continent? Looking at the potential mating material in this particular hotel suggested probably not.

The next day, unclear as to the must-see sights of Finland, we decided to head into Killipsjarvi national park for an opportunity to witness Europe's borders for ourselves. The leaflet for the national park showed a large white cairn which marked the spot where the borders of Finland, Norway and Sweden joined together. A small boat would take us across a lake and into the middle of the park where we could then admire the multi-country cairn at the lake's edge, before marching back through the Lapland forest. A brief Oscar tantrum ensued when he realised he was expected to jump from the quay onto the boat – post the Trollheimen trauma, he wasn't planning to go anywhere that might involve a sudden immersion in water. Chris was forced to carry him across the gap whilst the entire boatload of passengers looked on in amusement at this dictatorial dog and his well-trained human porters.

The boat chugged slowly across the water and within a few minutes of disembarking we had arrived at a cairn with Scandinavian words engraved around it. We dutifully took photos standing by the cairn with our feet in various countries, although something was clearly still puzzling Chris.

'Don't you think it looks a lot smaller than in the photo? I'm sure the people looked a lot shorter than the cairn in the leaflet.'

'Maybe they were very little people,' I suggested smugly. 'But, now you mention it, it does look a bit smaller.' Is it something to do with foreshortening and the way they took the photo? Perhaps all the people were standing a lot further from the camera? Or is it nearer? Well, anyway, you know what I mean.'

Feeling slightly diddled by the whole multi-country cairn experience, we continued on our route, only to arrive at a much bigger cairn which looked exactly like the one in the leaflet. We'd been duped by an impostor cairn. Unsurprisingly it was all a bit of a let down after this fiasco, but I'm sure at some point we were all standing in different countries, even if we couldn't quite manage it for the camera. What was more intriguing was the graffiti scrawled around the monument. A Swedish girl translated it for us as Norway + Finland + Sweden = Sapmi, the name the local people use for the area we know as Lapland. The native people in this area are called the Sami and over the coming days we were to realise just how hard they are fighting to retain their culture and traditions in the modern world.

The rest of the walk was un-eventful, just miles and miles of trees in gently rolling landscape. Most of the trees were birches, which would normally be in full, fluttering leaf in August. But Finland had recently been attacked by a tree eating moth, which had munched its way through the leaves of countless birch trees. All that was left now was a landscape that looked oddly like a winter scene, with bare branches and a handful of leaves clinging determinedly to each tree. Initially, the gently swaying branches and rolling moorland seemed a pleasant and relaxing landscape, but as time wore on I began to realise that you can have too much of some things, even trees.

Looking at the Finland guidebook a few days earlier, we'd come up with some sketchy plans for longer hikes through the forested national parks, and so the following morning we headed deeper into Finland. Arriving at the start of our first walk, we climbed out of the van to be hit by a wall of flying things. And not just small things, but mosquitoes the size of elephants, intent on sucking the blood from any flesh they could find. We exchanged nervous glances and headed into the local tourist office. As usual the staff spoke better English than we did and we proceeded to have a long discussion as to how we could complete a 4-day hike and then get back to the van, which we wanted to leave at the start.

'Don't worry,' the friendly woman reassured us, 'many people do this and we have a special service here, where you can arrange for someone to drive your van down to the other end of the trail for you.'

Chris and I looked at each other in horror. Were they suggesting we should inflict the torture of driving the Fuckit Bucket on someone else? How would we explain the lumpy porridge gears, the clouds of smoke from the back, the leaking oil and general unreliability, coupled with the lingering smell of damp dog and pasta sauce? And as if that wasn't all bad enough, the steering wheel would be on the wrong side for whichever poor soul got this job.

'Are there any buses we could get back to the van if we didn't do that?' Chris asked, gingerly.

'Not really, you'd probably have to change 3 times to get back to the start.'

So far this wasn't looking good, so I changed tack.

'I was just wondering about the mosquitoes, are they particularly bad round here or is the whole trail like this?'

'Oh they're not bad round here. The rest of the trail is worse. It's funny, for three years we've had no mosquitoes and then suddenly this year there are millions.'

Marvellous. Although I wondered if this was similar to the tourist offices at home that I sometimes overhear telling bedraggled tourists that it doesn't normally rain this much in Scotland.

Slightly depressed we thanked the woman for her help and headed back to the van. Unsure what to do, I figured we could take Oscar for a walk whilst we tried to make a decision. As we left the car park the cloud of mosquitoes around my head got gradually thicker and thicker until I could hardly see through them. I'd lathered repellent on my hands and face but it didn't seem to put them off. Standing still wasn't an option so I half walked, half ran round the path, with Oscar stopping for regular rolls on the ground as he struggled to get the flies away. After the briefest of marches we hurled ourselves back into the van with sighs of relief all round. Inspecting my arms I then discovered that these mosquitoes were so big they weren't even confined to exposed flesh. No, these bastards could bite through clothes and had merrily chewed their way along my T-shirted arms and shoulders. Realising that tents and clothes would offer no relief, the idea of a 4 minute walk was starting to seem unbearable, let alone 4 days.

Before we'd even put the kettle on we'd made a decision. Walking was off the agenda for now. Instead we decided to head north to the Sami villages, figuring that a short swap of physical activity for cultural immersion wouldn't do us any harm and would help us avoid giving a blood transfusion to the Finnish mosquito population.

We rattled north on bone shaking roads, innocently described by our atlas as 'secondary roads', but which turned out to be little more than farm tracks. I tried not to think about what the break-down company would say if we rang them from a dirt track in

Lapland, somewhere north of the Arctic Circle. If they couldn't cope with Glasgow we were really going to be on a hiding to nothing. To my amazement the van resisted the opportunity to test out this theory and we arrived in the town of Inari slightly battered, with bruised bottoms and the remains of our bottles of gin and tonic remarkably well mixed.

As it turned out, our decision was the right one. We visited a Sami-run reindeer farm where the farmer gave us a tour of his herd and explained the mysteries of reindeer farming. In parallel with British livestock farming he complained of the difficulties of getting a decent price for the meat from the supermarkets, especially now there is so much competition from New Zealand. And as it turns out – and don't tell Father Christmas I said this – Rudolph does make a rather good sausage.

Which is all the more surprising given that their staple winter food is lichen – the grey-green scrubby bits that you see hanging on trees. Bales of the stuff are collected throughout Europe and the first harvests are then picked over by commercial flower arrangers. After they've selected the finest cuts for use in table arrangements and buttonholes, the less aesthetically pleasing lichen is passed on for the reindeer to munch. After spending the winter chewing on the florists' cast-offs the reindeer then head out to their summer pastures, although my experience so far suggested they were keener to hang around on the road than anywhere else. In the autumn, they are herded back to the farms with the assistance of the mosquitoes, which drive the reindeer to distraction and cause them to run for cover as fast as their Rudolph legs will carry them. Undoubtedly cheaper than having to train sheep dogs, but I can't see them stringing a whole TV series out of 'One man and his mosquito'.

Despite the focus of the farm visit on the process of producing reindeer meat, I came away more interested in the local Sami culture and the efforts being made by so many young people to maintain their traditions. The reindeer farmer was only in his early thirties, but after working in Helsinki for a few years he had decided to return to Lapland to raise his children within the Sami culture. The children attended a Sami day centre, listened to Sami radio and learnt Sami folk songs from their grandmother.

We also visited the local museum, and found an enormous modern building of the size and style I'd expect in Glasgow or Edinburgh rather than this small northern town. It seemed the Finnish government and the local people were determined to nurture this culture, rather than leave it to be neglected in an area where the people faced such harsh physical challenges. We were visiting during the summer, when the temperatures were mild and the daylight continuous, and yet we were still struggling with the barrage of biting insects determined to turn us into their supper. When the farmer told us he could remember a recent winter when the temperature dropped to minus 57°C, I had to respect his determination to make a success of living here.

This respect for the Finnish people was increased when we woke the following morning to a grey sky and the sound of rain bucketing down on the roof of the van. We'd opted to park for the night in a picnic site next to a lake, which suddenly didn't seem such a good idea. Deciding we should head on before we were forced to test the van's sea worthiness, I nipped for a last visit to the nearby compost toilet, which involved togging up in full waterproofs. By the time I reached the small hut the sky was so leaden that the tiny window in the roof couldn't provide enough light for me to disrobe. As there'd been no other visitors to the picnic site, I figured the chances of a queue for the loo were unlikely and left the door wide open whilst I proceeded to roll layer upon layer of waterproof clothing around my ankles. I installed myself on my throne, with an appropriately regal view of the lake and passed the point of no return. At which moment, an astonishingly handsome man appeared around the corner and entered the small hut. My options were limited. Even if I'd been at a stage in proceedings where I could run for cover, my legs were so wrapped up in waterproof clothing that I would only have managed a step or two before crashing to the ground. I decided my only remaining hope was to brave it out and act casual.

'Hello!' I sang out as if I usually started chatting to handsome Finnish men with my trousers round my ankles.

'Ahh. Hello!' he replied, quickly recovering a nonchalant appearance after his initial reaction to the loony on the loo. 'I'm so sorry, I didn't see you there.'

'No problem, don't worry. Terrible weather, isn't it?'

'Yes, yes, very wet. Well, I'll return later.'

'Thanks, I'll give you a shout when I'm out.'

What a civil conversation. He politely left, I completed my tasks, headed back to the van and gave him a quick nod on my way past.

'Enjoy your day,' he called after me and I almost managed to make eye contact, but the memory of my waterproof trousered ankles was just a little too fresh in my mind.

We spent the next few days driving south through Finland. We stopped at regular intervals to look at the scenery, wondering if it might have changed yet. Every time we were rewarded with the same view of very slightly rolling countryside, covered in uniform-ly-coloured conifer trees as far as the eye could see. I have never seen so many trees in my life, stretching from wherever we were standing into Russia and beyond. Chris succinctly captured the only way to describe it – MAMBA – Miles And Miles of Bugger All.

Driving through it evoked only two emotions: boredom and terror. Boredom at the never changing view and the feeling of being hemmed in on both sides of the road by the tall conifers. And moments of terror at the sudden appearance of reindeer on the road, causing me to slam on the brakes and hope I could skid to a halt before the reindeer came through the windscreen. The van's engine is in the back, so when you sit in the front seat there is no bonnet in front of you, just the windscreen and a sheet of metal, bringing you eyeball to eyeball with over-confident reindeer. It didn't make for the most relaxing travelling conditions, although the roads were so straight that Chris was able to work on his thesis whilst I drove.

We re-crossed the Arctic Circle, this time heading south and for the first time in six weeks we saw darkness again. Or we would have done, had I not parked us directly under a streetlight that night, thereby negating my chances of finally getting some deep sleep. Because we were spending so many hours in the van we met remarkably few Finnish people, although I spent one day walking in a national park near the Russian border, where I shared my lunch and a fire with a local walker. Somehow my impression of Finnish people is now linked with him, a slightly overweight and pale man who seemed quite accepting of the monotonous Finnish landscape and the harsh vagaries of the climate.

The convenient lay-bys with toilets that seemed so popular in Lapland gradually disappeared as we headed further south and we stayed in more and more campsites, with the result that we met more Antipodean tourists than Finns. Increasingly we were meeting people who I naively thought were my age, before they'd suddenly drop into the conversation the words 'university' and 'vacation' and I'd realise that they were at least 10 years younger than me, and nearly 15 years younger than Chris. In some particularly frightening cases Chris was old enough, in a legal sense, to be their father, a fact which seemed to be causing him some concern. At the other end of the spectrum were the retired travellers – the ones who were keen to tell you they were spending their kids' inheritance as they showed off their brand new campervans. It seemed that the British approach to travelling – do it when you're 19 or 65 and not in-between – existed in much of the world. Those aged between 25 and 50 had so far been conspicuous by their absence. They really were the 'missing generation'.

Then, somewhat unexpectedly, we pitched up at a deserted

campsite to discover only one other vehicle – a British caravan and car. Excited at the potential for replenishing our rapidly-diminishing Marmite supplies, we peered out the window, twitching our curtains in an attempt to demonstrate our nationality. Later in the evening, one half of the British caravan came over to visit. She was in her mid-forties and had clearly gone to a frightfully good school. Despite the mis-match of social class, I was excited to think that we might have finally met a fellow traveller from the missing generation. Intrigued, I worked the conversation around to how long they'd been away.

'So, have you been in the caravan long?' I asked, struggling to sound innocent and non-committal.

'Well, we've been away for about 12 months now. We need to pop back to London at some point to see the tenants in our house, then we're hoping to travel for another couple of months' she replied. Aha, I thought. So they're on more than a holiday and she looks young enough to still be at work – maybe we've finally found some dropouts. I carefully worded my thoughts:

'Does that mean you had to give up jobs and stuff to leave – or are you on some sort of sabbatical deal?'

'No, my husband's retired – he was in banking you see, so he's made enough to be able to retire early and I figured if he was retiring, I might as well join him. Of course, I did insist on a little bit of luxury – I mean, it's one thing to go travelling, but I wasn't planning to slum it. So I said I'd only come if we bought the Volvo and the caravan brand new, so we'd know they were up to the job.'

Oh. So we weren't moving in the same social league. Suddenly I became acutely aware of the van's inherent scruffiness and the pervading smell of damp dog. And technically I wasn't sure if they were part of the missing generation anyway –if they'd retired early it meant they weren't having to worry about how, or if, they'd rejoin the jobs market. A few moments later, she continued to explain their stunningly secure financial set-up:

'We've got a reasonable size house in London you see – it's in

Kensington, don't know if you know it? Anyway, we're renting it out whilst we're away and the rent is enough to cover the cost of the trip. How about you?'

I wondered how I was going to explain that we had a tiny house in an obscure part of Scotland that she certainly wouldn't know, and that the rent we were receiving was barely sufficient to cover our mobile phone bill each month, let alone the mortgage payments. Glossing over this as best I could, I decided it was time to cut to the chase, before she came to her senses and realised she was talking to a couple of country peasants.

'Don't suppose you've got any Marmite have you? We've got a spare book here if you'd be interested in doing a trade?' Out of the corner of my eye I could see Oscar putting his head in his paws in embarrassment. But to everyone's surprise, the lure of an English book was enough to persuade her to return to her caravan and reappear a few seconds later with some, slightly out of date, Marmite. Once our dodgy deal was concluded she retreated to the safety of her caravan – our styles of travelling were clearly rather different and I think she was worried about spending too much time in our van in case she caught something nasty.

After she'd left we debated whether or not they could become honorary members of the missing generation, but it seemed they had to join the ranks of the other retired travellers, who were all travelling without the nagging worry of whether or not they'd ever be employed again. So far the missing generation had remained just that – missing.

Chapter 9

Russian raspberry

One of the more exciting things we'd discovered whilst researching pet passports was the list of other countries that Oscar could visit besides the European Union – places like Chile, Montserrat, Fiji and Russia. Given that we were driving down the Finnish – Russian border, it seemed an ideal opportunity to extend our tour into part of Russia. St Petersburg was only about five hours drive from Finland and struck me as a pretty exotic destination for both the van and someone reading 'War and Peace'.

I'd assumed that if we could get Oscar into the country then getting visas for us wouldn't be a problem, but our first visit to a Finnish travel agent soon told us otherwise. We were politely, but firmly told that our only option would be to head to Helsinki and wait two weeks, when we might receive visas to travel into Russia. Tempted though I was by the thought of being able to send a postcard from Bagpuss in Russia, we both knew that two weeks in Helsinki would be expensive and would give us less time in other countries on the way to Spain.

Bitterly disappointed, we had to accept that St Petersburg wasn't an option on this trip, but I wasn't quite ready to give up the idea of a Russian stamp in my passport. So far Oscar had managed to get more stamps in his passport than either of us and I could just see him bragging to all his friends when we got back. I decided I needed to compete, so we headed to Lappenranta, a small Finnish town connected by the Saimaa canal to Vyborg, an equally small town 40 kilometres inside Russia. According to the Finnish travel agent it was possible to get a visa for a day trip to Vyborg, which looked like my only hope for visiting the land of 'War and Peace'.

When I checked with the travel agency in town I only had to

wait 48 hours whilst my passport details were sent to Russia for checking. Then all being well, I would be allowed over the border – provided it was on an organised trip – for a whole 12 hours. Although that meant hanging around in Lappenranta for 48 hours, which wasn't the most exciting town in Europe, Chris decided it would be a good opportunity for him to catch up on some thesis-writing. It would also be a chance to visit some Finnish garages to see if anyone could deal with Bagpuss and its continuing oil leak and billowing smoke issues.

Once I'd provided my entire life history for faxing to Russia, we headed off on a tour of the local garages. Sadly, no-one was keen to take on the challenge that was the Fuckit Bucket, but Chris did find a new gasket seal, which he was confident would fix at least one of the oil leaks.

The day of my Russian odyssey dawned and I leapt aboard a coach bound for Russia – full to the gunnels with slightly too chirpy Finns. This included a rather lecherous old man sitting next to me, who insisted on leaning over to speak to his pal and placing his head in my chest at regular intervals. To my relief we soon arrived at the Russian border, which I naively assumed meant an impending arrival in Vyborg. But I'd underestimated the power of Russian bureaucracy. As we entered the border zone, a guard boarded the bus, and walked the length of it, checking we all had passports. Just as I was starting to feel slightly diddled at the lack of a passport stamp, the bus lurched forward a few paces and then drew to a halt outside another building.

The driver explained (fortunately in Finnish and English) that we had to get off the bus, line up first by nationality and then subdivided into Russian alphabetical order and wait for our passports to be checked. The Finns went first and very, very slowly filed through the small booth to have their passports checked and stamped (hurrah, at last I could compete with Oscar). All other nationalities went next, and I discovered two British holiday makers in my section of the queue. We dutifully arranged ourselves in the appropriate alphabetical order (with the help of the Russian speaking driver) and waited patiently for 45 minutes until we were called forward. The woman in the booth spent some time carefully considering my passport and typing importantly into a computer, before finally hammering down stamps in officious Post Office style and curtly nodding me through.

We then all filed back onto the coach and drove on a few more paces, where a third border check was taking place. Another customs officer boarded the bus and carefully checked that everyone still had a passport, and that each passport had the appropriate stamps in the right places. After this we were allowed to drive forward as far as the real, actual border, where the bus was checked again and we were finally allowed into Russia. At some stage whilst I was planning the Russian jaunt I'd considered taking Oscar with me to give Chris some space to get on with his thesis. But given that it had just taken two hours to get me through the border, I was beginning to realise that whilst in theory Oscar ought to be able to travel to Russia, putting it into practice might require more patience than either of us possessed. For the time being I was glad we'd decided to limit him to EU countries. Maybe the trans-Siberian trip should wait until dog passports have become a bit more of an international commodity.

I passed a pleasant, if rather grey, day in Vyborg, taking in the tourist sights (which were limited to looming Lenin statues and a rather ramshackle castle) and being silently impressed by the shop assistants' ability to ignore customers for hours on end. The contrast between visiting state run shops and the local farmers market couldn't have been starker. In the state run shops I waited patiently for about 10 minutes, waving my roubles in a more and more agitated manner until eventually a shop assistant would sigh deeply and deign to make eye contact. If I was quick enough I could just squeeze in a hopeful point at the item I wanted before they lost interest and returned to shuffling papers.

In contrast, the farmers' market showed capitalism in all its glory. Most of the stalls were run by formidable Russian ladies of a certain age. They were selling raspberries for only a few pence, so I approached the least scary looking lady and waved hopefully at the raspberries, trying to indicate that I wanted just a handful for an evening dessert. It turns out that only wanting a few of something is a difficult thing to communicate in sign language, especially to someone who thinks you are a walking wallet and can easily afford every item on the stall. She enthusiastically tried to press a couple of kilos of raspberries onto me and I, initially equally enthusiastically, tried to mime a smaller pot. I suspect she thought I was trying to haggle the price down instead, and not surprisingly, she didn't find this an endearing trait. She called round a gang of her friends who all headed over with surprising speed given their statuesque nature. Suddenly I was surrounded on all sides by mildly irate Russian ladies jabbering at me and pointing to my bag and the raspberries. It suddenly felt a lot more like war than peace and I saw no sign of a handsome Count coming to rescue me. Deciding that discretion was the better part of valour, I took the enormous bags of raspberries, passed over what I hoped was enough roubles and made a break for freedom.

I didn't stop to look back until I was several streets away, just in case. Then I had to figure out how to pack half a field into one small rucksack. But after being forced to buy them, there was no way I was planning to dump the raspberries now, so I squashed them in and figured we could eat pavlova for a few days.

I continued to wander around town for a while and whilst exploring various small alleyways I unexpectedly found myself in the farmers' market street again. I was just about to make a second dash for freedom when the original raspberry lady spotted me and rushed over. Panicking, I tried to back away, but she forced a 50 rouble note into my hand and then headed back to her stall. Now I was thoroughly confused. Had I overpaid or did I look poor? Given that she spoke no English and I spoke no Russian, I was never going to find out, so I decided to take the money gracefully, assume she thought I was really dim (and to be honest I wasn't providing her with much evidence to the contrary) and head back to the bus.

Returning to Lappenranta was an altogether quicker process. Yet the evidence I'd seen so far suggested that if you were an illegal immigrant you'd be much better off aiming for Finland than Russia. That didn't seem to trouble the Finns, who gave the rubbed off outside of my passport a cursory look, before waving me through and into their country. Once I got back to the van, I asked Chris how his day had gone.

'Complete disaster. I've tried to do the gasket, but it hasn't worked. It's leaking more oil than before and there's a huge patch on the ground. We'll have to stay here another day and I'll see if I can do something about it. And it was windy all day and it's blown a tree down on the blokes' loos so I can't even wash the oil off.'

This didn't seem like the best moment to tell him he'd got to eat raspberry everything for the next week, so I hid the raspberries in the fridge and tried to make sympathetic noises.

'Maybe it'll look better in the morning. Perhaps it's just the last bit of oil from under the old gasket and it'll have dried off soon.'

In the morning it was abundantly clear that it didn't look any better and the patch of oil under the van was starting to resemble the Exxon Valdez slick. Even more worryingly, the Russian raspberries had started to ferment and had blown the top off the plastic container, causing a minor raspberry slick in the fridge. Both determined not to be beaten by inanimate objects, Chris began on changing a second gasket and I rummaged around the van, emptying out food until I'd produced a small jam jar collection. I laid them out on the draining board, took the raspberries from the fridge and dug out the remains of a bag of sugar from the corner of a cupboard. Chris looked at me in horror.

'You aren't planning to try and make jam out of that lot are you?'

'Why not? We've got pans, we've got two oven rings, and some jam might be useful.'

'Tamsin, those raspberries must have cost pennies. Why don't you just throw them away?'

'Because it's a point of principle. Because I got steam-rollered into buying them, so I'll deal with them.'

Chris shrugged and headed outside with a spanner and a bemused look on his face. I took a deep breath, emptied raspberries and sugar into our camping saucepans and lit the gas.

Should you be planning to repeat this experiment in your own campervan, I'd like to warn you that pouring boiling hot jam into small jars with no oven gloves and only removable handles on your pans is a tricky operation. It will result in you getting large amounts of jam spread in a thin layer around the van and several significant scalds. On the plus side, the smell of boiling raspberries will linger in the van for days and make a pleasant alternative to the smell of damp dog. And you will make enough jam to last you all the way to Germany. But in the process you will use swearwords you didn't even know existed and, should your husband be trying to repair the engine at the same time, there is a good chance you will end up taking the jam to the divorce court as evidence.

As it turned out, once I'd finally cleared up, the Russian raspberry was pretty good and helped to improve the heavy Finnish bread. The second go at the gasket wasn't such a success and the van continued to belch oil at regular intervals. But all the garages for miles around were booked up for weeks, so we continued on our journey, trying to ignore the Hansel and Gretel style trail we were leaving behind us. Useful if we wanted to find our way home, but not a long term travelling strategy.

Having added a stamp to my passport and some jam to our cupboards, there wasn't much else I wanted to do in Finland. The scenery wasn't catching our attention and we were both starting to feel a bit treed-out. We headed into Helsinki to see the city sights and for Chris to connect with a new part for his computer, which he'd bought on Ebay and asked the seller to mail to Helsinki Post Restante. This really was travelling in the 21st century. Although in a sudden reversal to my student days we were also hoping to connect with an emergency mailing of Marmite, to supplement the supplies provided by the posh Brits. Some things will never change.

The city of Helsinki is built on a peninsula, surrounded by small islands and it's a surprisingly compact and neat place. It suffered heavily from Russian bombing during the Second World War, but it's been tastefully rebuilt and now feels friendly and cosmopolitan. This impression was accentuated by the presence of the World Athletics Championships, which coincided with our visit. Although the tickets for the stadium events were out of our price range, watching the marathon was free, so I made Oscar a paper Union Jack to wear and we headed out to cheer on the British athletes. Oscar's flag-flying caused quite a stir in Helsinki and he probably made it onto more photos than some of the athletes. For a while he was even stalked by the paparazzi as a couple of photographers began trying to catch him from different angles. Of course in true starlet style Oscar continued to plough his doggy furrow through the middle of his admirers, refusing to pose for pictures unless his full Bonio fee was paid, in advance.

Chapter 10

Safe as houses

Our plan from Helsinki onwards was less clear. We knew we could get a ferry across the Baltic Sea to Tallinn in Estonia and after that it all went a bit hazy. It was becoming uncharted territory in Oscar terms as well. We'd spoken to a few people who'd taken animals into Western Europe, but couldn't find anyone, either in person or on the internet, who'd yet ventured into Eastern Europe. This had only been an option for UK dogs in the last few months, so it had taken our vet some time to research the potential threats. The guidebooks for the region suggested it was filled to the gunnels with aggressive rabid dogs, lying in wait to catch the first passing tourist, let alone a passing tourist dog. So it was with some trepidation that we rang the ferry company and booked us all onto a one way ticket to Estonia. The ferry company's response did not inspire confidence.

'Yes, madam, we can book you on tomorrow's ferry. But dogs are only allowed on the ferry if they are muzzled.'

'But he doesn't have a muzzle. He doesn't need one. He's a pet dog, not a guard dog.'

'I'm sure, madam, but if he doesn't have a muzzle he can't travel on the ferry.'

It wasn't looking good. Oscar has never worn a muzzle in his life and we don't even own such a thing, so we certainly didn't have one packed away in a small corner of the van. During our time in Helsinki, Oscar had acquired his first Continental tick – truly horrible creatures that burrow into skin and suck blood, occasionally passing on nasty diseases at the same time. Oscar has had his fair share of ticks in Scotland, but tick-borne diseases are, so far, relatively rare in Scotland. In mainland Europe the variety and potential deadliness of tick-related diseases increases dramatically, so Oscar was being regularly anointed with tick repelling chemicals. Despite this, Heather had included a cunning tick pulling device in Oscar's first aid kit. These are basically glorified paperclips which help you pull the tick out of the dog's skin without either losing your grip on the tick, or losing your finger to the dog. Somehow in our packing we'd managed to lose the paperclip, so the discovery of Oscar's first tick meant a trip to a Finnish pet shop.

Unbelievably, a glorified paperclip retails for nearly 8 Euros in Helsinki, which implies that someone, somewhere is making an absolute killing. 'Vet' may have been struck off my list of future careers once I'd tried the thermometer trick, but a lucrative career reshaping paperclips was looking more attractive by the minute. Once we'd passed over enough Euros to buy three bottles of wine in Spain, we took our paperclip and yanked out the tick within seconds. But the experience of Finnish pet shop prices didn't encourage me to think about buying a muzzle here. A decent muzzle would presumably require a bank loan, and anyway I could see Oscar packing his rucksack and heading for home if we even thought about it. So we tried a makeshift job with a rucksack strap, which seemed to work OK if you ignored Oscar's look of hatred, sufficient to curdle milk at 40 paces.

Suitably armed with a de-ticked and potentially muzzled dog, we headed to the ferry and prepared to face the worst the East could offer. Once the guidebooks had finished their doom-mongering on the rabid dog army, they moved onto car thieves. According to most sources every foreign car was a target and campervans were potential targets even whilst you were driving. Trying not to panic, once we'd driven onto the boat we locked all our worldly possessions into the safe – Chris's laptop with the draft thesis, credit cards, money and all our documents. With a deep breath, we braced ourselves, picked up the part-time rucksack strap cum muzzle, the more than slightly peeved dog and headed upstairs to the rest of the boat.

To our surprise, we were met by friendly smiles and a chorus of ahhs as most of the passengers rushed over to pet Oscar. Who stood there with his crowd of admirers, occasionally glancing over at the two wallflowers standing with his makeshift muzzle dangling uselessly in their hands. I've never seen such a good line in smug from a dog.

The rest of the journey was spent on the back deck of the boat, basking in the sunshine and answering questions about where Oscar was from, what sort of dog he was, did he always roll on his back and expect his tummy tickled and so on. As we pulled into Tallinn Oscar allowed himself to be escorted back to the van, dodging his paparazzi as we went and, under his baleful stare, we sheepishly returned the rucksack strap to the cupboard, where it would languish, unused, for the remainder of the trip.

Suitably admonished by a dog who would soon be expecting to sell his shedding hair to admirers, we drove away from the ferry and into the former Soviet Union state. As an initial counteract to our stereotypes, we weren't met by a rush of car thieves; browbeaten women in headscarves or the smell of cabbage and dumplings. Instead we drove into a bustling city with smart shops, swanky cars and the usual confusion of lanes and signs, none of which seemed to mention campsites.

We headed out of town and after a couple of miles found a small handwritten sign pointing to a campsite next to the main sports stadium. Pulling in, we discovered the entrepreneurial spirit alive and well with an informal campsite set up in the car park of the stadium. It had all the usual facilities of showers and toilets, providing there weren't two teams playing that night. The entrepreneurial spirit also seemed to be alive in the prices, with a £10 charge levied on all dog campers. Suddenly we reverted to teenage gap yearers, pushed the dog down onto the floor and insisted there were just two of us. Of course that meant we had to keep the dog hidden for the next two days. Which involved a complicated procedure of chest wracking coughs every time Oscar chose to bark, probably causing untold lung damage and certainly negating any small cash saving. It seems you can take the pack out of the backpacker, but you still won't get the moth out of their wallet.

After carefully hiding the dog under a pile of clothes, I returned to the campsite 'office' to check on buses into town and spent some time browsing the brochures that were haphazardly strewn around the room. A small notice caught my eye – written in Estonian (I assume) and English, it informed me that I had now entered a Wi-Fi zone. The whole campsite was set up to enable campers to use their wireless internet connections at any location in the car park. Strange as it seems now, back in the dim and distant past of 2005, Wi-Fi zones were still reasonably rare in the UK and certainly hadn't got as far as temporary campsites.

'Do all Estonian campsites have Wi-Fi then?' I asked the "camp-site owner".

'Not yet, but soon they will. All garages have it you know.'

'Garages as in petrol stations? I can check my email whilst we get fuel?'

'Yes, and town squares and shops and bars and usually some other places too. Isn't it the same in your country?'

'I don't think so. At least, round us they don't. Well, they didn't, two months ago.'

Suddenly I began to wonder if we'd been away too long. Maybe it had all changed and rural Scotland finally had high speed internet and a decent mobile phone signal. Perhaps the days of hanging out the spare bedroom window to make a phone call were over. Somehow, it seemed unlikely.

And of course, with Wi-Fi zones still so rare in the UK, it hadn't been our top priority to install a wireless card in the laptop before we'd entered Eastern Europe. We'd been more focused on basic security measures and topping up our loo roll supply. I was starting to wonder if we were hopelessly out of date and had just left the slow lane of the UK to enter the real technological highway of Europe. Perhaps the European Union was wrong. Perhaps Europe isn't a melting pot of countries all looking to achieve similar living standards. Maybe it's more of a two-horse race between west and east in which we were being overtaken by the horse with the sprint finish.

My ruminations on the state of Europe were interrupted by the sight of Chris's backside emerging from the van, wiggling from side to side as he repeatedly thumped something on the floor. Concerned that he'd finally lost the plot, I asked the protruding backside what seemed to be the problem.

'I can't get the bloody safe open. It's jammed and the key isn't working – it won't turn at all.'

A brief flashback of the morning spent stuffing all our things into the safe flickered through my mind. With the exception of our passports, absolutely everything else of value was locked into that safe.

'Have you tried taking the key out and starting again?'

'No, because the key won't come out. It's jammed in. It won't twist and it won't come out. Any other thoughts, Einstein?' Resisting the temptation to seek out the dog's temporary muzzle and use it on Chris, I stayed calm.

'Can I have a go, maybe it's just the angle you're at?'

With an audible huff, Chris backed out from the van and gestured for me to take his place. So that the safe was hidden from the prying eyes of burglars, we'd bolted it to the floor between the front seats, and put the dog's seat over the top of it. Our theory was that any burglar keen enough to crawl around in the dog hair on the floor would probably deserve to get something in reward. It seemed likely that the combination of hairballs and the gentle aroma of my trainers, shoved in front of the safe, should be enough to deter all but the most determined of thieves. A good theory, but we'd forgotten that we would also have to run the gamut of the furballs every time we needed something from the safe, which meant we avoided using it as much as possible. It also meant that whenever we did tackle the safe, we'd end up dangling upside down over the edge of the seat, breathing in eau de dog and trainer and usually culminating in some short sharp exchanges between the two of us.

This one was no different. I wedged myself onto the seat and hung my head over the edge and into the valley of certain asphyxiation. I fumbled with the key, tried wiggling it this way and that, speaking to it nicely and swearing at it. No joy. Our worldly possessions were carefully locked into a small metal box, firmly attached to a clapped out van and there seemed to be no way of retrieving them. Without documents to prove we owned the van we couldn't get home and without money we couldn't get replacements. We had a handful of Estonian Kroons to our name and that was it.

'OK, let's swap, I'll have another go.'

I extricated myself from the floor of hell and Chris slid into my place. Trying to appear under control, he gently wiggled the key in the lock. A nasty splintering sound came from the safe, followed by a deep sigh.

'Bollocks.'

He sat up slowly, holding one end of the key in his hand. The other end was still firmly wedged in the lock.

'Big dog's bollocks,' I agreed.

Sometime later, when we'd finished picking sufficient dog hair off Chris to maintain the dog denial routine, he headed to the campsite office and spent a happy half hour with the Estonian Yellow Pages. Fortunately the campsite owner (or maybe 'organiser' would be a more appropriate title for someone who seemed to be temporarily borrowing a car park and changing room) spoke good English and, after his initial laughter, he found us the Locksmiths page and gave us directions to the nearest shop. By then it was too late in the day to catch anyone, so we spent a quiet evening in Tallinn, squandering a few of our measly Kroon collection on pizza and beer.

In the morning we drove to the first of the locksmiths, allowed the dog to come back out from his hiding place, and made an attempt at cleaning the floor around the safe. We entered the shop and looked around hopefully for an English speaker. To my relief, the owner spoke excellent English, and quickly cottoned onto our dilemma. In no time at all, three locksmiths were crawling round the floor of our van, whilst we stood around like spare parts, apologising for the dog hair and general grime. A fourth locksmith came across to take on the key role of dog entertainer and passed the majority of his working day throwing the squeaky toy collection around the car park. I could see a number of parallels between his task and my former employment – certainly a squeaky dog toy would've been more than enough intellectual stimulation for my former boss.

After 30 minutes with pliers, trying to extricate the half key, the owner took us aside, and in the tone of voice usually reserved for news of a life threatening illness, gently revealed that they would have no choice but to drill out the lock. Realising we were stuck between a rock and a locked place, Chris tried not to think about the drill coming out the other side and into the laptop and camera and silently nodded his assent.

With extreme reverence a large drill was brought to the van and the screeching, dentist noise began. A shout told us when they'd got through and by some further mechanical jiggery pokery they were able to take the entire lock out and then remove the door from its hinges. Suddenly our worldly possessions were revealed in all their glory, with only some metal dust to show for their recent high risk existence.

After the initial drilling there were cheers and handshakes all round and even Oscar paused in his toy chasing to check that his rabies certificate was still safe. But beyond the initial euphoria came the recognition that we no longer had a safe. Instead, we had an open plan set of shelves, which might not deter your average burglar – unless they were offended by the dubious Feng shui of having them on the floor. Our locksmith in shining armour soon had an answer. Although they didn't have a replacement barrel, they would drive round the other locksmiths in town until they found one and then fit it for us. The only downside was that it would probably take most of the day, so did we want to go sightseeing in town and then pick it up later?

Slightly surprised that we could take over an entire company for a day with one lock, and verging on the suspicious because they were just so nice, we looked for reassurance from the dog toy supervisor. Surely nobody could be this nice to a dog and then filch his rabies certificate? It seemed a reasonable premise on which to base the decision to leave the contents of our lives with a stranger and so we headed into town. As a parting shot, they gave us a recommendation for a good cake shop and the judgement was confirmed – anyone who likes cakes and dogs is alright in my book.

Tallinn was serenely beautiful, full of medieval buildings that had been tastefully and, I can only assume, expensively restored. We'd been warned that it might be full of stag parties, but arriving mid week we met only genteel, middle class tourists reading worthy accounts of the architectural styles on display. Climbing to the top of the city walls I saw a town of two halves – the half that's visited by tourists, full of immaculate buildings, which could easily grace any chocolate box. And the half left from the Soviet Union days, full of utilitarian, square buildings, demonstrating what we in the UK now view as the very worst of 60s and 70s architecture. Compared with the genteel parks and polite information boards of the historic centre the contrast was sharp and I wondered how the Estonians will eventually bring these two halves together to make one city. Will the ugly grey boxes one day be viewed with the same historical interest as the turrets and towers, or will the only solution be a bulldozer and a blank sheet of paper?

After a pleasant day spent admiring beautiful buildings and eating fine cakes in the park, we returned to the locksmiths. Both of us were slightly nervous that we'd find only an empty room and no sign of a locksmith or a van ever having existed. But no, we weren't about to become another story in the 'Worst Travel Disasters' book. Or at least, not yet. There was the locksmiths shop, still looking as solid as ever and there in the corner of the car park was Bagpuss, with an unnaturally clean floor and a safe in full working order.

The locksmith came outside to chat to us and after the usual discussion of our route and older than expected age, it became clear just why they had spent the whole day working on our van. Despite the apparent economic prowess of Wi-Fi zones in garages, some of the country's new found wealth had yet to trickle down. The locksmith obviously wasn't poor by Estonian standards, but the total charge for a day's labour from 3 people would be about £25. To me this represented substantially better value than two and a half nights of camping for Oscar, but for the locksmith it represented a more salutary amount. We asked him what the country had been like when it first gained its independence.

'It was hard. Very hard. We had a new currency and all our old roubles were almost worthless. They had to be changed for the new Kroons, but nobody could have more than 150 Kroons, no matter how many roubles they had saved under the bed. My aunt lost all her life's savings.'

A quick calculation in my head told me that 150 Kroons then was equivalent to about £6 now. Whilst that was in 1992, when £6 might've bought more, and even though times had undoubtedly changed, there was no doubt that our £25 was still a significant amount to an Estonian locksmith in 2005, and well worth him prioritising over other work.

And yet he hadn't ripped us off. Given our precarious state, deprived of all valuables without his help, he could easily have charged us 10 times that and we would have had little choice but to pay up. I wondered why he'd stuck to such a reasonable price. Talking to him further, it seemed that the very fact that we were, to his eyes, rich Westerners, was also part of the reason why he hadn't charged an excessive amount. I asked him about Estonia's recent

101

entry into the EU.

'I voted against it, my wife voted for it. It's difficult to know what is right. Prices are rising here, but wages don't rise as quickly. But land and houses are still cheap. I think many western Europeans will buy up cheap land here for holiday homes and Estonians won't be able to compete.'

'But isn't it better than being part of the Soviet Union?'

'Of course. Last year, I went back to Russia for the first time in 15 years. And I got the old feeling again, the one I used to get here when we were part of the Soviet Union. I'd forgotten how it felt. But I think Estonia should make its own way for a while. We have already been involved with a superpower, I'm not sure we should rush to be linked with another economic giant. We should just do our own thing. I think the grants from Europe will come at a price.'

I admired his independent spirit and wished that he could be heard by those in Britain who remain convinced that all Eastern Europeans want to come to the UK and live on benefits whilst doing the minimum work possible. Whilst one locksmith and a campsite entrepreneur aren't enough to judge an entire nation, it seemed to me that mostly these people wanted to work and improve their lot, whether in their own country or elsewhere. There seemed to be little interest in sponging off the goodwill of others.

As a final gesture, he gave us an old copy of the Estonian Yellow Pages because it was full of town maps, a handful of boiled sweets and sent us on our way, newly locked up and ready to face the East again.

Chapter 11

The arrival of the missing generation

We entertained ourselves for a further evening in the Tallinn camp-site, admiring our newly locking safe door and debating putting the dog inside it to avoid having to sit on him when anyone came past. But by the morning even the novelty of a lock was starting to wear thin and we packed up with a plan to head east towards a national park and the Russian border. As always happens, because we were trying to hide the free loading, unticketed dog in the van, we suddenly became the most popular people on the campsite. Everybody wanted to come over and ask us about the van, or about Scotland, or that nasty sounding cough I had that was so bad I almost sounded like a dog barking.

Our first visitors were an Antipodean couple, in the midst of their 'overseas experience' and heading north with a van almost as old as ours. They asked various technical questions about spares and filling gas cylinders and once we were confident in their skin-flinty nature we allowed Oscar out from under the bed to subject them to his routine security measures (nose in crotch).

Despite a common interest in the van and how to survive the astronomical prices of Scandinavia they still seemed incredibly young. In reality they were probably about 19, but part of me wanted to ask them if they'd got proper insurance and had they rung home recently. I limited myself to a few generalities about eating properly and not drinking too much before Chris bundled me into the dog's recently vacated under-bed spot. But my social deficiencies apart, there was no denying that there must be a good ten years between us. We were worrying about whether or not the rent on our house would cover the mortgage payments and if ageing parents would hold up until we got back to the UK. And they weren't subjects which I would have been interested in discussing at 19 and I couldn't imagine these 19 year olds were any different.

After a few minutes they politely made their escapes, probably wondering if the van was big enough to fit our Zimmer frames and bedpans. Just as Oscar was adjusting to life in the daylight, a German couple from the adjacent campervan appeared.

'You are from Britain yes?'

'Yes, we live in Scotland, it's in the north,' I began, about to start on my usual explanation.

'Ah, Scotland, it is very beautiful. But I wondered, is it as expensive to visit as people say?'

'Not if you like macaroni pies and Irn Bru,' I shot back, in a non-Tourist-Board-approved answer. Fortunately, Chris managed a more constructive response and we launched into the usual traveller exchanges of where we'd come from and where we were heading.

To our surprise, we discovered they were planning a similar route to ours, and had started travelling in Norway only a few weeks after us. They were also aiming for Spain and planned to take about a year for the whole journey. What unnerved me further was their hair – they both had sprinklings of grey and one of them definitely had a bald patch developing. But they certainly weren't old enough to be retired and I figured they were probably in their late thirties. They turned out to have given up jobs as well and were going through similar concerns about whether they had permanently consigned themselves to the HR Manager's 'dropout' pile when the CVs were sifted.

After countless campsites and thousands of other 'Vannies' we'd finally found the only other two thirty-somethings in Europe who had decided to jack it all in and hit the open road. Nearly three months into the trip, the missing generation had finally decided to put in an appearance. The only surprise was that the missing generation was pink.

The image of a gay German couple in a campervan isn't one that instantly springs to mind. But there they were and if, as it seemed, the only attendees from the missing generation at this party were either gay or with a dog, well so be it. We swapped emails and mobile numbers and headed on our way with promises to meet again soon, heaving a sigh of relief at the knowledge that we were not alone.

~

After only a short drive we found our national park destination, and spent a couple of days hiking in the trees. Sadly we were greeted again by the Finnish elephant mosquito which had discovered the absence of the iron curtain and spread into Estonia. In another striking demonstration of the strange mix of old and new that had so far typified this country, we stayed in a field at the back of someone's house. Described as a campsite with full facilities, it was a piece of grass with the world's shortest long-drop toilet. Not to put too fine a point on it, it was a pile of shit with a seat above it. Now picture that in 30 degree heat, and you'll understand my sudden move to a diet consisting entirely of eggs. Sanitary facilities seemed fairly low down on Estonia's development list and yet the following morning an entire film crew moved into the field, where they were shooting an advert for national television. State of the art television cameras whirled around and stressed TV executives shouted into mobile phones. And in the middle of it all sat the pile-of-shit loo, un-fussed and unchanged for dozens of years. Part of me wondered if they'd got their priorities in the right order, but maybe they wondered the same about us. As I was to learn later in our trip, you can get used to a lot when it comes to bathrooms.

The remainder of our time in Estonia passed in a similar manner. Driving through the countryside we saw a mix of rapid technological advancement combined with a lack of development of basic facilities. Many Soviet era collective farms had been left to rot – huge concrete blocks of buildings with dangerous looking roofs and clanking machinery, followed by state of the art hotels only a few hundred metres away. We even had a hectic eight minute walk up the highest hill in the Baltic countries, all 318 metres of it. From the top, there was a dramatic view of not a whole lot – trees and flat land with occasional concrete blocks. A deeply under-whelming view, and yet many of the towns contained staggeringly beautiful churches and monuments. It seemed to be a country of contrasts – the mix of technological wizardry and old fashioned plumbing (if you can call a hole in the ground plumbing); utilitarian buildings mixed with opulent orthodox churches and a people who wanted to deny all previous links to the Soviet Union whilst selling Russian dolls in every tourist town.

~

A few weeks into the trip we'd made an arrangement to meet my parents in Germany in late September. The plan was for them to hire an apartment and for us to stay with them, enjoying a week of luxury and the opportunity to be able to turn round without hitting a cupboard. This meant we were committed to making it to Germany by the third week in September, something which went slightly against our dreams of an open, unconstrained road. But the promise of a small amount of luxury had been more than enough to convince us to compromise our ideals. As we pottered around Estonia in late August, we realised we'd have to start to make significant progress south in the near future, and so we headed for the Latvian border with new determination.

And of course, the moment we realised we'd got some serious mileage to cover, the van decided to up the stakes on the smoke-belching, oil-dripping, van-on-the-verge-of-nervous-breakdown act. Finally, deciding that we really couldn't drag it much further, we persuaded a helpful campsite owner to book Bagpuss into a garage on the edge of Riga. Both of us were beginning to prepare for bad news as we left the van with the Latvian mechanic and headed out to see the sights of the Riga.

I'm sure I wasn't in my most receptive mood, but Riga completely failed to captivate me in the same way as Tallin. There were beautiful buildings aplenty, but there were also lots of beautiful people. People who seemed to feel they owned the pavement and that you should get out of their way, preferably as quickly as your scruffy little legs would carry you. No one stopped to fuss over Oscar, or even slowed their pace. Instead, they whisked straight by us, glaring crossly if we didn't haul Oscar out of their path instantly. I'm sure some of this stemmed from the heat – Oscar was getting slower and slower by the second and had to sit down in the shade every five minutes. And probably the people of the city were also hot and bothered and just wanted to get to work without tripping over dim tourists. But somehow it made the whole place seem horribly unfriendly.

It wasn't helped by the city's horrific history over the last century. Occupied by the Germans in 1941, the city's Jewish population was pretty much exterminated. Estimates of the number killed vary between 45,000 and 100,000 and even today the Jewish population in the city has still not returned to its pre-war levels. After the war, Soviet Union repression took over and forced deportations took place, with many citizens relocated to Siberia. Residents were no longer able to visit the city's Freedom Monument, erected in the 1930s and representing the three regions of Latvia, although an alternative statue of Lenin was built conveniently nearby. The Freedom monument became a focus for the Latvian independence movement in the late 1980s but a further five people were to die with hundreds injured before independence finally came in 1991. Whilst the city is a bustling hub now, it's hard to forget that sort of a past and perhaps sometimes you just can't airbrush history.

~

Later on that day, we trudged our way slowly back to the garage and the mechanic delivered his damming verdict. £700 and two weeks of repairs, or you've only got 200 kilometres left. So there we were. No longer the international jet setters of my imagination, but the grungy dropouts who were going to have to hitch hike to Aberdeen. Or spend a heck of a lot of cash.

Not an easy choice, especially as both of us felt slightly uneasy with the mechanic – there was something about his manner that meant I didn't quite trust him – probably because he'd yet to make eye contact with either of us. It's always impossible to tell if a garage is ripping you off and I'm sure I've paid for a lot of work to cars that wasn't essential, but now it was even harder to tell. To this guy we were presumably two rich Western Europeans who could afford not to work and to drive round Europe instead. Hence we must be loaded and maybe he saw an opportunity to talk us into expensive repairs that didn't really need doing. But on the other hand there was no denying that the van wasn't looking healthy – it was causing significant air pollution and could no longer be left in car parks without an oil slick appearing. Should we admit defeat and resign ourselves to a huge bill and the opportunity to see every single sight in Riga at least twice, or should we take the risk and push onwards? Or should we abandon our plans completely and head back to Scotland, hoping the van would last as far as Aberdeen. Or abandon the van as well and test European compassion by attempting to hitch hike with a smelly dog.

Eventually suspicion got the better of us and we agreed to take the van away and think about it overnight. We drove to an uninspiring city campsite and headed to the nearest supermarket to fill up on cheap beer – on the grounds that as alcoholic overindulgence had got us into this mess to start with, it could damn well get us out again.

We spent the evening sitting in the van, drinking cheap beer and worrying. It was another roasting night so we gave up on shorts and sat around in t-shirts and knickers, with a slowly increasing pile of bottles on the floor. It was too hot to have the door closed, but the mosquitoes were out in force, so we were reduced to spreading the mosquito net across the door, turning the lights out and sitting in the dark, half cut and half dressed. We must have made a merry picture as we gradually became more morose, but just as we began to think about going to bed and waiting for it to look better in the morning, two beaming faces suddenly popped up on the other side of the mosquito net.

'Aha, we found you again. How is your travelling? And where is my friend Oscar?'

Like two sudden rays of pink sunshine, Kris and Wolfgang, the other half of the missing generation, had arrived late at the campsite, and had decided to do a quick wander round just in case we'd made it this far. Without batting an eyelid, they came into the darkened van, stepped around the beer bottle collection, ignored our semi-dressed state and insisted we came to their much larger van to drown our sorrows instead. They spent the remainder of the evening listening to our woes, making sympathetic noises and helping us to see the funny side of our predicament. By the time we finally went to bed, much, much later, it all looked a lot less bleak and we were beginning to feel brave enough to stagger on.

In the morning we compared guidebooks and discussed where we wanted to visit in Latvia and Lithuania. Our lists had some places in common, so we agreed to meet up at various locations over the next few hundred miles, to check we were still on the road. Because when the shit hits the fan, the missing generation have to be there for each other – ready and waiting with a cup of tea and a ride to the cheap beer shop.

~

I felt slightly reassured now that we had some semblance of a back up plan, even if it only went as far as The Boys (as we now found ourselves calling them) giving us a free ride down the road. And so we decided to bite the bullet and see if we couldn't have a good time for the next 200 kilometres, even if that was all we'd got.

Later that morning we collected the van, shunned the dubious mechanic and headed off towards an impressive sounding palace near the Lithuanian border – only an hour's drive away, but using up 60 of our precious last kilometres in the process.

Pilsrundale Palace was built by Rastrelli, an Italian master who also created St Petersburg's Winter Palace. It was originally designed as a summer residence for the Duke of Courland and was certainly a step up on your average holiday cottage, containing a total of 138 rooms. It stayed in private ownership until the 1920s, when it was passed over to the state and used at various times as flats, a school and, incredibly, a granary. It fell into disrepair after the Second World War, but restoration work began in the 1970s and has now reached the stage where about a third of the rooms are open to the public. It turned out to be every bit as impressive as we'd hoped – showing the lives of the Russian nobility in all their glory. I suspect that a British heritage expert would have thought the whole thing was hugely over restored, but for me it worked just perfectly. The rooms were lavishly furnished with draped beds, room height ceramic stoves and other wonders that you just don't find in Ikea.

I'd made it all the way through War and Peace during the somewhat less visually stimulating Finnish weeks, and had now worked my way further into the good book collection by starting on Anna Karenina. The harmonica lessons may not have taken off, but I'd got seriously into Russian literature. As I stood in the palace ballroom I felt I could imagine Anna and all her counterparts dancing the night away around me. In the same way as Pride and Prejudice and Colin Firth are now inextricably linked in my head, so Tolstoy's books and this opulent old Russian palace had also formed one image. I'll never know whether this was just good timing, but in spite of its over-restored and probably not entirely authentic touching up, the rooms of this palace had bought history to life for me in a way that a set of incomplete ruins somehow couldn't achieve.

Chapter 12

The name's Bagpuss,
James Bagpuss

After taking our fill of Russian aristocracy, we headed further south and squandered more of our limited kilometres in a meandering route across the Lithuanian border.

Passing through borders had become almost routine now. After the initial struggle to get Oscar into Norway, interest had since declined to such an extent that when we handed over our three passports, the customs official would hand the dog passport straight back.

But, of course, Oscar wasn't content with taking such a backseat in formalities, and he soon dreamed up a new plan to ensure he remained star of the show. As we cruised up to the Lithuanian border we were slightly flummoxed by a request to see our vehicle registration document, safely hidden away in the re-modelled safe. And carefully installed on top of the safe was one special travelling dog seat, complete with one special travelling dog. The simple solution would've been for Oscar to leap off his seat and out of the way, so we could get to the safe with minimal fuss. But when does a dog ever take the simple solution? Oscar was struck by another of his 'primadogga' moments and refused to budge, causing frazzled nerves for us and mild amusement for the waiting inspectors.

After a few minutes of fruitless dog shoving, the amusement began to turn to frustration and the queue of waiting cars behind us started to build. Sensing the need for a quick resolution, I grabbed Oscar, hauled him off his seat and plonked him on my lap. At which point Oscar seized his opportunity for stardom, pushed his full 25 kilos of weight backwards into my chest and thrust his head and shoulders out the window and into the face of the waiting official. The customs guy looked slightly bemused, but then, as we were beginning to learn was standard practice, he succumbed to Oscar's charms and began to pat the emergent head.

And as usual, Chris and I were left to clear up behind Oscar. Confusion and dog slaver reigned as I failed to get Oscar's head back in the van and the appropriate certificate out. By the time it finally reached the customs man, I could tell he was wishing he'd never asked for it in the first place. I have to say I wouldn't have blamed him if he'd refused entry to these two travellers and their dictatorial dog. But to my surprise, he waved us through, brushing dog hairs from his jacket as he turned and shrugged to a colleague.

Once we were all back in our respective seats, including Oscar's ego, we headed a few minutes down the road in search of one of Lithuania's most famous sights – the Hill of Crosses.

The Hill of Crosses is a place which does exactly what it says on the tin. It's a hill. Full of crosses. Not a huge hill, but nevertheless a big enough rise in the ground that it requires steps to reach the top. And the entire hillside is covered in crosses. Small ones, big ones, ornate ones, plain ones, old ones, new ones. Covering an area equivalent to two football fields, the site has survived despite frequent attempts to remove it. During the Soviet occupation, the hill was bulldozed and the crosses removed on several occasions. But mysteriously, in an almost comic way, as soon as they knocked them down, people would steal out in the darkness and start to rebuild. Crosses would reappear until the whole process re-started and the site would be razed again. Now that Lithuania has its independence and people are free to worship whatever god they choose, the site has grown and grown, with recent estimates putting the number of crosses at well over the 50,000 mark.

We arrived at the Hill of Crosses on a Saturday afternoon and expected to find only a handful of tourists there. To our surprise, the place was heaving and we had to fight for a parking space.

'What the hell's going on?' Chris muttered as he tried to shoehorn the van into a space designed for a Ford Fiesta. 'I don't think I've seen this many tour buses anywhere else in the Baltics. Why are they all here?'

'No idea. I wouldn't have thought it was a huge tourist draw at this time of year. In fact, I wouldn't have thought there were this many tourists in Lithuania right now. Where've they all come from?'

'Look at the hill though, it's crawling with people – they look like ants from here.'

Squeezing ourselves out through the tiny crack between adjacent cars, we walked over towards the hill. Only as we got to the base did I realise the buses weren't for tourists – they were for photographers of a very different variety.

'Look, over there, that's got to be a wedding party. That girl's definitely wearing a wedding dress.'

'Let's hope so, otherwise we've really under-dressed for being a tourist here' Chris warned.

'There's another group over there as well. In fact, they're queuing up. It's like some sort of Hollywood chick flick – there must be about 10 brides running round here.'

For reasons which I assume are ingrained deep in the Lithuanian psyche, the Hill of Crosses was clearly THE place to have your wedding photos taken. The handful of tourists visiting the site was completely outnumbered by the wedding parties, complete with chilly brides and drunken uncles. Every time I tried to walk up the hill itself I would head off along what looked like a bride free path, turn a corner and find myself bumping into the back of a charmingly posed family group. There may well be several Lithuanian families who've since looked at their wedding photos and questioned how exactly they are related to the slightly scruffy girl at the back, the one standing just behind the bridesmaids.

I wondered why they might have chosen this site as a venue for photos. It was undoubtedly a striking place, but it wouldn't have been my first thought if I was challenged to come up with a beautiful Lithuanian background. To me it seemed a slightly macabre place, like electing to have your wedding photos taken in the middle of a graveyard or next to the war memorial. Maybe it serves as an act of defiance. If this place had been destroyed so many times, then surely there is no better way of thumbing your nose at the old occupiers than recording the site in a thousand and one photographs. Or maybe it's just tradition. Perhaps it seems odd to the Lithuanians that we choose to have old churches and castles in photos. If I'd spoken more Lithuanian (OK, if I'd spoken *any* Lithuanian) I would've liked to ask a passing bride. But sadly I had neither the linguistic skills nor the confidence to butt into a family celebration and we left the site still wondering. Later investigations revealed a visit by Pope John Paul to the site in the early 1990s, which may have started the trend, but until I bump into another Lithuanian bride, I guess I'll never know.

After meeting most of the population of the country in one afternoon, we decided to head towards a National Park in the evening, looking for the quieter side of Lithuania. We arrived at the outskirts of the park late in the evening and searched fruitlessly for a campsite. After much driving in circles, we were both excited to suddenly spot 3 or 4 tents, pitched together by the edge of a small lake. A few hundred metres away were some old farm buildings, with a track leading in from the road. Assuming this was the campsite entrance, we screeched in and found ourselves in the middle of a rustic farmyard. Faces appeared at the door and peered out at us. Guessing they were perhaps low on tourists now that it was later in the summer, Chris stopped the engine and jumped out to pay our allotted fee. The owner of one of the faces left the door and walked nervously towards him, whilst Chris tried to smile in an encouraging, non-psychopathic kind of way.

'Do you speak English?' he asked, with a polite smile. The man shook his head.

'Lithuanian. Russian,' he answered. Hmmm. Chris' ability in either language was non-existent, so he moved into sign language.

'Camping?' he asked whilst trying to make a gesture that I think was supposed to be a tent, but could also have been 'It's a play' in a game of charades. The man looked confused, surprisingly so for a campsite owner, but after some further gesticulating from Chris he seemed to get the general idea and shrugged his shoulders. Capitalism didn't appear to have made it out here, but the owner spent some time wandering round the yard and eventually found a flattish spot which he pointed at, then pointed at the van, presumably suggesting it as a parking spot.

'Toilets?' Chris asked, hopefully. This was then followed by various gestures which I won't describe here, in case his mother ever reads this. Unsurprisingly the man cottoned onto this question rather more quickly and took Chris to one of the farm buildings, and solemnly showed him a hole in the ground, with a makeshift seat above it.

'OK. And dog OK?' I got Oscar out of the van and held him up in an 'Exhibit A' kind of way. The campsite owner looked mildly shocked, then shook his head firmly and pointed at the suddenly growling farm dog tied up in the corner. This was followed by gestures which I think were supposed to say:

'If you put that dog within forty paces of my dog he will eat it alive and only leave you the tail.'

This didn't seem such a good idea, so we all made polite shrugging signs, smiled nicely and Chris and I beetled back to the van. As we drove back down the road, I suddenly spotted the fence that ran between the farm and the lake.

'You know…I'm not sure they're anything to do with those tents – there's a fence all the way along the edge of the farm buildings with no way through.'

'Oh God, you're right. Maybe those people have pitched their tents there because they thought it was a nice spot, rather than because it's a campsite.'

'And that man must've thought we'd just driven in and asked to camp in his garden, use his bathroom and let our dog run round his yard – without even being polite enough to speak his language!'

'So he's probably in there right now, telling his mates about the rude Brits who demanded to use his house, in sign language' Chris moaned.

'Still, it's impressive that he even thought about it. I mean, if it wasn't for Oscar I think he would've let us stay. I'm not sure I'd be so helpful if a vanful of Lithuanians pulled onto our drive and demanded to use the facilities.'

'Do you think we should go back and try and explain?' Chris asked.

'In sign language! Yeah, right. It'd take you all night. We'll just have to put it down to experience and hope he manages to dine out on the story for a few nights.'

So far our Lithuanian camping experiences weren't going well and it was starting to get dark. From out of nowhere a small campsite sign appeared and in our enthusiasm we raced straight in, paid a hefty chunk of money, texted Kris and Wolfgang to tell them about this great site in the National Park and then, and only then, went to use the loos. Or loo, singular. Or, more accurately, heap of ….. well, you get the picture. We appeared to have paid good money for the privilege of experiencing a small shed enclosing a heap of shit. Without even a seat. Marvellous. A second text to The Boys followed, warning them to head elsewhere. By then it was completely dark, so I decided to pick the nearest patch of short grass and risk mooning at the world. Only in the morning did I discover I'd peed all over their makeshift tennis court.

Lithuania had a lot to do to make up for our first night's camping experience. And a former nuclear missile site doesn't seem like an obvious tourist attraction for someone trying to find the scenic side of a country, but that's where we ended up. In amongst the details of beaches and cities, our guidebook contained a short paragraph about a former Soviet nuclear missile site, which was open to visitors. Whilst this sounded a bit mawkish, it also sounded like something we wouldn't see every day, so we followed the somewhat sketchy directions and drove down a bumpy track and into the middle of a forest. Just as we were about to give up and go elsewhere, Chris spotted a rusty gate further up the track, with some oddly symmetrical bulges in the ground behind.

We parked by the gate and got out of the van to a deathly silence. The gate was locked and the whole place seemed deserted, until a young woman appeared from the small hut nearby.

'Hello. How are you? You want tour of site?'

We agreed that we did, passed over a small number of Litus and waited whilst she unlocked the gate. To begin with she walked around on the grass, pointing out bits of decaying building and using military sounding terms, most of which meant nothing to me. Then, she unlocked a small, half sunken door, and invited us to follow her down a narrow passageway. Once we entered, the floor began to slope down into the ground and the temperature dropped dramatically. I tried to ignore the small shiver running down my back as our footsteps clattered in the silence.

We followed our guide into various rooms, past some pipes that were even rustier than the van and into more corridors that gradually took us lower and lower. Finally she opened a hatch in the last corridor and motioned for us to climb through the hatch and up a small ladder. Chris went ahead of me and I heard a low whistle followed by a 'Bloody hell' as he came to the top of the ladder. I squeezed through behind him and followed his exclamation with one of my own. We were perched on a small balcony which ran round in a circle, halfway up a cylindrical hole in the ground. Our guide informed us that the hole was 26 metres deep, six metres across and lined with metal.

'In this area, the missiles. Roof, slides back. Missiles launched once roof back.'

Looking up we could see that the domed roof was indeed designed to slide back, in true James Bond style.

'Missiles pointed at different places. Change all the time. Could be launched in few seconds.'

That'll be your four minute warning then. A strange sensation ran over me as I looked at this metal lined crater. I remembered those nights I'd spent as an over imaginative small child, worrying about the Russians dropping a bomb on us. And now I was standing where those very missiles had been. According to our guide, even the Lithuanians didn't know it existed – they only found the site after the Russians had left.

In some ways, now that the site had fallen into disrepair it was even scarier. Bits of metal clanked and creaked and water dripped down intermittently. But, with very little effort, you could imagine the place a hive of activity, with Sean Connery sneaking through whilst soldiers marched in the corridors and pressed significant looking buttons. Somehow, as I've got older, and the Cold War has thawed, I've begun to think that these kind of places only ever existed in films and that my childhood worries were irrational. And yet, here, in cold, damp, dark detail was just such a place. And in my lifetime this very place *was* full of soldiers, *did* have significant looking buttons, and could've bought civilisation to its knees. No wonder Bond spends so much time drinking vodka martinis. I felt like a stiff drink myself.

After thanking our guide we both left the site in silence. I imagine that as health and safety law is tightened in Lithuania they will either stop people visiting, or the whole site will be cleaned up and sanitised. And in doing so it will probably lose some of its power. But in its raw, unedited state it was a dramatic and powerful testament to the very real chill of the Cold War and its frightening proximity.

In an attempt to lighten the tone, I entertained myself with Bond girl impressions in the van as we drove out of the forest. Of course, screeching round corners whilst looking impossibly glamorous was difficult in a clapped out campervan with black smoke belching out the back and a wardrobe of only two pairs of grotty hiking trousers. But I made a sterling effort and I could see that Oscar was certainly shaken, not stirred.

~

Surprisingly, even after my Bond girl driving, we'd managed to rack up nearly 170 kilometres and so far there'd been no sign of the terminal decline predicted by the Riga garage. We were now on the western coast of Lithuania and had planned a quick visit across to the Curonian spit – a long strip of sand that separates the Baltic Sea from the Curonian lagoon. The spit was reputed to have some of the Baltic's finest beaches, but also to have some of the Baltic's highest prices, with the 7 minute ferry across to the spit priced eye wateringly high. To reduce costs and to try and avoid a van breakdown with only some sand for company, we arranged with The Boys that we'd all pile into their swish van for the visit to the Spit. So for two days we got to live it up in campervan luxury – admiring the décor, revelling in the idea of an electric water pump and other luxuries (our water had to be pumped through a filter by foot pump, which required so much pressure it made the entire van rock, giving the impression we were undertaking an athletic bedroom session every time one of us wanted a drink).

Oscar of course had the time of his life – not only were there four people to give him attention now rather than a measly two, but he also got to spend all day jumping around through sand dunes, his favourite landscape. He threw himself down dunes with enthusiasm, ensuring he got sand into every part of his fur so he could then flick it across the posh van with a single shake of his coat. Kris and Wolfgang managed to turn a blind eye to his attempts to trash their home, mostly because they were also excited by the miles of beach and dune. But Chris and I struggled to find much enthusiasm for it – the dunes were reminiscent of the ones on the Aberdeenshire coast and, whilst the weather was undoubtedly better, to us coast dwellers it all looked rather familiar.

It seemed The Boys had a bit of an advantage by living in the middle of the continent: not only were they genuinely excited by the prospect of sand in their sandals, but they could also call in at home halfway round their trip. As we were all about to head into Poland and then Germany, they could see the upcoming excitement of catching up with family and friends.

Once we'd all got over the novelties this short trip had offered, we did take the chance to have some serious conversations about the missing generation – wondering why we were out here, where everyone else was and why the only ones on the road were either gay or with a dog. Should we be at home with a proper job and a mortgage, forever grateful to our employers? Was that the right thing to be doing? Was this the wrong thing to be doing? And if so, why were we enjoying it so much?

~

Returning from the Spit we planned to drive across to Vilnius, capital city of Lithuania and to use the drive across the country to make a decision on where to go next. As we passed the Riga garage's fated 200 kilometre mark, the van showed no signs of further deterioration, so we needed to decide how to head south. The safe option was to keep to the coast, following close behind Kris and Wolfgang so we had a back up vehicle that could help us out if Bagpuss decided to give up the ghost. We could then turn left at the end of what used to be East Germany and head south to our rendezvous with my parents by using the main German auto-bahns, where we stood a better chance of getting a breakdown vehicle.

The alternative plan was to head south first, crossing through Poland and making a line for Krakow, followed by the Tatras Mountains and Slovakia, before heading west towards the Czech Republic and Germany. This would take us a long way from anyone we knew, and would leave us more exposed on the breakdown front, particularly as we spoke no Polish, and only a few words of Slovak and Czech (and they mostly consisted of toilet, vodka and bar). It would also mean we'd need to cross the Tatras, involving the van in a laborious uphill climb that would result in billowing clouds of black smoke.

But the north of Poland didn't appeal – whilst the beaches were probably beautiful, we'd conclusively proved that we got our fair share of beaches at home, even if they weren't quite as warm, and the idea of visiting the city of Krakow was more attractive. We were also both starting to feel a need to see some mountains again – there'd been no real mountains since Norway and the relentlessly flat landscape was beginning to take its toll.

We discussed the choice at length and in the end decided to use the drive to Vilnius as a test. If the van cruised the 150 kilometres across Lithuania we'd decide the Riga garage was wrong, head into Poland and maybe look for a garage there. But if it died on the Lithuanian highway, we'd call in the German cavalry and use The Boys as a high class back up vehicle.

With bated breath, we set off on the super highway. And maybe it was a super highway. The driving was smooth, quiet and – dare I say it – almost pleasant. We looked around and admired the rural scenery, rather than constantly checking the thickness of the belching smoke behind us. We were even able to appreciate the gentle irony of the flashy Mercedes parked on the side of the road, with a driver trying to ease two milk churns out of the boot. And in less time than we'd expected, we'd arrived on the edge of Vilnius. At the last minute Bagpuss had finally come up with the goods and acted like a proper, grown up van rather than the temper tantrum prone teenager we knew it to be.

And so the decision was made. We would head south through Poland and see what the mountains would bring. But our first port of call was a quick trip into Vilnius to see the sights of the capital city. Despite the sweltering heat and road works, we managed to admire a few buildings before heading back to the van, parked on the side of the road in what we'd been told was one of the safer districts of town.

As we walked back towards it, the sun was just catching the back door, illuminating its thick layer of dust, as well as some strange looking handprints in the grime.

'Chris are those your handprints on the back?' I asked.

'I don't think so, they're too big. And they're all round the lock, which….,' Chris tailed off.

We both had the same thought at the same time and set off down the road at a sprint. Sure enough, when we got to the back of the van, it was clear someone had tried to prise the lock open. But it was also clear, much to my surprise, that they'd failed and had either given up or been disturbed. Our worldly possessions were still in the back of the van, and other than a slight dent in the bodywork by the lock, everything had survived unscathed.

In the space of a few hours, the van had gone from being the poor cousin of the proper campervans, to our hero – outlasting the 200 kilometre doomsday deadline and even fighting off burglars. Maybe we had misjudged the van. Maybe we would come to love this saggy old, baggy old thing one day and maybe it wouldn't stay the Fuckit Bucket for ever. Time would tell – but for now – we were heading south by the high road.

Chapter 13

Kaput in Krakow

We said a sad goodbye to Kris and Wolfgang and promised to meet up with them in Germany, particularly as my parents would be staying near their hometown. They'd been travel agents before they joined the missing generation so we figured they ought to be able to offer us the full guided tour when we were on their home turf.

And then we headed out of Vilnius and onto the main road south. But we had one more port of call before we left Lithuania, one which seemed slightly at odds with our normal itinerary of city culture and National Parks. We were heading to a theme park. But this wasn't just an ordinary theme park – no Disneyland or Alton Towers for us. No – we were headed to Stalinworld, a theme park dedicated to the Soviet Union's impact on Lithuania.

Arriving at the park and unconvinced that such a paradox could exist, we parked up and headed towards the main entrance. Stretched along the side of the pavement were a series of notice-boards, plastered with newspaper articles about the place we were intending to visit. And it was clear that it was a controversial place, where the boundaries of good taste were being systematically explored. The owner had made a fortune in mushroom farming. Even more impressively, it appeared to have been made in the legal kind. He'd then decided to give something back to his country by using his fungal cash to buy up old Russian statues. These mostly consisted of Stalin, Lenin and others frozen in macho looking postures, and, not surprisingly, after Lithuanian independence, they weren't in much demand for town centres. But rather than consign them to the scrapheap of both town and history, Mr Malinauskas, the mighty mushroom mogul, had collected them in his back garden and spotted an opportunity to make a quick buck. At least, that's the less charitable explanation. His more charitable view was that he was preserving Russian culture so that the Lithuanians would never forget what had happened to their country. According to the newspaper biographies his father had been deported by the Russians, so it wasn't hard to imagine that he might have a grudge against them. But on the other hand, he seemed to have made his fortune during the time of the Soviet Union, implying that he could've been batting for both teams, so to speak.

But whatever his reasons for creating Stalinworld, it was certainly a bizarre place. A small path led us through a conifer forest and every hundred metres or so, we'd find a clearing amongst the trees that had been filled with another group of statues. In some cases these were Russian greats that I didn't recognise, but in other places there would be four or five different statues of Lenin or Stalin all grouped together. Interspersed with the statues were buildings containing Russian artefacts, from soldiers' uniforms to propaganda posters. Most of the statues and artefacts had some accompanying explanatory text, some with English translations, which gave us a clearer steer on Stalinworld's view of the Soviet Union. To complete the image, loudspeakers around the park played stirring Russian music, which drifted through the statues, giving them a faint air of music hall theatricality.

When we'd completed our 'theme park' tour, I still felt something was missing. The displays had been unequivocal in their damnation of the Soviet Union and the damage it had done to Lithuania. But nowhere was there a monument to those who had lost their lives as part of the occupation. Undoubtedly countless Lithuanians had been tortured and killed by Russian troops, and even as recently as 1991, thirteen people were killed as the country struggled to achieve independence. Surely in a theme park dedicated to the evils of this regime, there should be some lasting tribute to these people and their suffering? Without it, the park felt trite and I could understand why so many people had criticised it for taking a lightweight angle on such a heavyweight reality. So was the mushroom mogul only trying to make a quick buck out of his country's history? Or was he, as he claimed, trying to make sure that the people of his country never forgot why his father and others had died? Is it possible to make a theme park out of history without it appearing shallow and even if you can, should you do it with such recent history? Perhaps using a theme park format served to lighten the historical load and allowed previously warring factions to look at one another more gently. Maybe it lessened some of the guilt and helped us all to move forward constructively to a new and better place.

In contrast, Kris had told me of their visit to the Holocaust museum in Vilnius. He'd explained how the information was presented in Estonian, German and English and admitted to only reading the English version because he felt too guilty and embarrassed to raise his eyes high enough to read the German version, located further up the wall. It is surely clear to anyone with an ounce of sense that the Holocaust must not be forgotten or tidied away. But should we find a way of presenting it that doesn't make the current generation of Germans feel guilty for something that happened thirty years before they were born? Particularly when you consider that Kris would have been an early target for Hitler's regime. It didn't seem to me that Stalinworld was necessarily the right answer to this problem, but I had to give the mushroom man credit for his creative approach.

Musing on these questions, we left the confusion of Stalinworld and headed back to the road south. A few minutes later, we headed into Poland, where we'd been warned to expect nothing but fierce dogs (cue Oscar standing behind me), potholed roads and car crime.

By now we'd met several German tourists who had travelled up through Poland and were more than happy to tell us how our van would be broken into instantly, shortly before the big dogs came to eat Oscar. Although one of those tourists was travelling in a campervan complete with eight dogs, which made me take his views with a pinch of salt. Eight dogs! I was struggling to cope with one – hair everywhere, late night farting and snoring (well, OK, that was Chris as well), random barking (although never when there was any actual danger) and limited entry to bars and restaurants. How anyone could cope with eight dogs in a space the size of a campervan was beyond me. And not only that, but he seemed to have three children in there as well. The van was bigger than ours, but not that much bigger. As we walked past we saw the whole van start swaying as the dogs began to bark and jump around – unsurprisingly the owner seemed a little deaf, even when he was away from the van.

But mad German dog lovers apart, the warnings about Poland were certainly coming thick and fast. And to start with, they seemed well founded. The main roads were potholed and difficult to drive, the other drivers were lunatics who would force you off the road if you travelled at less than eighty miles an hour and there did seem to be an unhealthy interest in the van from spotty teenage boys whenever we parked.

After a particularly stressful couple of hours on the main road we decided to take it easy for a few miles on a country road. I assumed that even if it was badly potholed we might at least be able to drive at van pace in peace. But after a few miles I started to notice something rather odd.

'Do you think this road is smoother than the main one, or is it just me?' I asked, gazing at the gently cambered tarmac in front of us.

'Yeah, it's definitely better, and there are far fewer cars on it.'

'And the ones that are on it don't seem to be driving quite as manically.'

'Well, I wouldn't quite say they were relaxed, but they certainly seem a bit more chilled out.'

'And the people on the streets in the villages are smiling at us, rather than glaring. It's almost like they're pleased to see us, rather than feeling like they're sizing us up.'

'Maybe rural is the way to go then,' Chris decided. 'Even if it's a bit further, I think I'm less likely to have a heart attack this way.'

And so for the remainder of our travels through Poland we stuck to the quiet back roads and discovered a Poland full of smooth roads; friendly villages and if not quite polite, then not actually aggressive drivers. As we pottered through the villages we had time to admire the colourful shrines strewn through the countryside, each with a central cross and brightly coloured streamers threaded around like ribbons on a maypole. The only drawback was the occasional horse and cart returning from the fields, but even this gave it all a relaxed, bucolic feeling, after the stress and bustle of the main highways. And made an entertaining contrast with the Tesco stores that suddenly began to spring up around us. In the space of a few hundred metres, Polish highways give you the opportunity to go from rural idyll to flashing neon, with little in-between. Shopping cart had a whole new meaning here.

The following day we made it to Krakow, putting the van well beyond its 200 kilometre expiry date, although the feeling that we were living on borrowed time still nagged at me. The bits of Krakow that I saw as we drove through to the campsite were every bit as beautiful as claimed. So beautiful in fact that it was hard to keep appreciating each gorgeous building as it came into sight round the next corner. Had you stuck each of the buildings into the suburbs of Swindon they would have stood out as dramatic pearls of architecture. But because they were all piled into together – without so much as an office block to break up the beautiful monotony – I found that I quickly became blasé and stopped noticing the awe inspiring wonder around me. The buildings were dammed by their own relativity – put them all together in one town centre and they became only relatively beautiful, as compared to their equally dazzling neighbours. I felt some central town planning organisation should take Krakow and share it out around all the soulless, concrete towns in the world, so that each little part of it can be appreciated by those truly in need of a decent building, rather than squandering it all in one massive outpouring and allowing visitors to become complacent in its beauty.

But perhaps I was jaded by the heat. Krakow showed no sign of realising we were approaching mid September and was basking in midsummer heat. Daily temperatures were in the low thirties, well beyond Oscar's comfort range. Despite his stoic contributions to sight-seeing so far, we decided city streets in 30 degree heat was more than could reasonably be asked of a dog who was only interested in the lampposts. Instead, we agreed to take it in turns to visit Krakow city centre whilst the other person lazed around by the van with Oscar, taking him for short walks in the suburbs when the temperatures dropped and allowing him to sleep during the midday heat.

Chris was first to hit the big lights and Oscar and I settled down for an afternoon spent sunbathing for me, and shadebathing for him. This was my first opportunity to try and work on my tan, so I planned to take advantage of the relative quiet of the campsite and see if I could even up the unattractive white lines on my legs. Undeterred by my lack of bikini, I whisked off my shorts, and flaked out by the van with bum and slightly holey knickers on display for all to see. Oscar settled down in the shade and I'd just nodded off when I was rudely awakened by his barking, followed by a quick leap over me to the other end of the van, using his dangling lead as an opportunity to give me a rope burn on the bottom as he went. Sitting up bleary eyed, I heard a Scottish accent:

'Hello beautiful. And how are you? You are a beautiful dog aren't you? Isn't anyone with you? Shouldn't you be out on a walk?'

Great. The only opportunity I'd had for sunbathing in the last year and I was being interrupted by someone who would be horrified that Oscar was stuck here by the van, apparently unloved whilst I fussed over my tan. Trying not to look sheepish I slunk round the corner of the van, uncomfortably aware that I wasn't exactly over-dressed for this meeting.

'Hello dear. Are you with this dog? Isn't he lovely? Doesn't he get bored just sitting there?' cooed Oscar's latest middle-aged female admirer.

'Errr…no, I think he's fine. He'll get a walk when it's a bit cooler.' Of course Oscar took this as his cue to rush off and find a toy, thereby demonstrating just how bored he really was.

'He's such a gorgeous dog. What sort is he?'

The usual conversation followed about Oscar's strange parentage and his different coloured eyes. In the midst of the conversation it transpired that Oscar's latest admirer was from Northern Scotland. Somewhat tentatively I asked whereabouts.

'A little village near Aberdeen. You won't have heard of it.'

'Try me.'

'It's a tiny place called Methlick, near somewhere called Tarves. No one's ever heard of it. Where are you from?' For a brief moment I debated lying. I have a nondescript accent, so I could've claimed anything. But honesty got the better of me.

'We're from a little village called Tarves. It's near a place called Methlick. But nobody's ever heard of it.' We both exclaimed over what a small world it was, before I made the fatal mistake of admitting that we used the vet's surgery in Methlick.

'Well, so do we. Do you go to Heather?'

'Yes, she did loads to help us get Oscar here – sorted out all his passport and stuff.'

'Well, I'm going in next week when we get back, so I'll tell her I saw you. I'll say Oscar was tied up by the van and you were sunbathing. I expect she'll be worrying how the poor mite's coping with all this heat.'

Marvellous. I'd spent months looking after Oscar, taking him on long walks, ensuring he was never bored or stressed out by this ridiculous trip. I'd convinced our vet that we were responsible owners who weren't just going somewhere hot to sunbathe whilst he melted. And now, the one and only time Oscar had been shoved in the shade whilst I sunbathed, I'd met someone from the next-door village, in Krakow of all places. And she was going to report back that our poor dog was being dragged from hot pillar to hot post whilst I paraded round in my underwear. As I looked down I could see Oscar glancing up at me and I'm sure he smiled. 'Just remember,' he seemed to be saying, 'I will always, always win.'

~

When Chris returned from his tour of Krakow I was delighted to head off the next day and leave him to manage the dog's ego alone. He muttered about some vague plan to drive out of the city and try a walk in the country, but to be honest, I was so excited by the idea of an entirely dog free day in the city that I didn't pay much attention. I figured I'd enter every café and museum at least once, just to prove I could, without having to stop and ask for dog entry permission.

And so my day passed uneventfully. I visited scenic sights, stopped for regular coffees and didn't once have to beg permission to leave dog hair on the floor. And yet it was all strangely soulless. Nobody came up to pat Oscar, nobody asked me in a mix of languages where he was from, nobody smiled at me and my strange dog. Of course there were pluses – I didn't have to try and remove Oscar's nose from the crotch of the resident drunk or muddy pawprints from the smart city suits. But somehow I didn't feel I got to know the people of the city. I saw the sights and did the tourist thing, but without Oscar's interpersonal skills my only conversations were commercial transactions. I felt further from Krakow's soul than any other city. I was beginning to realise how dependent we were on Oscar's language transcending communication skills and that without him, we would have spoken to only a handful of people in each country.

Feeling oddly bereft I travelled back to the campsite on the commuters' bus. Just as the bus had deposited me at the campsite and driven off in a cloud of dust, a text message came through on my phone.

'Broken down. Gone 2 garage. U need 2 get off bus 3 stops b4 campsite. Love, C&O'

I sighed. But there wasn't much point going into the campsite without something to camp in, so I patiently waited for a bus back into town and got off at what I hoped was the right stop. After wandering up and down the road, I spotted Chris approaching and ran to meet him.

'So what's gone wrong with it this time?'

'I think it's the turbo. The smoke just got worse and worse, so I went to the VW garage.'

'And they said they were far too busy to do it' I said, repeating what we'd heard in countless garages so far.

'Yes, but this guy was really helpful and he rang round the local VW specialists as well and one guy said he'd take us, so it's down this road here.'

'Are you sure? This is all houses.' I was beginning to sense something slightly shifty in Chris' manner.

'I know, but this guy's got a garage in his garage if you see what I mean. And there are loads of VWs there.'

'OK,' I said, suspiciously. 'Does he know what's wrong with it?'

'Well, I think he might, but he doesn't speak any English.'

'Right,' I said, more suspiciously.

'But he speaks German, so we've been talking in German.'

'Chris, you haven't spoken any German for 20 years. You can't know what he's saying.'

'Well, I can sort of get the idea and anyway, I think he can fix it and we can stay on his drive overnight so it's fine, I'm sure,' Chris tumbled the words out, working on the principle that if he said it fast enough I might not notice.

'OK, Chris – I'm hot, I'm tired, I've got period pain and I really, really don't want to sleep on someone's drive.'

'Ohh. Well the engine's in bits, so we can't go anywhere else. We can use the mechanics' toilet though.'

Based on my experience of Eastern European plumbing so far, the idea of a mechanics' toilet in Poland was not remotely appealing.

131

'Fine,' I spat out and we walked the rest of the way to the house in an uncomfortable silence.

As we entered the residential cul-de-sac my suspicions appeared well founded, but at the bottom of the road was a large house with abandoned VW campervans and Beetles strewn around the garden. If it was a fake business then the guy had at least made some effort at camouflage. A remarkably smiley, round man came out of the house and enthusiastically pumped my hand, whilst I floundered around for any words of German.

'Errr...Guten Morgen?' I stuttered.

Not a great effort for six o'clock in the evening, but I think he appreciated the sentiment.

A complicated English / German / Polish conversation followed, with the mechanics pointing at various parts of the engine whilst Chris looked on in confusion. After a vague attempt to follow I lost interest and wandered off with Oscar, only to discover that all the neighbouring houses had BIG dogs that threw themselves manically at the fence as we walked past.

When I returned, Chris attempted to distil the essence of the conversation for me.

'It's the turbo.'

'And it just took you twenty minutes to find that out?'

'His nephew's here tomorrow and he speaks English, so he's going to translate for us.' Chris replied, ignoring my unhelpful questions. 'So we'll stay here tonight and I'll start dinner now.'

A quiet and uneventful night on the driveway followed. The mechanics' loo was no worse than your average UK garage loo, but with fewer page 3 pictures on the walls. The neighbouring dogs quietened down as darkness fell, leaving us to the surreal situation of book reading in a campervan on a suburban driveway.

In the morning the quiet suburban peace was soon shattered by the arrival of the mechanics in a collection of Volkswagen vehicles, all in varying stages of decay. As the van's engine is directly below the bed there wasn't going to be much of a lie in for us, so we took the hint, got up and tried to perform at least minor ablutions in the mechanics' toilet. By the time I'd finished brushing my teeth, I came out to discover my bed pulled onto the ground and bits of vehicle splattered across the lawn. The Fuckit Bucket clearly wasn't going anywhere in a hurry. Oscar and I entertained ourselves by wandering around the neighbourhood, returning each time to discover more bits of engine on the grass and fewer inside the van.

At the end of our third trip round the block, I figured it was time to work out what was going on. By this time the famous nephew had arrived and there were some complicated multi-language conversations going on around me. After a brief burst of arm waving and teeth sucking, Chris came over and explained the latest plan:

'They still think it's the turbo that's broken. They've taken it out, but it would need to be re-machined to be properly fixed and they can't do that here.'

'So what are we supposed to do?'

'Well, they could send it away to be machined, but it'd probably take about 10 days.'

'10 days! And can we use the van in-between?'

'No, the engine won't work without the turbo, so we'd have to stay here.'

'But what about meeting my folks in Germany? That'd only leave us two days to drive there.'

The conversation deteriorated into plans for Oscar and me to continue to Germany on the train, leaving Chris to collect the remains of the van when it was fixed and follow on later. But neither of us was particularly keen on the idea – I didn't fancy negotiating dog and train in countries where I didn't speak the language, and Chris wasn't enthusiastic about spending ten days by himself on someone's drive.

After exhausting the possibilities, we returned to the gaggle of mechanics around the van and, relying heavily on the nephew translation services, began to look at other options. After more hand waving, and gestures at Oscar and me to demonstrate our inability to get ourselves to the end of the road, let alone into another country, the mechanics conceded that there just might be another option. The nephew outlined the plan to us:

'He has another turbo in garage. It's not new and he doesn't know the history but it might not leak as much as this one. He can put that on and it might stop the smoking. It won't last forever, but you might get back to the UK.'

'And how much, roughly, would we be looking at for that?' Chris asked, his nervous tic reappearing.

'Not too much. Maybe 500 zloty.'

A quick calculation told us this was about £130, roughly one fifth the cost of fitting a new turbo at home.

'And what about the cost of all the other work you've done – the suspension and the fuel injectors and stuff?'

'Oh, that's included. He can't guarantee it works, but it'll take a couple more hours.'

'And we can keep the turbo that's on there at the moment, in case we can get it fixed somewhere?'

'Of course, it's your turbo.'

It looked like our only hope, so we agreed to the plan and the mechanics excavated the 'new' turbo from a heap of engine spares rotting at the back of the garage.

In the meantime, I'd returned to the delights of the mechanics' loo. But when I pressed the grease covered flush handle, it was clear that all was not well with the plumbing. Rather than flushing stuff away, the water bubbled ominously, and I watched in horror as the contents of the sewer beneath began to rumble back up the pipe and into the bowl. After a few seconds, the bowl had become a swirling, bubbling caldron of horrors. Just as I was debating what I could climb on to avoid the flood as it swept onto the floor, there was a horrifying burp from the pipes and the process stopped. The contents of the bowl continued to teeter on the edge of flooding over, but – for now at least – it seemed to have stopped increasing.

But I had the feeling this was only a temporary stay of execution and that the future for the mechanics' loo and, more particularly, for our continued use of it, wasn't looking so rosy.

For a while I hid in the small dark room, wondering how to raise the alarm. I had a sneaking suspicion that I was responsible for the damage, being the only female with period pain on the premises. But exactly how you explained that in Polish was quite, quite beyond me. To make matters worse, after negotiating the turbo deal the nephew had headed off to college, so there was no way of passing the buck to the messenger and forcing him to explain the problem. A horrible knot of embarrassment and fear began to settle in my stomach.

After spending some time resting my head on the wall waiting for inspiration, I decided all I could do was take a deep breath, head outside and own up. As I came out, I met Chris on the drive and tried one desperate plea to make him go and talk to the owner. But I was met with an unhelpful look of bewilderment and it was clear that if I wasn't using the sort of words you'd expect to hear on Top Gear, it simply wasn't going to register in his brain.

So after thinking long and hard about that bloody anniversary bottle of wine and all the trouble it'd got us into, I headed into the house and went in search of the owner.

'Err…hello..' We looked at each other and smiled uncomfortably, both unable to communicate.

'OK. So…' Suddenly I was struck by a moment of inspiration. The Polish word for toilet was toaletty. I had at least learnt that.

'Toaletty…err.'

'Ahh!' He smiled in recognition and began to point me in the direction of the toilet. Then he looked confused as it dawned on him I'd probably already found it sometime in the last 16 hours that I'd spent on his drive.

'So…it's like this. Err…toaletty….' Some deeply buried German suddenly floated to the surface of my brain, in a process that had striking parallels with the current toilet bowl situation.

'Toaletty es kaput!' There, a multilingual sentence which neatly and succinctly captured the current situation. If this was an exam I'd be an A grade student by now.

The owner looked at me in bemusement, but sensed my agitation and followed me through to the small cloakroom. Silently I pointed to the offending bowl and watched as his brow furrowed and his nose wrinkled. Some communication doesn't need language.

After looking perplexed for a while, he walked over to the toilet and put his hand on the flush. No, no, no I tried to scream, don't do that, it'll overflow, stop, stop, stop. But of course it was all in English and in a horrible slow motion moment he pressed the flush and watched the consequences. Some communication, it seems, does need language.

We both backed out of the room as the contents of a Polish sewer began to spread itself across the floor. I took to doing that little dancing hands, shrugging shoulders, minor grimacing routine which indicates someone who feels guilty about something, but can do absolutely nothing about it. As the owner headed back in with a plunger and a mop I decided the time had come to beat a hasty retreat and check progress on the van.

Out on the drive, chaos continued to reign, with more bits of the van flying around the garden and Chris learning some useful Polish swearwords. Suddenly the comforts of home seemed a very long way away. And I couldn't remember just what was wrong with my nice job, my nice house, my nice bathroom and my nice normal car. Bring it all back, I thought, I'm happy to swap this travelling lark for a pension fund statement and something decent on the telly.

But, as I knew only too well, once you've started on the road to being a dropout, you have to follow it through. So Oscar and I headed out for another turn around the block and continued to hope, against all evidence to the contrary, that this whole bloody fiasco might somehow resolve itself.

Sheepishly, we returned an hour later to discover the owner looking a little pale, but with a fully working toilet, and fewer bits of engine on the lawn. After I'd spent several more hours with a book in the shade of a tree, the van was loosely back together again, and Chris was instructed to take it for a short test drive. Sensing a slight glimmer of light at the end of the tunnel, he hopped into the driver's seat and headed off into the sunset, with strict instructions to only drive it for a few minutes, just to see how it went.

Forty five minutes later the light at the end of the tunnel had indeed turned into the headlights of an oncoming train. There was no sign of Chris or the van returning. Oscar and I were left on the drive, making confused shrugs at the mechanics as they looked at their watches and debated if they should go out and look for him. I was beginning to wonder if living together in a small space had taken its toll and Chris had seen this as an opportunity to make a break for freedom without the hassle of waiting for a divorce court. Surely he'd have given me my passport before he did that? He wasn't that mean, or mad – was he? As I wondered if the UK embassy in Poland had ever got an emergency dog passport, the mechanics continued to fret amongst themselves, every so often casting sympathetic looks in the direction of the jilted wife.

And then suddenly, as if by magic, I heard the roar of dodgy engine at the end of the road and the van swept onto the drive. Chris climbed out to a barrage of questions, Polish and English, about both the state of the engine and the state of our marriage. Fortunately the nephew had reappeared from college, and was able to translate the engine related remarks to the mechanics. And he also had the sense to realise that he wasn't going to need to translate some of my questions, but that he should maybe stand between us anyway, just to be safe.

'Where the bloody hell have you been? They said a few minutes. It's been nearly an hour!' I roared, slightly louder than the engine.

'I got stopped by the police.' Chris admitted, and I noticed the wilder than usual roll of his eyes.

'Oh no, what for? Are you OK?'

'For doing a u-turn at the lights. I was turning round to come back quickly like they said, and the guy in front had done it, so I assumed it was OK.'

'And what did they say?'

'He only spoke Polish, so I don't know what he said, but I think he wanted a fine. On the spot. He wrote the number 250 on a notepad.'

'Did you have that much cash?'

'No, I only had about 25. So I tried to look confused and waved the paper bit of my licence and stuff and eventually he gave in and told me to get lost. Well, I think that's what he said.'

'Blimey, well done. Do you have to take your papers in or anything?'

'I don't think so. Well, maybe I do, but I have no idea what or where, so I guess I won't be doing it.'

'Surely it ought to start getting easier soon.' I groaned, as we collapsed onto the lawn in a heap of despair.

And finally, it did. The mechanics continued to poke around in the back of the van, but it was starting to look like they might almost have a plan. I braved the loo and found it to be more or less fully functional, although I noticed the owner looking twitchy when he saw me heading that way. And as darkness began to fall over Krakow we finally had a van that seemed to be working, with slightly less smoke billowing out the back. Although I couldn't in all honesty say there was no smoke, it was at least possible to see the car behind now.

We headed to the cash machine to boost our zloty supply, then handed them over to the finally relaxing owner, who waved us off with a parting shot, translated by the nephew.

'You know, one of my customers tells me that the only people who will always have work are the undertaker and me. There will always be Volkswagen vans that need repairing. Good luck on your travels.'

And with that we headed out into the night and prepared to try our luck with the rest of the journey south.

Chapter 14

No dogs allowed

By the time we left Krakow it had been nearly six weeks since Norway, and in all that time we hadn't seen a small hill, let alone a mountain. It was beginning to take its toll – my lungs were burning if I met a road bridge whilst out running and both of us had an indefinable longing to see a different horizon.

So we headed from Krakow to the High Tatras, having heard that they offered spectacular views and great walking. The edge of the mountains was only an hour's drive south from Krakow, so it would make a good test run for the van, with the regional centre of Zakopane big enough to have a garage if it all went wrong.

Miraculously, the surgery on the mechanic's drive appeared to have given us a stay of execution, and as we headed south the van was running smoothly. But after fifty minutes of driving, there was still no sign of mountains. Confusingly, the road signs showed we were only 10 kilometres from Zakopane, but I had to resort to checking the guidebook to make sure we'd got the right town. And there it was, down in black and white, lots of highbrow prose talking about the beautiful mountain vistas. Surely even we couldn't have managed to lose an entire mountain range?

Finally, five kilometres from the edge of the National Park, some blurry mountain shapes appeared on the horizon. I'd been noticing the hazy air for several days now, but I'd assumed it was just around the van and wasn't a nationwide phenomenon. But the weather had been hot and sunny for several weeks now and Poland's industrial heritage was starting to show: we were surrounded by full scale smog. It was only at the very foot of the mountains that we could finally see the new horizon – hardly the mountain vistas for which we'd been hoping. It did give me a pang of guilt though, as I looked at the air pollution and remembered what we'd been churning out of the van. Whilst we hadn't caused all of this, it certainly hadn't helped. Perhaps our next trip should be by bike, although how Oscar would take part in that I wasn't sure. One dog's run around Europe sounded like hard work to me.

We found a small campsite in a village nearby, then headed to the nearest information office to find out the best way to head into the hills. Several leaflets later I was just getting excited about finally stretching my hamstrings when the tourist officer dealt a fatal blow.

'That's not your dog outside is it?'

'Why? What's he done now?' I answered, like a despairing parent.

'Nothing. But you know dogs aren't allowed into the National Park?'

'What? Anywhere?' I sensed a significant flaw in the plan.

'Nowhere in the whole park I'm afraid. It's because the Polish have such big dogs and they can do such damage to the wildlife.'

'But Oscar doesn't chase wildlife, he's been trained to leave it alone. He's never chased stuff.'

'I'm sorry, but that's the rule.' I was beginning to protest when I realised I was, again, starting to sound like a parent with a spoilt child. So I shrugged and was about to walk away, when I suddenly had a brainwave.

'Is it the same in Slovakia? I mean, it's the same mountains, but I just wondered....?'

Grudgingly, she admitted through gritted teeth that it was completely different in Slovakia. Slovakian dogs could go anywhere.

'But its only five kilometres to the border – we could walk there. Although obviously not with the dog,' I said, with unnecessary sarcasm.

'You could. Or you could drive round there and then you can walk where you want with the dog.'

And so our stay in Poland ended with a quick drive over the border to Slovakia, all for the sake of a dog walk. So far no one has written a dog travel guide (the Ruff Guide perhaps?), so there's no way of knowing in advance the different dog walking rules. Or the particular idiosyncrasies of dog-encumbered travel, which mean that if you want to go hiking in the Tatras, make sure you are in Slovakia before you try the approach.

But the extra drive was worth it. Slovakia seems to have struggled to shake off its image as the poor partner in the old Czechslovakia and the mountain campsites certainly weren't over-run with tourists. But we had a fantastic day's walk, through meadows bursting at the seams with bright blue gentian flowers. Cue lots of stops for Oscar to be shoved into a patch of flowers and told to look scenic for the camera, so that the grandparents could have more photos for their wallets. You do have to wonder when you discover your parents carry more photos of your dog than photos of you, but as he sat in the gentians – complete with his co-ordinating blue eye – I had to agree he's more scenic.

Of course just as I was starting to believe he really was a sweet and intelligent dog, Oscar insisted on ruining the image by sinking to a new low in the guard dog stakes. At some point in Norway, we'd parked overnight in a scenic layby, only to be awoken at 6am by the arrival of a bus full of exceptionally drunk people. They'd all poured off the bus and spent some time wandering around the layby, peeing everywhere and occasionally banging on the side of the van. We'd lain in bed, terrified that the van was about to be broken into by 45 people. And what had our faithful guard dog done? Had he leapt to our defence and thrown himself at the window, gnashing his teeth and snarling? Of course not. He eventually deigned to wake up, turned over, looked back at us to say, 'Blimey, sounds a bit scary out there, you ought to go and tell them to keep it down a bit,' and then promptly went back to sleep.

So as I headed out for a run in the Slovakian foothills, I wasn't expecting much defence from Oscar the Also Ran. And according-ly, we met various lone males wandering suspiciously in the woods and Oscar either ignored them or rushed up to them, tail wildly wagging as he inserted his head in their crotches. Then just as I was heading home, Oscar suddenly spotted a threat to my survival. Without realising it, I was about to be in very real and present danger. Without my dog at my side, barking and snarling, who knows how I'd get past the obstacle that now faced me? What was I going to do, staring into the black abyss of horror? Storming down the path to meet us was that most frightening of sights – a solitary nun. Whether it was the black habit or whether Oscar is an ardent atheist, I'll never know, but he saw this woman as a major threat. So much so that he had to throw himself at her, madly snarling, whilst I attempted to restrain him so the terrified nun could sidle past. Still, good to know who you can rely on. Next time I'm attacked by a passing convent, I'll know who to call.

~

After a few days enjoying the hills and finally feeling my quad muscles work again, we leapt back into the van, took a large right turn and headed west towards the Czech Republic and Germany. The downside of the Slovakian mountains appeared later that day. On an earlier walk, the sight of a small hut selling drinks part way up a large hill had been too strong a temptation and we'd rashly drunk a lot of orange squash, assuming that the water ought to be fairly clean. Which turned out to be a mistaken presumption that resulted in an evening curled up in the back of the van, rushing to the campsite loos every half hour.

From Slovakia it was more or less all downhill to Germany, so we headed onwards, still checking the exhaust at regular intervals. It was smoking less, but it was also lacking power in the engine. We were beginning to get a sneaking suspicion that the new turbo didn't leak oil because it didn't actually *do* anything at all – turning our turbo diesel van into just a diesel van. But we had more time than your average commuter and it meant we'd at least stopped belching smoke, so we decided we weren't overly fussed. If we'd paid £130 to get a giant cork put in the oil leak, well, so be it. At least we were still moving.

142

The new travelling pace did mean that we needed to make a concerted effort to get to Germany on time, so we saw relatively little of the rest of Slovakia and the Czech Republic. Our entry into the Czech Republic was marked by driving into the middle of a local harvest festival. Seeing the crowds and being fundamentally quite nosy, I insisted we should stop and see what you get in your average Czech harvest festival. Somewhat confusingly, it turned out to involve a lot of dancing by some mature ladies who were dressed like the Teletubbies. Now I'm guessing that a Teletubbies outfit doesn't look good on anyone, least of all me. But when the incumbents are slightly larger ladies who are completing a complicated dance that involves a lot of bobbing up and down, it's hard to appreciate its finer artistic points.

Slightly bemused by the local culture, we decided to bring it all down to our level by heading for Czecky Budwiche, home of Budweiser beer (the real one, not the American one). We hoped this would be an opportunity to stock up on a few alcoholic essentials at Eastern European prices, and so our final night in the Czech Republic was spent in a small and somewhat dubious campsite outside an equally dubious hotel with just one lone tent. The tent owners turned out to be from Scotland and included a trainee Church of Scotland minister on his holidays. Further questioning revealed that he was the grand old age of 25, and had been married and training for the ministry for the last 4 years. I couldn't decide if I was impressed or scared – here I was, several years older and unsure of where I'd be sleeping the next night, let alone my future career path and religious views. And yet this relative youngster seemed to have not only his own life mapped out, but also that of his future parishioners.

Just what was I doing with my life? Why was I not this sorted? Why do I still feel 14 inside, even if the crows' feet appearing around my eyes make it clear that I'm a lot older? Was there something wrong with me, or was there something wrong with the 25 going on 66 minister? And how were we going to explain to him that we were only there for the beer?

So much navel gazing could lead to only one conclusion. It was time to lighten up and hang out with some equally confused, equally undirected representatives of the Missing Generation. It was time to go pink.

And so we crossed the border into Germany and there were Kris and Wolfgang. Still travelling, still unemployed, still worrying about being jobless and broke for ever more, but managing to work through the worry by heading out for a coffee and a quick sightsee. They came into their own as former travel agents should, giving us guided tours of various German towns, even going so far as to circle places of interest on the German map, like the undisputed kings of tourism that they are.

They even took us to their former town of residence and showed us the sights of the local sculpture trail. These included a large and shiny laughing cow, placed incongruously in the midst of a suburban shopping street. Maybe it was great art, but to me it just looked like someone had decided to melt down old car parts whilst taking some really good drugs. I could see that The Boys wouldn't be overly keen on my Philistine view of their local meeting point though, so I kept my thoughts to myself. It was interesting to watch the effect of this hometown visit on their normally cheerful and sunny dispositions. Repeatedly they told us how much they would've liked to invite us to their house – except now they had no house in this town and their only true 'home' was their campervan. Given the size of their van, we still thought they were living palatially, but I could see they felt somewhat rueful at being visitors in their own town.

They also introduced us to Germany's most appealing habit. All my fears of German efficiency not allowing us to leave a single dog hair turned out to be misguided. Rather than being ruthlessly efficient when it came to dogs, the Germans, in fact, couldn't be more helpful. Dogs were allowed everywhere. Cafes, bars, restaurants, stations, trains, buses. Anywhere you could think of, the presumption was that dogs were allowed unless you were specifical-ly told otherwise. In fact, I wouldn't be surprised if there is a Ruff guide to Germany. If it rained, all three of us could head into the nearest café, sit down and eat cake and drink coffee until it stopped. Or head into a bar and have a few beers until the clouds cleared. We didn't have to stop and ask, or look appealingly and beg to be allowed entrance for the dog, or take him back to the van first. We just had to walk in and sit down. I was so excited by this concept that we spent most of our first few days in Germany entering cafes and bars, just to test the theory out. And of course, once we were there, well – it would have been rude not to have a drink.

We pottered around a variety of German towns, admiring the half timbered houses, each painted a different colour and looking like the top of a chocolate box. We called in on the city of Regensberg, full of dramatic stone buildings and medieval style turrets – in many ways reminiscent of Tallinn, but without the nice locksmiths. And we learnt of the German campsite's Nachtstell-platz, designed for those campers only planning to stay one night, but complete with all the facilities of the main campsite for half the price. The trade off for the 50% price cut appeared to be their location on the edge of the campsite, usually with a view of the back of a building, but I was more than prepared to take a hike to the bathroom if the price was right.

After a few days, I was beginning to wonder about emigrating, but my lack of language skills looked like something of a barrier. Perhaps it was going to be back to Scotland after all. But in our newly emerging 'perfect European country', there was no doubt that the dog policy of Germany would be a pre-requisite.

By this stage in our trip, we'd developed a pretty good idea of which elements of the various countries could be cherry picked to make up the perfect European country. So far, we'd added the scenery of Norway to the pubs of English villages to the cakes and cafes of Germany, with a good sprinkling of Finnish forests and reindeer at Christmas time. Previous visits showed that the coffee and wine of Spain could be added to the mix and if you threw in the road maintenance of Shetland with the party sense of the Scots, we knew visas for such a country would be in hot demand. In fact, I'm surprised I haven't received an invite from the European Commission to create such a country. Now that would make Brussels popular.

A few days after we arrived in Germany, my parents flew into Stuttgart and we headed down to the Black Forest to meet them. They weren't due to arrive until lunchtime, so we passed a leisurely morning at a small forested campsite. I'd planned to take Oscar for a run, just to take off his slight edge of mania before he threw himself into my parents' waiting arms. But when I left the van, fully resplendent in not a lot of running gear, it took me several seconds to figure out what was different. As I ran across the grass towards the conifer trees, it seemed to be making a strange noise. Each step was echoed by a small crunching sound and my thighs were seizing into a spasm. Suddenly, it dawned on me. This was frost. I'd forgotten all about the concept of cold weather in the last couple of months. Ever since our Arctic Circle heatwave we'd been experiencing fantastic luck with the weather, with a never ending succession of hot, balmy days, constant sunshine and only occasional showers of rain. But now we were into the second half of September and the weather was reminding us that winter wasn't far away. And if the weather was starting to get a bit chillier, that meant the van would soon be testing our resistance. During our Ireland tester trip the temperature had dipped well below zero and I'd noticed a slight tendency for ice to accumulate on the inside of the windscreen. When it had only been for a couple of days, it had seemed quite a novelty. But as I crunched through the grass I wondered if we were really ready for the chilly times ahead.

Fortunately, we weren't going to be jumping straight into our thermal underwear. My parents had rented an apartment in the southern part of the Black Forest and a quick check on arrival soon ascertained that it had that most essential of items – a heater. Not

146

only that, but – luxury of luxuries, excitement of excitements – we also got to sleep in a normal sized double bed! And have a shower where you didn't need to wear flip-flops to avoid the veruccas and stray hairs. And use a proper table to eat dinner. And use a washing machine. And an electric kettle. Such excitements! I guess my folks may have been slightly concerned at my new materialistic outlook on life, but I suppose they could take comfort from my limited goals – if I was this excited by an electric kettle it was unlikely I'd be splashing out on a new Ferrari in the near future.

After a teenage experience as an au pair, my Mum speaks good German, so we were able to rely on her for communication whilst we were there. Which was fortunate, as I needed a blood test to keep an eye on my thyroid problems. Because the hormone levels hadn't completely stabilised, I still had to have regular checks at Aberdeen hospital. I'd now reached the stage where I either needed to get it checked out in Germany, or I'd have to head home for a check up in the next couple of weeks. It seemed fairly pointless flying all the way back to Aberdeen for what's a reasonably routine job, so I decided to brave a German doctor.

Bright and early one Monday morning, my parents and I trooped off to the local doctor's surgery. Kris and Wolfgang had prepared some extra notes for us, so we were hoping we had all the right German phrases. Arriving in the surgery, my Mum had to do all the talking for me – which made me feel about eight and a half. Any minute now the Tixylix would be coming out and if I was lucky I'd get a Mr Bump plaster as well.

After handing over our 10 Euro fee, we sat in the waiting room and watched as others came and went. We soon realised our social faux pax – when entering the waiting room it was clearly customary to say Guten Morgen to all the waiting patients, before heading in to see the receptionist. Of course, as rude and insensitive Brits we'd just marched straight through, probably giving everyone an opportunity to raise their eyebrows in a significant manner.

Finally, we were called in to the consulting room. As I heard it, the conversation went something like this:

'Guten flugen, yurdy ancht stull'

'Errr…flurdey, foudrk haben stuck wieden Thyroid,' replied my suddenly fluent mother.

'Ja, upsil, murdy gruten,' continued the doctor, launching into a diatribe which meant nothing to me, and which I suspected didn't mean a whole lot to my Mum either. Then there was silence as the doctor busied himself collecting shiny and painful looking bits of equipment.

'So, what did he say?' I asked nervously.

'Something about taking the blood and the analysis will be done at the hospital and won't take long. You know, the usual.' Then she slipped in the killer line. 'And he's going to need four tubes of blood.'

'He's going to need what? Four tubes! What's he doing with it? Selling it on the black market?' I exclaimed. Fortunately, there was no time for answers, as I was shoved onto the adjacent bed by the doctor, whose bedside manner clearly needed work. Before I had a chance to say anything he began stabbing what looked like a screwdriver into my arm.

'Ummmm…are you sure he knows what he's doing,' I mumbled, as my tongue stuck to the roof of my mouth.

Stab, stab went the screwdriver.

'I think you need to tell him he needs a vein to do that,' I yelped. 'It's no use just stabbing wildly and hoping he'll hit something eventually.'

'Err..yes dear. Now, what was the word for 'vein'? I think 'artery' is 'pulsader', but I suppose you don't want him to hit one of those. Let's see.' And my mother began leafing through the pages of her dictionary, apparently quite relaxed at the idea of her younger daughter being stabbed to death by a mad German doctor.

'What I want is for him to stop hitting me with a DIY instrument and get a proper needle instead. Oh..yuck.' I petered out, looking in horror at my arm. The doctor was now trying to push

148

the blood back up my arm, presumably in the hopes of filling a vein with sufficient blood that he could continue his archery practice. I realised my palms were covered in a cold film of sweat.

Eventually, several stab wounds later, he decided to give up on that arm and headed round to the other side to repeat the whole process again. Finally he struck gold and began sucking out his four tubefuls, ready for auctioning on EBay later in the day. Halfway through, he turned to my mother, uttered a few words of German and chuckled.

'What did he say?'

'Something about how normally the nurse does this, but she's away today. He thinks it always takes doctors longer to take blood as they get so little practice.'

'No shit, Sherlock.'

A few seconds later and we were free to go. I raced to the waiting room, keen to escape this German torture chamber. I'd planned to try and resurrect myself with the waiting room crowd by remembering to say Cheerio. But when I got there, they all seemed to be taking part in a strange German dance routine, whirling around the room at breakneck speed. I made it as far as the car park but, discovering that the cars were taking part in the same whirling routine, I opted for what looked like the only safe place – the floor. I sat down with a plop, and two seconds later, so I'm told, my head hit the tarmac.

I came round to discover both parents standing in the car park, each holding one of my feet in the air, whilst cheerfully chatting about whether to buy bread now or later.

'Umm...feufliimbliy,' I stuttered feebly.

'Don't worry, you fainted, that's all. We'll just stand here with your legs up till you feel better' my Dad responded, far too cheer-fully. 'It's alright, we'll just pretend it's normal and that we always stand in car parks holding feet in the air.'

Marvellous. I've never been great with the sight of blood (well, more particularly with my own blood – I don't mind if other people

149

want to bleed to death around me, I just don't want to do it myself), but it'd been a good few years since I'd hit the ground. How humiliating! On reflection, it was starting to look like a trip back to Aberdeen would've been easier. I'd certainly never had an Aberdeen nurse take repeated stabs at my arm like it was some sort of dart board. Was there some German policy about making sure it was painful? Or had I just caught the doctor on an off day? Either way, I wasn't planning to find out – next time, I decided, I was sticking with the Aberdeen option – flight or no flight.

In the morning I returned for the results, which fortunately were fine. But despite all their efficiency in returning the results in 24 hours, as far as I was concerned, give me the NHS any day. At least they don't try to take blood with something they bought in B & Q.

Fortunately, the remainder of our time in Germany passed more pleasantly, with plenty of long walks on the wooded slopes for Oscar and lots of café stops for me. But all too soon our spell of luxury had passed and it was time to hit the road again. This meant back to the UK for my parents, having reassured themselves that Oscar wasn't being mistreated, and further south for us, having taken the opportunity to wash absolutely everything in the van. Kris and Wolfgang had a similar spell of luxury with their friends and family in Germany, demonstrating one of the essentials of being a grown up gapper living in a campervan – every few months, you just need a break. Preferably with a tumble dryer.

Chapter 15

Picking up Popeye

We left Germany via Switzerland, then headed full steam towards Spain. Autumn should have arrived and we figured it would be cool enough for Oscar to cope with the Spanish weather. Our vague plan had been to spend the winter in Spain, getting our Spanish language closer to fluency and generally hanging out until Aberdeen had warmed up the following spring (in as much as Aberdeen ever warms up). But that was as far as we'd got with a plan. And as a plan it had seemed quite reasonable when we were still at the other end of the continent and had no idea if we could expect the van to make it to the end of the street, let alone to Spain.

But suddenly it was all frighteningly close. We were a four-day slow drive from Spain and we were beginning to realise that we needed a little more of a plan. Just crossing the border and then stopping and waiting for the world to come up and start speaking to us in slow Spanish might not work. As we wove our way through rural France we debated our options.

'Maybe we should do a language course first. Just to remind ourselves a bit. We haven't spoken any Spanish for months now,' I suggested.

'We should look for work as well though. That's the only way we'll really get to learn. And figure out what the country's like as well. Any sort of work would be OK.'

'But what about Oscar? We can't work all day and leave him in the van – it'd be too hot and he'll be bored to death.'

'Maybe farm work then, or fruit picking, or something where he can come with us.'

And that was about as far as our planning went. In the end we decided to stop in Girona for a few weeks, because we'd been there before. It wasn't far from the border and we knew there were some vineyards nearby that might be looking for grape pickers at this time of year. Not the most comprehensive plan in the world, but at least it was a stab in the right direction.

But first we had to make our way through the south of France. We hadn't planned to stop much in France – mostly because I learnt French for years at school and find it can easily displace my recently learned Spanish. Whilst being able to speak good French is undoubtedly a useful skill, the one time it wouldn't be too helpful was on arrival in Spain. So I planned to drive through France humming loudly, with my hands over my ears. The theory of zipping through France as fast as the van would allow was aided by the appalling signposting we found every time we strayed off the main road. A simple trip to look for a campsite would take on mammoth proportions when we had to pick our way around the suburbs of small towns, circling again and again in the hopes of finally being able to follow the signposts to their supposed destinations.

Our only successful stop was in the Cervennes National Park, an area of dramatic gorges and old stone villages. Spotting a sign for 'One of the most beautiful villages in France', we decided we'd give French signposting one last chance, and turned off the main road. After a few hundred metres we found ourselves in a small car park on the outskirts of what looked like a walled village. The roads were clearly designed for something slightly smaller than the French onion man's bike, so we abandoned the van in the car park and headed into the village on foot. We were quickly immersed in a labyrinth of tiny cobbled alleyways, wending their way between beautiful stone buildings, which leaned over the alleys until they almost touched above our heads. In the centre of the village we found a small church, a square with a couple of haphazardly strewn benches and a disarmingly friendly tourist office, who gave us directions for an easy 8 km stroll to a nearby gorge.

Setting off towards the gorge, we took a second wander through the village, which seemed picture-book perfect, but just slightly eerie.

'Have you seen any people here yet?' I asked. 'I mean people who live here, not just tourists?'

'Not really. Everywhere seems very quiet doesn't it? I don't know if anyone does actually live here.'

'It's like it's been preserved as a museum and nobody can live here in case they mess it up. I feel like I'm walking round the set of a stage play or something.'

And there did seem to be a complete absence of actual residents. Undoubtedly the village was beautifully preserved and quite possibly was one of the most beautiful in France, but without any villagers, it seemed to lack a soul. Even a few stray crisp packets and a loitering teenager would've added some life and might have been preferable to this sterile museum piece.

Debating the need for a bit of scruffy human nature to liven a place up, we headed out towards the gorge. The walk had been billed by the tourist office as an easy, short walk. So I wasn't expecting to discover that not only did it involve visiting the gorge, it also involved scrabbling down one side, jumping across the river running through the base and then crawling back up the other side, mostly on hands and knees. If this was short and easy I was glad we hadn't gone for a long and hard option – we'd probably have needed full climbing gear and oxygen supplies. It was an interesting contrast to some of the walks we'd taken in Finland. One called the Little Bear's Ring had been described in the park leaflet as a 'very demanding trail which will test the hiker's condition.' With a certain sense of trepidation we'd embarked on this walk with rucksacks stuffed to the gunnels with muesli bars, extra clothing and mobile phones – just in case. But either the Finns weren't very fit, or their health and safety committee was taking life very seriously. In fact, the majority of the walk was no more difficult than your average stroll in some fairly flat woodland. It seemed the French had a much more laissez faire attitude to hikers – which perhaps wasn't that surprising, but I did wonder how the European

153

Commission planned to bring about European integration of walking standards. Would we all have to take part in some routine fitness tests so that common EU standards could be established? Or would we soon find trails marked with differing ability levels depending on your nationality – if you're Finnish this is a difficult trail, but if you're French then you can probably squeeze it in before lunch?

One highlight of our canyon crawl was the discovery of a perfectly sized campervan parking place on a dead end road, which provided us with a peaceful home for the night. In the morning, we packed up and prepared to head further south, aiming to reach the Spanish border by nightfall. But we'd reckoned without the heat, and the acquisition of some dubious German hitchhikers.

Leaving a non-descript town shortly after lunch we spotted two young hitchhikers, complete with backpacks, and, remembering our own days of penniless hitchhiking, we stopped to give them a lift. After exchanging the usual pleasantries I asked their names, and suppressed a smile at 'Popeye and Julia'. He certainly didn't look like a Popeye, being short and weedy with blonde dreadlocks, but then she bore little resemblance to Olive Oyle. They weren't part of the missing generation, being the ripe old age of 19 and between school and university. I asked about their plans for the next few months.

'I want to live without money,' Julia sang. There was a dreamy look in her eye, but the unfettered spirit effect was spoiled by rolling a cigarette at the same time.

'I see,' I responded, perhaps a little too curtly. 'And how are you planning to pay for the tobacco then?'

'Someone will provide,' Popeye answered. I sensed he was struggling to understand my over practical outlook on life. Our conversation faltered fairly quickly, but part of me was again desperate to ask them if they were suitably insured and had packed some warm clothes. Our distance from the late teenage gap year kid was strikingly apparent – we had insurance for the van, the dog and ourselves as well as for the house in Aberdeen. In fact, we were an insurance broker's wet dream.

But despite feeling old enough to be Popeye and Julia's parents, we gave them a slow ride through the south of France. Although it was nearly October, the weather was suddenly scorching and we had to stop at regular intervals to cool down both van and dog. The roads seemed to be constantly busy and as we continued to try and push south we all felt a bit frazzled around the edges. By six o'clock we decided that our chances of making it to Spain that night weren't great, so we pulled into a soulless campsite by the beach, with unfriendly service and exorbitant prices. Popeye and Julia, needing to live without money, went for the cheaper option of sleeping on the beach. To complete the stress, Oscar decided it would be a good evening to throw up all over the front seat, leaving us trying not to think how that would smell in the morning, coupled with the full heat of the sun and four sweaty bodies in the van.

After a short dog walk along the beach in the morning, we continued on the road south, and arrived at the Spanish border just before lunchtime. As we got into the queue to pass through the border checkpoints, I was suddenly struck by a horrible realisation. Popeye and Julia had been happily smoking a spliff when we all got back into the van. By itself, that wasn't a problem – unlike Clinton, I have inhaled in the past, so I wasn't bothered if they were now. But now we were approaching the border it occurred to me that this meant they had a stash of hash somewhere in their bags. If we were stopped at the border and searched, would they leave it in their bags, or would they take the road of least resistance and swiftly conceal it somewhere in the van, for us to explain away?

I felt my palms go sweaty as I considered our options. To a passing customs officer we were four young (OK, young-ish) people, in a VW campervan, complete with Popeye's dreadlocks, juggling clubs and guitar sticking out the window. We couldn't have looked more stereotypical if we'd tried. All it needed was the addition of some Bob Dylan on the radio to make us picture book perfect. To be honest, I'd have stopped and searched us. Popeye and Julia had fallen asleep in the back, so I switched the radio off and muttered my fears to Chris. Who looked back at me like a rabbit in headlights.

'Shit,' he murmured. 'You might be right. But what can we do? We can't chuck them out now, we're already in the queue and it'll look even more dodgy if we do that.'

'I know, but how pissed off are we going to be if we make it all the way to Spain and then get stopped at the border. All our plans are going to be scuppered.'

'OK, OK, I know, but we can't do anything now. We'll just have to try and look innocent. Maybe Oscar can charm them if we get stopped.'

'Great. What a plan.' I sighed, then tried to arrange my facial features into those of an unquestionably innocent person.

As the queue crawled towards the customs booth, a smartly dressed woman approached the van. I felt the sweat running down the middle of my back and tried to stop my hands shaking. We both stared straight ahead, trying to ignore her, but there was no denying she was approaching our vehicle. Slowly I wound down the window, struggling to make eye contact and smile, whilst at the same time wiping my sweaty palms on the seat covers.

'Hola' I squeaked, hoping an attempt to speak Spanish might make her friendlier. She glared back at me and I felt my heart sink. We were stuffed. But just as I began to brace for the impact of disaster, she thrust out her hand, pushed a leaflet through the open window and marched on towards the next vehicle.

'It's OK' I exclaimed, 'it's just a leaflet for a restaurant on the other side.' A few seconds later, the border guard emerged from his booth, waved us through and we drove into Spain as fast as we dared, heaving a collective sigh of relief as we rolled across the border.

~

As soon as was decently possible, we deposited Popeye, Julia, guitar and juggling sticks on the side of the road, wound down the windows and laughed ourselves stupid at our own naivety. Then we stopped in the first village, looked around us and took in the fact that finally, on the 1st of October, three and a half months after leaving Aberdeen, we had rolled across the Spanish border. If only we'd kept an address for the Latvian garage we could've sent them a postcard. But then if we started writing postcards to all the doubters, we'd never have time for anything else. We had to be content with a small celebratory round of applause for the van, followed by a much needed trip to the local wine dealers for us.

A valedictory bottle of wine to counteract that first rash anniversary one was unquestionably required. Just as we'd planned on that long drunken night, here we were, the three of us, in the van, in Spain, watching the sun set over the Mediterranean.

Just sometimes, and probably not in the way you expect, dreams do come true.

~

The initial shell shock of a dream coming true takes a bit of adjustment though. For several hours the next day we wandered around the villages on the Spanish coast, not quite brave enough to ask about work or language courses, or even for the time of day. As the lunchtime siesta approached, we settled down on the terrace of a nearby cafe to plan our next step. And to my surprise several people came over to pat Oscar and generally pass the time of day. They weren't long conversations and they often ground to a halt after the obvious questions about Oscar's strange colouring and dubious heritage. But they were the kind of conversations we have in the UK (although obviously not in Spanish).

'I think folks are assuming we're Spanish, because of your colouring and the dog. That's why they're talking to us, because they don't think we're tourists. I don't think they expect anyone to be taking a dog on holiday.' Chris reasoned. He looked jealously at my dark hair and complexion which has led people to ask if we had an Italian milkman in my Mum's younger days.

'I guess they must do. It's quite comforting though, isn't it? I'm not getting every word they're saying, but I do at least feel I can communicate a bit.'

'Does that make you brave enough to go and ask for work then?' Chris asked.

'I'm not sure about that, but if you want, I'll try in the tourist information office this afternoon, see if they've got any ideas.'

'Blimey, that's a bit rash isn't it?'

'Well, let's see how I'm feeling at the end of siesta break.'

Two hours later, as rural Spain woke up again, I was still riding high on my wave of enthusiasm and set off for the office before my courage deserted me. Swallowing hard before entering, I launched into my prepared speech about our search, whilst trying to make sure I used the right tenses in all the right places. As I reached the end, I waited for the woman to start laughing, or look at me in confusion before switching to perfect English. But she just nodded, thought for a minute and then fetched a map and began marking off the locations of possible vineyards and orchards.

Flushed with success we headed to the first vineyard, where Chris decided it was his turn to step up and be counted.

'OK, I'll go and ask in here,' he offered.

'Sure?'

'No, but if I go now, before I have a chance to think too much, I might be alright.'

'OK. Buena suerte,' I said, relaxing back into my seat.

'Let's not get flashy now' Chris cautioned, as he hauled himself out of the van before bracing himself to head into the main office. Several minutes passed and Oscar and I waited nervously, wondering when we should start worrying. Eventually a slightly shaky looking Chris emerged, clutching a phone number on a battered piece of paper.

'Well, there was no joy there, but they said to try this other place. And they understood me and they didn't laugh so I feel pretty good, even though I'm still unemployed.'

And so the next few days progressed in a similar manner, as we visited more and more vineyards and offices. The answer was always no, or not at the moment, or the harvest's finished, or something similar, which in some ways was deeply discouraging. But the thrill of managing to communicate more than basic details stayed with us, and helped us ride out the lows of continuing unemployability.

One thing we did learn was that it was difficult. Really difficult. And anyone who says that foreign migrants to the UK have an easy life should be forced to try a couple of days of job hunting in a different language. It's anything but easy. And we weren't desperate. Work would have been nice, but if we didn't find any, it just meant we might have to head home a month earlier than we wanted. We weren't on the breadline. We didn't have children who would starve if we didn't get work – even Oscar would still get fed, whatever the outcome. And it was still hard going. I can feel an anti-Daily Mail rant coming on here so I shall move on, but all I can say is don't knock it till you've tried it.

After a few days of job searching it was clear that we weren't going to find anything amongst the remnants of the grape harvest, so we reverted to the language course plan, putting our plans to join the world's workers on hold for a few weeks.

We headed into Girona, a university town with a healthy sprinkling of language schools. In a few minutes we'd booked ourselves into a two week course at a school that would allow the dog in for lessons as well. Not that Oscar needed the language practice (he was already fluent in Spanish lady dog communication), but at least he wouldn't have to wait in a hot van whilst we tried to catch up on his linguistic skills. Next stop was to find a campsite for a couple of weeks and finally we were all set.

As the two weeks of lessons passed we got to know our fellow campers, marooned on the campsite outside the main tourist season. It didn't take us long to meet the resident Brit, Dave, who – despite being a big chap – was passing his nights in a tiny tent, set up a few hundred metres from our van. A few days into our stay we discovered he'd been planning to spend several months of the winter in Spain with his wife, but shortly before their departure she'd casually dropped into the conversation that actually she'd prefer a divorce. Oh, and she was keeping the dog and the house.

Dave had decided not to be downhearted at his substantial change of circumstances and had headed to the nearest camping shop, bought a tent and gone anyway. He certainly didn't seem to be losing any sleep over it. His snoring echoed around the campsite and frequently kept us awake, despite the metal wall between us. In our bleary eyed mornings, it was hard not to twitch when he told us he couldn't understand why his wife had left him. It didn't take long for us to name him the Roncador, once we'd learnt the Spanish verb for snoring was roncar. Sadly his similarities to the Spanish matadors ended at the name – he wasn't a guy you wanted to imagine in a tight-fitting spangley suit, waving his cape at an approaching bull.

After two weeks we reached the end of our language course, and decided that any more lessons would put too much of a hole in our budget. It was time to be unleashed on the Spanish speaking world again. But our stay at the campsite had to be extended for a few days whilst Chris flew back to the UK to discuss the final draft of his thesis with his tutor. As I was still fighting second gear (yes, still) I was nervous at being left in sole charge of the van and dog. But other than being hooted by a few irate lorry drivers who didn't like my speed up hills (and to be honest, I wasn't too chuffed with it either) both Oscar and I lived to tell the tale.

Chris returned just as Northern Spain was hit by its worst week of flooding in ten years. The sky took on a uniform leaden grey and the rain fell in sheets, quickly overpowering the road drainage and flooding our campsite. We were parked at the back of the campsite, several feet higher, so whilst the threat to our immediate safety wasn't too bad, the road in and out of the site was closed. Unable to escape the van or the campsite, cabin fever began to spread through the van. In no time at all, Chris and I were bickering about the slightest thing and tempers began to fray. As Charles Dickens once said 'aggravation in a campervan is SO aggravating'. Well, I think he said it about carts actually, but you get the idea. Chris has a tendency to share Oscar's stubborn streak and with almost comically poor timing, he decided this was the moment to get on with the final tidy up of the thesis. Being away from friends and colleagues seemed to have robbed him of all sense of perspective, with the brain-rot fuelled by the all pervading damp. Day after day of 'tidying' followed, with the laptop out at all hours. Obsession is closer to us all than we realise, and over the course of the next week I watched my relatively normal husband turn into a bad-tempered, insensitive, obsessive perfectionist. That's not to say I was completely blameless, but there seemed to be no persuading Chris of the need to finally let go and hand in.

Matters came to a head as the waters rose around the campsite and our hundredth row of the week boiled up into a froth of tantrum and bile. Finally, provoked beyond belief, I stormed out of the van and into the rain, dragging a less than enthusiastic dog with me. With a surprising presence of mind I grabbed not only my walking boots, but also a pair of flip flops to wade through the flood.

'It's not just the dog' I called over my shoulder as I flounced out. 'This shouldn't happen to a wife.'

Determined to get away from the campsite and my bastard of a husband, I waded through knee high floodwaters with Oscar paddling beside me. Arriving on the other side we squelched determinedly along the pavement, sick to the back teeth of the rain, a small van and my marriage. Stomping round the village, I found a phone box, called my parents and demanded they check the prices of Eurostar tickets.

Fortunately, my mother had seen it all before, and had the

presence of mind to tell me to calm down and wait a while. Give him another week was her sage advice. Then book a ticket home if it doesn't improve. But give him a bit more time.

After moaning for a full half hour, I hung up and debated my options. If I wasn't getting on the first train back to the UK I'd have to go back to the van and wait in the dry. Storming out is all well and good in principle, but it works better when you've already packed, the roads aren't flooded and you've got somewhere to go. Squelching back in your flip flops is difficult to carry off with much style.

A sullen silence reigned in the van for the remainder of the week. Somewhere in Chris' psyche he had convinced himself that success in his MSc would overwrite his previously middle-of-the-road academic record. And once he'd become fixated on achieving the highest grade possible, he couldn't quite let go of the idea. No matter how much I tried to persuade him people wouldn't care what grade he'd got and they'd probably never even know, it had become the Holy Grail of his existence. And nearly became the end of our marriage.

It was made worse by a passing visit from some Edinburgh friends, in the midst of a city break in Barcelona. As we settled down for a meal in a Girona restaurant, they launched into an account of their most recent house purchase. Their new house, it transpired, would be in the right school catchment for their son, had five bedrooms and had only set them back a few hundred thousand. Chris and I offered polite, but strained congratulations and I suspect our lack of enthusiasm was more evident than either of us would normally have allowed.

Just what the fuck were we doing with our lives? It wasn't that long ago that we were on a social and financial par with these people. Now they were buying a house with *five* bedrooms whilst we bickered in an over-sized cupboard. We were watching as our life's savings drained out of our bank account and considering ourselves lucky that we at least had our shabby cottage awaiting our return. And our friends were moving into a house with a different bedroom for every day of the working week. This was the very tangible reality of what our decisions meant. We were getting a sharp reminder of the old adage – 'you pays your money and you takes your choice'. Our friends had worked hard to afford their house and were demonstrating a level of commitment to raising their family that we were incapable of replicating. In contrast, we'd blown a lot of money on this trip and lost a lot of earning power. So we wouldn't be moving house in the near future. We would have to be content with our two-up-two-down shack for some considerable time. And in the meantime, our friends who'd made the effort to stay in gainful employment would be moving up the house and possession ladder ahead of us. We'd made our bed and now we had to lie in it, even if it was cramped and had slightly mouldy sheets, not to mention a degree of marital tension.

But even bad things usually come to an end, and the day finally dawned when Chris posted his thesis to the UK and the sun re-emerged. The van steamed gently in the sunlight, the Spaniards came back out to play and we were free of commitments. People stopped to chat to us on the streets again, as Oscar wagged his language-transcending tail and our decision to exchange possessions for experiences didn't seem so foolish. And after our language course, we felt linguistically ready to hit the road. For now, the only remaining problem was that we weren't quite sure which road to hit. We knew we needed to find some work, partly to put our linguistic prowess to the test and partly because without some form of work, we would have to return home in early January. And the thought of returning to Aberdeenshire in the middle of winter wasn't an appealing prospect – we wanted to hang on until the beginning of March so that at least there was some daylight back home, even if we'd still be freezing to death.

Undaunted by our first failure to find grape picking work, we opted to take advantage of the fact that once upon a time we were proper grown-up people with jobs and credit cards. In our heady days of regular salaries, I'd become a little too keen on ordering a crate or two of wine from a wine dealer in the south of England who worked with organic vineyards in Spain. So I sent a quick email to Vintage Roots, explaining what we were looking for, and to his credit, Lance responded almost instantly with some names and phone numbers. This seemed all the more generous given my explanation of our current status must have indicated that we were unlikely to be making any significant purchases in the near future. Clutching our list of names we headed into the Rioja region, found a campsite and settled into another trawl of the vineyards.

Chapter 16

There but for the grace of a preposition

The Rioja region is home to over 130,000 acres of vineyard, so it seemed reasonable to hope that at least one of them might want some cheap labour, especially when it came with extra "fertiliser" courtesy of a grey dog. We'd arrived in the region just after the grape harvest, but hoped there might be work in the forthcoming pruning season. In order for a wine to qualify as a Rioja wine, the grapes must have come from vines which are pruned regularly to ensure they only have a carefully controlled number of stems per acre. By limiting the number of stems produced by each vine, the farmers also limit the total number of grapes produced, enabling the plant to produce a smaller number of better quality grapes, rather than a larger quantity of mediocre ones. This ensures that the underlying quality of Rioja wine is maintained, something which is taken very seriously by the Rioja Regulatory Council, who certify the genuine Riojas. To accommodate this, the pruning of the vines in the Rioja region is usually done by hand to allow for careful control of stem numbers.

Entering the region, we headed for the town of La Guardia, nestled on the border between the Rioja and Basque areas, but surrounded on all sides by acres of vines, stretching as far as the eye could see. La Guardia itself is a beautiful old walled town, built on a rocky outcrop that towers above the surrounding vines. From the town walls we had a heart stopping view out across the vineyards, where the vines were just beginning to glow an autumnal red as the leaves prepared to drop. The red glow of the vines contrasted against the bright blue sky and pale soil to give a postcard view that we stood and gazed at for hours. Inside the town walls we found a maze of narrow cobbled streets, tall stone buildings and brightly coloured window boxes. Within a few minutes we were standing outside the local estate agents, wondering if this could be the moment when one of us invested in a new life.

Fortunately for our bank balances the estate agents remained firmly shut, so we mooched around town checking out the quality of the local cafes. And in doing so, we unearthed a divide in the local hostelleries. The majority of the cafes fell into the category of a standard Spanish bar, with alcoholic drinks on offer, plus the obligatory coffee machine. Food options generally included some great savoury tapas, but the sweet menu was restricted to some dubious looking pre-packaged sponge cakes. Each bar contained anything from one to five Spanish males, propping up the bar and exchanging gruff pleasantries with each other.

After cruising past a few of these 'standard' cafes, we rounded a corner and entered a parallel universe. Wandering down an innocuous cobbled street and in need of more caffeine we opened the door of an adjacent café, stepped down two steps and realised within seconds that we'd entered the 'women's domain.' A gaggle of ladies in black were stationed around a small bar, behind which lurked the requisite coffee maker, a few wine bottles and a world class collection of cakes. Not a savoury tapas to be seen – these women weren't wasting time on the pointless savoury course when they could head straight on to dessert. As I stepped down into this new universe not an eyebrow was raised, but as Chris followed behind me a deathly hush settled across the café. Chocolate cakes stopped midway between plate and mouth as the assembled ladies assimilated the concept of a Y chromosome entering the room. Our steps rang out in the silence as we walked to the nearest table. Shoving Chris down into a chair I assessed our options.

'OK,' I whispered, 'I don't think you're supposed to be in here. So I'll go and order at the bar, you stay here and do not under any circumstances talk about cars or gadgets. You'll have to eat cake and try and pretend you're getting in touch with your feminine side or something.'

Dumbstruck with nerves, Chris nodded silently before quickly turning his gaze to the interesting pattern on the floor. I sidled to the bar, trying to make shrugging apologies for having inadvertently allowed a man to enter this female domain. Eventually the ladies shuffled sideways to allow me space at the bar, and in my most high pitched voice I falteringly asked for two coffees and six cakes. An audible sigh of relief ran around the room and the conversation returned to standard female fare – namely, the daily struggle with ever increasing male inadequacy. As I listened to the conversations around me I had to agree that it was a further tick for the European Commission – when it comes to women, chocolate and conversation, borders mean nothing.

The discovery of the womens' café turned an already beautiful village into something not far off perfection for me, but depressingly, it still seemed to lack the vital ingredient of paid employment. We even asked at the campsite in case they needed any extra workers, but given the presence of only three campervans (one of which was us) it wasn't unexpected when they said no. After a few days of fruitless searching around the vineyards we returned to La Guardia for a Saturday morning of drowning our sorrows in coffee and cake. On our earlier visit we'd seen a notice for a harvest festival, taking place over the weekend, so we thought we'd call in and see if a Spanish harvest festival also consisted of children bringing tins of Sainsbury's baked beans to church. The posters had advertised a procession and marching bands – which seemed rather a lot for a small town – but it sounded like an entertaining way to pass a weekend, so we abandoned van and dog outside the town walls and headed back to the women's café.

Surprisingly for a harvest festival the town was much busier, with a keen sense of anticipation and excitement in the air. It certainly seemed to promise something more exciting than the annual dirge through 'We plough the fields and scatter' which marks

167

harvest festival in our home village. Intrigued, we ploughed our way through several cakes before scattering into the streets to await the marching band. Whilst we'd been adding to the day's calorific value, the good people of the town had been putting up waist-high metal barriers at strategic corners, and the local version of the St Johns Ambulance had also pitched up.

'Seems a bit much for a marching band.' I wiped the chocolate crumbs from my mouth. 'I mean, unless it's the Beatles or something. I hardly think we're going to be throwing ourselves at them and screaming the place down.'

'Yeah, it does seem a bit over the top. Maybe it all turns into a huge riot afterwards or something,' Chris agreed, as we squeezed between a barrier and an unforgiving stone wall. 'Everyone seems a bit worked-up. I wonder if there's something else going on.'

The words had hardly left his mouth when a loud cheer rang out from a few hundred metres away. An old lady grabbed my arm and rather crossly yanked me through the narrow gap, then firmly clanged the barrier shut behind me, before folding her arms across her chest and glaring at me.

'Alright, alright, I get the idea. What's she think I'm going to do? Rush a tuba?'

Suddenly the small group around me pressed forward, pushing me back towards the barrier. I turned to follow their gaze up the street and found myself facing straight into a medium sized pair of horns. Behind which was a distinctly pissed off, medium sized bull.

'Shit,' I cursed.

'You know,' Chris said helpfully. 'I think it might not be a marching band. I think it might be a running of the bulls.'

'Really? You think?' I yelled sarcastically as the crowd pushed me forwards again. The grumpy old lady who'd dragged me through the barrier now lifted her walking stick and brandished it at the unfortunate animal, shouting angrily as she tried to persuade it to take a bit more interest in the running part and a bit less interest in us.

After a few uncomfortable minutes of being pushed and shoved with the wildly yelling crowd, whilst trying to avoid getting my nose picked by a passing horn, it was clearly time to beat a hasty retreat. We ran back to the van as fast as we could, then drove back to the campsite without so much as a backward glance, hoping we weren't being pursued by an irate bull.

~

Apart from the harvest festival episode, the region seemed to be hunkering down for winter. All the vineyard owners were polite to us, but we didn't seem to be striking gold anywhere. Just as we began to lose hope, Chris saw a small hand written sign pinned on a telegraph pole, seeking the help of a pruner and a tractor driver. It sounded perfect and the idea of settling down to some light pruning work, basking in the autumnal sunshine before heading indoors to a few glasses of Rioja seemed to fit us just fine. All we had to do was rake up enough courage to call the phone number on the advert.

After several days of bickering and trying to pass the buck between us, Chris eventually banished me from the van, took a deep breath and rang to find out further details. I didn't hear the conversation, but when Chris re-emerged he seemed remarkably relaxed.

'So how did it go?' I asked.

'Fine, he was really nice. I said my Spanish wasn't great and he spoke slowly for me. I didn't understand everything, but I got most of it.'

'And what's the deal?'

'I'm not sure. I think he said the work was still available, although it sounded like he said he was still available, but maybe I missed a bit. Anyway, he's called Fernando and he wants us to meet him tonight, in the village square and we can talk about it there.'

'Uh oh, that sounds a bit scary. Did you tell him about the dog?'

'Yeah, I said we'd have Oscar with us, so he'd be able to spot us easily.'

We spent the rest of the day trying to make ourselves look presentable for a job interview and as if we regularly spent time pruning and tractor driving. We figured they'd probably be more reassured by the idea of Chris driving and me pruning, so I tried to look like a tidy and efficient pruner, whilst Chris worked on his farmer tan arms.

As the appointed hour arrived we headed into town, complete with identifying dog, and waited – somewhat nervously – in the square. Being a Spanish village, the square was still a hive of activity, even in the evening, with people taking their evening constitutional walk before beginning to think about a pre dinner drink.

'How are we going to spot him?' I asked nervously.

'I guess we're not. We'll have to hope he spots us. Or more to the point, we'll have to hope he spots Oscar.'

'I can't see any single blokes. Its all couples apart from those two blokes over there.' In the corner of the square were two shifty looking men, who seemed to be casting suspicious looks in our direction. I wondered if this was going to be one of those ghastly group interviews and if the vineyard owner had invited a variety of potential pruners and tractor drivers to meet him that night.

'Do you think they're trying to get work as well?' I asked.

'I don't know. They look a bit dubious though. I'd definitely employ us instead. We look a lot less dodgy.'

A few more minutes passed and the couples taking a turn of the square swapped with more couples, who all walked past us without a backward glance. The two men in the corner continued to eye us up moodily and we continued to try and pretend we hadn't seen them. A few moments later, the larger one approached us. Oscar rushed in for the customary crotch sniff, but his routine security measures failed to have their usual effect. Rather than stopping to pet him, the large man made a beeline for Chris, looked him firmly in the eye and said:

170

'You are Chris, yes?'

'Yes. And you are Fernando?' Chris stuttered in bad Spanish. He cast me a meaningful glance – somehow this man didn't look much like a vineyard owner.

'So, you are new to La Guardia?'

'Yes, just arrived last week. We were hoping to find some work for a few months to stay for the winter.'

'You are *looking* for work, not giving work, no?' Fernando clarified. The smile vanished faster than a pickpocket down an alleyway. 'It is the wrong way round. We are looking for work. I thought you have work, but you are looking for it as well, no?'

I felt a rush of blood to my face as I realised we'd made a fundamental mistake with a preposition and read 'looking for an offer of work' as 'looking to make an offer of work'. This guy would've heard Chris's broken Spanish and thought he was sorted – a naïve English vineyard owner ringing with an offer of work and probably no idea of local prices. But instead of the cash-cow he thought he'd found, we'd turned out to be just as much in need of work as him. If I hadn't been so embarrassed by our fatal blunder, I would've been slightly peeved that he'd felt able to judge our financial status on looks alone. Was it so very clear that we were job seekers rather than rich ex-pat vineyard owners? Even vineyard owners must have dressing down days? But it appeared that discretion was the better part of valour in this situation and we made our rapid apologies.

Back at the van we debated our mistake. How had we managed to be so dim? Was our linguistic capability really this hopeless? It seemed we were hardly safe to be out by ourselves in this place. Had we just dragged some poor guy on a wild goose chase because we were too stupid to understand the difference between offer and give? We discussed it at length, but we were both sure we'd read the sign correctly. We were convinced it had said offering, not looking for work. Faced with the not inconsiderable suggestion that we were completely losing the plot, we headed to bed – hoping we

171

wouldn't get run out of town in the morning.

In the cold light of the morning, I went back to check the sign. And discovered it had been doctored slightly. At some point after we'd left the night before, the dodgy man and his pal had realised that their sign gave the wrong impression and had attacked it with a biro. It now quite clearly stated that they were looking for work, but crucially for our pride, they had changed some significant prepositions.

At last, vindication! We weren't quite as stupid as we thought. Just for once, it hadn't been our mistake. Being constantly on the back foot in a language means you are inclined to take the blame for any misunderstandings, but just this once, we'd been in the right and the native speaker had ballsed up. Whilst that was vaguely comforting, the fear of running into the guy in daylight lingered in my mind and it wasn't long before we decided it was time to give up on the vineyards and try a different tack.

Chapter 17

Oscar learns to WWOOF

Our search for work had so far been an unmitigated failure. And so, like all good grown up gappers, we decided to resort to technology. Could the Internet come up with a solution? Given the number of emails I got offering me the opportunity to view celebrities in compromising positions with farmyard animals, as well as more v:@gr@ than it is possible to need in a lifetime, it didn't seem unreasonable to assume that the web might also be able to offer some useful suggestions for finding work in a strange country. Some of our friends in the missing generation had been able to find life partners on the web, so surely it wasn't too much to ask it to provide us with gainful employment for a few weeks.

Several trawls later, we'd made little progress on the paid employment front, but we'd come up with some options for voluntary work in exchange for bed and board. Whilst this wasn't an ideal solution, we reasoned that it would still help to balance our finances by reducing our outgoings, even if it didn't increase our income. And we'd get to practice Spanish, but would have slightly more bargaining power in terms of fitting working hours around the dog and our other constraints.

On a previous escapade to New Zealand I'd joined an organisation called Worldwide Workers On Organic Farms – better known as WWOOF. It had started life as 'Willing Workers On Organic Farms – but the organisers had recently realised that the days of willing workers were long gone and changed it to the more enigmatic Worldwide. The organisation provided a linking point between Worldwide (and possibly Willing) workers and local organic farmers, the theory being that the workers provided four or five hours of free labour each day in exchange for the farmer providing all

173

food and accommodation. The farmer got some labour and you gained experience of work in a rural setting, without a significant outlay of cash on either side.

The New Zealand farm experience hadn't worked out too well – the farmer turned out to have been recently abandoned by his wife and it was clear he was looking for assistance of a slightly more personal nature than I was prepared to provide. The chances of a repeat of that particular problem seemed unlikely– I was now older, wiser, wrinklier and also planning to take a husband and dog with me, which should be sufficient to put off all but your most ardent suitor.

The organic farm work seemed to be a good solution all round – with our 'proper careers' being in the environment sector we might even be able to turn it into something productive-looking on our CVs. It would also mean Oscar could have the run of a farmyard, rather than being cooped up in the van. So I printed off a list of Spanish farms looking for workers and we tried to draw up a shortlist of possibilities.

There are about 300 participating farms in Spain and the list covers all the areas of the country. But being very slightly older and wiser than most other volunteers (well, certainly older anyway) we found ourselves using a pretty harsh set of criteria for weeding out (no pun intended) some of the farms. A surprising number of places were run by people with names like Giles Marshall or John Smith, so the chances that we'd speak much Spanish at any of these didn't seem that high. Having come all this distance to practice Spanish, I wasn't particularly keen to start spending time with someone who'd recently emigrated from Surbiton.

Once we'd cut out all the ex-pat farms, we then had to weed out all the clearly barking elbow-patch-and-sandal farms. I'm happy to support the organic movement and enthusiastically munch my way through an organic vegetable box at home, but that doesn't mean I want to complete sun worship exercises before I start on the weeding, or hold hands and bless the leeks on a nightly basis. So any farms that talked about optional rain dance sessions had to be zapped from our list as well. Ditto any ones only offering a vegan diet or banning alcohol consumption on the premises. I certainly didn't plan to pass my time in Spain munching on tofu and lentils whilst seeking spiritual enlightenment.

Once the tree huggers with 'farms' the size of your average suburban garden had gone as well, our list was getting down to single figures. We composed a careful email that explained our situation and sent it off to a handful of potential farms, then settled back to wait. And wait. And wait.

Most of the farmers turned out to be so laidback they couldn't even manage to answer an email to accept the offer of free labour. Which does kind of make you wonder. Eventually we got two responses, but one was from a farmer who was just moving to his new farm on the outskirts of Malaga. Previous visits to the Mediterranean coast had left us wondering where all the Spaniards had gone. The area seemed to be full of British hotels, serving British food and selling British newspapers to, you guessed it, the Brits themselves. The opportunities for a sun tan would be great, but I thought we'd probably speak more Spanish in Aberdeen than in Malaga.

Which whittled our list down to just one farm located in the centre of Galicia, in the top left hand corner of Spain. This sounded more hopeful, so I rang to check the details. It was run by a three quarters Spanish, one quarter English family which seemed like a good compromise. If we were about to do something dangerous with some farm machinery then the English quarter (Joe) could shout at us in English, but he assured us that they spoke only Spanish in the house and that his wife spoke no English at all. Some of their neighbours spoke Galician, but we were promised they would revert to ordinary Spanish with us. They needed help with some fencing, something we'd both done in the past (that's the post and rail variety, not the dancing around with a sieve on your head version) and also with looking after the resident flock of

175

sheep. Cunningly we'd packed a spare sheepdog (OK half sheep-dog) so I was sure something would stir deep in Oscar's genes and he'd be running around, One Man and his Dog style, in no time at all. The deal was done and, like the good shepherds we were soon to become, we followed yonder star and headed to a stable (and, as it turned out, not much else).

~

In our brief discussions with Joe we'd arranged to arrive at the farm on a Sunday afternoon, which gave us a few days to make our way across the north of Spain. We'd planned a brief trip to the Lago de Sanabria park on the way, based on the promise of several campsites that our guidebook categorised as open all year. By the time we'd made it across to the western half of Spain, Chris had gone down with some form of cold bug (or man flu as its more commonly known) and was spending his time huddled under the duvet, shivering and blowing his nose. Things didn't improve as we got horribly lost on the way over and finally arrived at the edge of the park in the pitch black and rain. Driving slowly up a deserted road we did our best to maintain a cheery front, despite the growing evidence that there was nobody in this place.

'So, how are you feeling now?' I asked.

'You know, not great, but I'm sure I'll be fine once we get to the campsite.'

'Yeah, you might feel better after a shower and we can put the gas heater on for a while and get the van really warm.'

'It shouldn't be long now, should it?' Chris sounded like one of those nasal train announcements.

'No, it's not far from here. It'll get busier when we're nearer. I expect these are all holiday chalets and that's why they're all closed.' But it wasn't working. As we followed the guidebook instructions down increasingly narrow and dark roads, we had to admit that the chances of the place being open weren't that great. Finally we swung round a corner and faced a depressing sight – two large metal gates which were firmly closed across the campsite entrance.

'OK, let's not panic,' I said, trying to sound chirpy. 'There's another site listed down the road. That might be open. I mean, maybe they just keep one site open in the winter if it's not so busy.' But Chris was starting to sink into a shivery despair

'Yeah, right. We haven't seen a soul for miles. They must all be shut and who can blame them, it's pissing down out there.'

Deciding it was best just to keep quiet I drove on, but his prophecy was soon proved right. After a few more twists and turns we had exhausted all the campsites in the area. Not one was open before April, which was going to be a long wait – given that it was mid November.

In mild despair we set off in search of a suitable layby. Whilst layby camping was fun and cheap during the summer months, with good weather and light nights, it had become substantially less fun now it was dark at 6pm. And it was looking even less fun in the pouring rain with Chris knocking back the Lemsips and the internal van temperature dropping like a stone as soon as we turned the engine off.

And it becomes worse still when you can't even find a lay-by. All the roads nearby seemed to be single track, so only had passing places rather than actual pull off areas. We tried the nearest village, but the only potential parking spot was full of teenagers, entertaining themselves by throwing bottles at each other. It didn't look like an inspiring stop for a ten minute break, let alone a whole night. The thought of waking up to discover the van on bricks wasn't appealing so we hit the road again, trying to stave off despair, hunger and – in Chris' case – significant amounts of phlegm.

Three or four miles later, we spotted a small hotel, set back from the road. We looked at each other in silence, neither of us wanting to be the first to make the suggestion. Gradually I slowed the van to walking pace.

'What do you reckon?' I asked gently.

'Well, it doesn't look cheap. And we won't be able to take Oscar in. And we haven't given in and gone for a hotel yet, in nearly six months of travelling.'

'But…'

'But, we don't seem to have many options do we?' Suddenly I was struck by a brainwave.

'Didn't Kris and Wolfgang say they'd managed to stay in a couple of hotel car parks by having a meal there first? Maybe if we had dinner here they'd let us stay in the car park and use the loos?'

'Well, dinner won't be cheap either.' Chris was struggling to find anything positive through his web of phlegm.

'No, but it's better than driving all night. And we don't have much to eat in the van anyway.'

'OK, give it a go. Try and park near the edge of the car park so they can't see how scruffy the van is. I'll go and ask, they might feel sorry for me if they see how bad my cold is.' I resisted pointing out that they'd be more likely to try and disinfect him than give him a parking space for the night and nodded encouragingly.

'OK, maybe don't mention Oscar until you have to' I suggested helpfully. Chris headed off, trying to look like a clean living, respectable person who through no fault of his own had been struck down by the double whammy of a bad cold and a rather scruffy van. Trade must have been bad that night because the hotel owner seemed almost pleased to see us and Chris soon re-emerged, looking just slightly more perky.

'He says fine, we have to go and have dinner in half an hour and we can stay here afterwards and Oscar can go for a walk over there.'

'Excellent. I'm starving now I come to think about it.'

Half an hour later we settled at a table in the completely empty restaurant. The owner reeled off a short list of possible dishes (well, list might be an overstatement) and we were soon tucking into the first of three courses, accompanied by a bottle of rather nice local red. After another half hour only one other table was occupied, and that was by the owner and his family, who'd settled down to their evening meal.

After an excellent home cooked meal, we somewhat regretfully came to the end of the bottle of wine (and we hadn't even committed to buying any ancient bits of scrap metal – who says you can't teach an old dog new tricks!). Nervously, we waited for the owner to finish his own supper and then asked for the bill. He headed over, stood politely by the table and very formally announced that it would be 20 Euros. Trying not to show our relief, we quickly handed over a note, left some loose change on the table and headed out to our handily-located accommodation. As we left the owner gave us directions to the outside door that we could use to get into the bathrooms if we needed them overnight.

By the time we'd walked the six yards back to the van, we were in full self-congratulation mode.

'That was only about six euros more than a campsite and we got a meal and a bottle of wine as well!' I exclaimed.

'And a private bathroom, don't forget!'

'That's true. We should try this again.'

'Definitely. If we weren't about to go and live on a farm in the middle of nowhere I'd say we should do this all the time. Although I suppose that would use up the cash pretty quick.'

'Might be more inspiring than having pasta and tomato sauce though. But if we ate and drank that much every night, we'd have to get a bigger van just to get us home.'

And with a contented giggle at the thought of our soon to be enormous backsides attempting to squeeze into Bagpuss' small seats, we were soon both drifting off into the land of Nod.

Even better, by the morning the only after effect seemed to be the clearing of Chris' cold in record time and the friendly owner putting on his flash coffee maker just to whizz up an early morning cuppa for us. Farm work was going to come as a bit of a shock to the system.

~

One of the positives of campervan life is that every night can be different. You aren't tied to one place and can park up any place you fancy. But whilst that can be hugely liberating, it can also mean that one good night is no guarantee of what's to follow. So you may find yourself parked up somewhere fantastic one day, then only 12 hours later you can be in the campervan equivalent of a dodgy backstreet Glaswegian B&B.

Which is precisely what happened to us.

Our night of hotel luxury was followed by a deeply unedifying night spent on the forecourt of the Repsol petrol station in a wild-west frontier town on a Saturday night. So apart from the boy racers doing trips round the block at 50 miles an hour in second gear and the groups of drunken youths and the crowd in the petrol station bar watching the football, it was a good night's sleep.

Unsurprisingly the shower options in the morning were also pretty limited and, in what would turn out to be an ironic moment of worry, I didn't really fancy turning up at the farm when I hadn't had a shower in days, with hair plastered greasily to the side of my face.

With our arrival at the farm due in a few hours, we decided to take the plunge and head to the town swimming pool for a general clean up. As Chris disappeared to use the loo, I realised that going to the swimming pool would be likely to necessitate the use of a swimsuit, which, in turn, meant turning my attention to that most ghastly of subjects, the leg hair.

I tried to think back to the last time I'd managed to wax my legs and realised it was probably somewhere around Lithuania, roughly about 2 months beforehand. Thinking about it further I also realised that the Spanish probably weren't quite ready for the King Kong look, and decided I'd have to make some effort at general maintenance duties. A quick draw of the curtains and, I hope, completely unbeknownst to the folks filling their cars with petrol, I whisked out the cold wax strips, undertook the necessary (with only a few minor winces) and was ready to go in less time than it took to

180

put 45 litres of unleaded in the neighbouring car. Superman has nothing on me.

We emerged from the swimming pool startlingly clean and blinked at each other in surprise. So we weren't quite as tanned as we'd thought.

'Blimey' Chris couldn't help observing, 'at least the folks on the farm won't be able to tell we spent the night at the Repsol garage. They'll think we're nice, clean, respectable travellers and they should be delighted to be giving us house room for a while'

'Yep' I agreed, 'there's no hairs on us, quite literally in my case.'

And so we were off, scrubbed and polished and ready to face sheep, fences and anything else the agricultural world felt inclined to offer us. A short drive later we arrived in the nearest village to the farm, which looked like it might not have changed since Franco's days. And most of the inhabitants looked like they might well pre-date Franco. I think we might've been the first foreign visitors since the Fifth International Brigade.

'Well, we'll certainly be getting the full rural experience I guess.'

'True' Chris agreed. 'It makes Tarves look like a cosmopolitan city.'

'And I think we might have inadvertently driven back through a couple of centuries. Don Quixote might pass through in a minute.'

Still, we weren't exactly city slickers ourselves, so we figured we could probably cope so far, even if the locals were all staring at the van like it might be the Tardis. Which, in many respects it was, to us. Deciding to save the full village tour for another day, we headed off up the hill and in the direction of the farm. About three miles out of the village the road began to climb steeply and as Bagpuss trundled up at a snail's pace we looked out for the bus stop, which was our signal to turn off.

'Well, it can't be that remote if there's a bus stop, I guess,' Chris said. 'Hopefully it'll go into the village every so often, so we can always go out for a drink in the evening. OK, this looks like it. Can you see a turn off on the left?'

'There's a track over there – do you think that's it?' I asked.

'You mean the one with all the potholes? Yeah, I guess that's it. Here goes…' And slowly Chris lurched Bagpuss off the road and onto the rough, bumpy track. After a few hundred metres we saw some tie dye style paintings on the rocks at the side of the track.

'Ah yes, this'll be it. There's probably a peace pagoda somewhere along here as well. Did you pack some beansprouts and a yoga mat by the way?'

'Don't be facetious, I'm sure it'll be fine. Maybe the kids were practicing for art class.' Shortly after the rock paintings, the track dipped down towards a tumbledown heap of rocks and a couple of abandoned houses, with a pile of rusting cars and other assortments outside.

'I think this is it,' Chris announced.

'Ohhh.'

We sat in silence for a while, looking at the ruined houses, which even the most hopeful estate agent would struggle to describe as anything other than derelict.

'Maybe it's round the corner a bit?'

''Fraid not, there's smoke coming from the chimney there.'

'Ohhh,' I said. Again.

As we debated our new home, a large Alsatian–crossed-with-something dog appeared from behind one of the adjacent piles of rocks and threw itself in our direction, bouncing onto the bumper and nearly coming through the windscreen.

'Whoa, whoa. I guess that'll be their dog then.' Chris said, as Oscar strained to throw himself out the window.

'Is it friendly, do you think?'

'Let's hope so. Otherwise Oscar's in real trouble.' As we sat and debated our next move, a large round man with hair in a Bob Geldof style appeared around the corner.

'Hi,' he said, as we clambered out of the van. 'I'm Joe.'

We shook hands politely and waited whilst he tried, and failed, to persuade the Alsatian to chill out.

'Sorry about Lua,' he apologised. 'It's just she's coming into heat, I think, and she's desperate to shag anything.'

Which explained why Oscar had suddenly developed eyeballs on stalks.

'Well Oscar's had the snip, so he should be fine'. I watched as Oscar struck Adonis poses in the windscreen. 'I'll let him out and see what happens.' What was going to happen was abundantly clear to all present. As I opened the door a grey streak of lightning shot through, rushed up to the Alsatian and, without even stopping to ask her name or buy her dinner, Oscar began a full-blown demonstration of his virility.

We watched in silence for a while, Chris slightly awe struck at Oscar's ability to be – how shall we put this – 'in there' with a chick in less time than it takes to say, 'Your dog's a slapper'. Joe sighed.

'Yep, guess she's in heat then.'

So far this wasn't going exactly to plan.

'I'll show you round first and then you can go and meet the rest of the family,' Joe said, making a brave effort to continue a conversation despite the Olympic scale humping now taking place beside us.

'OK,' I agreed, 'we'll maybe leave Oscar here. I think he's kind of busy right now.'

A full tour of the derelict village ensued. It had once had maybe 14 or 15 houses separated by narrow alleyways, but now only four of the houses were occupied. One of these was being filled by Joe and family and the one on the opposite side of the alley was for working guests. Which meant us. Technically, 'house' was a bit of an overstatement. In reality it was more of a room – with two beds, a wood-burning stove and a small sink with a tap that would intermittently spout water. The water itself came from the nearest river, so its colour changed with the weather – rainy weather bringing brown water whilst sunshine bought clear water.

After a quick glance around our abode we headed across the 'street' to meet the family. Entering their also derelict house, we stepped down two steps and into the darkest, smokiest room I'd ever entered. Even Tarves pub on a heavy Saturday night had never been this smoky. Once my eyes had adjusted, I squinted round to see who was puffing the 60 a day that must be causing this smog. But no one was smoking, and the residents were calmly sitting at the table. Did they not realise their house was on fire then? What were they doing? They should be outside finding their assembly point, doing a roll call and waiting for the fire brigade to appear, not sitting here eating when they were about to die from smoke inhalation.

Just as I was about to start rushing round yelling 'Fire', a small dark haired woman stood up from the table and came over to shake hands. She introduced herself as Sabela and the two children as Alba (the older) and Paz (the younger). It slowly dawned on me that the smoke was coming from the wood burning stove in the corner, and that the family had grown used to it, so much so that they could even open their eyes, a feat I was still unable to achieve.

After a few minutes' polite conversation we beat a hasty retreat and headed to our room to unpack and suggest to the dog that he should take a break every so often. Joe headed over with us to give us instructions on the idiosyncrasies of the wood-burning stove. Just as he was leaving, I asked the all important question:

'And where's the bathroom?'

'Ahh.' Uh oh. This wasn't looking so good.

'Well, you see….'. This really wasn't looking so good.

'Well, we don't have one. As far as a loo goes, if you want to pee do it anywhere around, but not too close to the house and if you want a number two, there's a bucket over there in that shed in the corner of the yard. There's some sawdust to chuck in afterwards if you want. Then we chuck what's in the bucket on that heap over there, with a few branches, every day or so.'

I've seen a poster that says something along the lines of stress being what happens when your mouth says yes and your brain says no. I now realised that stress is also what happens when your mouth says 'ok, that's fine, thanks' and your head says 'what the frigging hell did he just say?'

We closed the door behind Joe's slightly sheepish figure and looked at each other.

'So, still think we could maybe stay till Christmas?' Chris asked.

'No. I'm not even sure I'm going to manage till Monday.'

'But that's tomorrow!'

'Well, at some point in the next 24 hours I'm going to have to use the bucket. And whilst I'm happy to take the shovel of shame and dig my own hole in the hills, the idea of a bucket full of someone else's ….. well, it just doesn't appeal.'

'And was it just me, or was it really smoky in there?' he asked.

'Yeah, it was horrendous. And so dark. I don't know how they could see anything.'

'OK, let's not panic. At least Oscar's having a good time.'

'He's going to be exhausted at this rate. Maybe we should get him in for a while. He's going to get repetitive strain injury soon.'

'Well, you can go and break up his fun. I'm sorry, I'm a bloke. It's bad enough that you made me get his balls snipped off. I can't go and interrupt the best sex he's had in years.'

'He's a dog Chris.'

'That's not the point.'

'Fine, I'll go.' I stomped out, wondering if this sudden rush of male solidarity was going to extend to Chris starting to pee up lampposts as well.

With some persuasion I convinced Oscar that he needed to lie down in a darkened room for a while, to rebuild his strength before the next humpathon. He strutted up the stone stairs to our room, and collapsed on the floor, hairy chest and ego on display for all to see. I made a mental note to buy him a medallion to complete the look.

Just as Oscar was debating whether or not to give Chris some tips on his pulling technique, Joe reappeared.

'I see. He's an inside dog is he?' he asked, a little nippily.

Now come on mate, I thought. You've just told us we've got to crap in a bucket, your living room is smokier than your average boozer and now you're going to get arsey about us getting some dog hair on the floor. I don't think so.

'Yes. He's an inside dog. He's house trained and if he's not inside, then neither are we,' I explained, trying – and failing – not to sound stroppy. Clearly it worked. Joe shrugged and wandered off. Chris raised an eyebrow at me.

'There's no discussion I'm afraid, Chris. Either Oscar comes into our room or we leave.'

'Alright, alright. It's not very clean in here anyway, I don't think there's much they can say. I'll try and get the fire lit.'

Several minutes and a couple of lung linings later, he'd got a small fire going and the room began to heat up, damp rising off the bedding in clouds of steam. I looked at the bedding options, but given that they'd all got dubious stains (some more significant than others) we decided to use our own sleeping bags. Later that night when the fire had died out and the temperature had plummeted to below freezing, using mountaineering sleeping bags indoors didn't seem such a bad idea after all.

Chapter 18

Not so idle in the rural idyll

The following day we embarked on our first day's 'work' – taking down the fence around the former chicken coop and recycling the wire for use in new fences. Other than not having any proper work clothes, we seemed to survive OK, although I was slightly uncomfortable with Joe's cavalier attitude to using chainsaws and strimmers within close proximity to someone's arm.

We'd only been able to fit a few items of clothing into the van, so I wasn't keen to trash any of them on bits of stray wire and brambles. When I asked Joe if he had any spare clothes, he looked at me blankly and then finally managed to come up with one old yellow mac. In the end I resorted to working in the yellow mac and my waterproof trousers, an unpleasantly sweaty combination. We soon decided that some overalls would be a useful investment, and after our allotted hours of work were completed, headed into the village to see what the local shops could supply.

I also wanted some work boots as I couldn't afford to ruin my reasonably expensive (and currently more or less leakproof) walking boots. But experience of hardware and agricultural supply shops in the north east of Scotland has taught me that women customers are looked on with something little short of suspicion and they certainly don't stock women's sizes of such manly essentials as boiler suits and safety boots. This prejudice even extended as far as the main stockist of health and safety equipment for the local Council. When I had enquired about getting a pair of Wellington boots with steel toe caps in a woman's size 6 for my last job (not an unreasonable request if your job involves sessions moving large rocks around a river to suit the whim of a passing salmon) I was told 'those things aren't stocked for women'. If I wanted a nice slip-on shoe with a steel toe cap they could probably help, but women certainly didn't use Wellingtons for anything other than light dog walking.

All of which meant I wasn't filled with confidence at my chances of finding suitable equipment for a slightly short woman in a DIY shop in a village slightly beyond the back end of beyond. I embarked on my painstakingly slow explanation with little hope of success:

'Excuse me, I'm looking for a boiler suit that will fit me, and some boots with iron toes,' (OK, I admit it, I'd checked that one in the dictionary beforehand)

'OK, what size?' the shop assistant replied, without skipping a beat.

'No, they are for me. To fit me. I will wear them.' I struggled to clarify what I wanted to say. Was that the right tense?

'Yes, OK, but what size?'

'Me, you mean what size for me?' The owner nodded politely and struggled not to raise his eyes skywards.

'Oh, err..,' I hadn't expected to get this far, so it hadn't occurred to me to check my European size.

'Well my feet are probably about a 40, but I don't know what size boiler suit.'

'OK, no problem. Wait a second,' and with a sprightly step he nipped off to the back of the shop, popped up a small ladder and returned with a boiler suit in my size and, even more surprisingly, with two pairs of steel toe capped boots – one set in my size, and just to really show off, a second set in a size smaller as well.

Why it was so simple here, I had no idea. Did the women of this area do more work in the fields than your average Scottish woman? This struck me as unlikely. Some of the farmers' wives I've met in Scotland quite clearly knew what they were doing when it came to fixing a tractor, and weren't the Latin countries supposed to have a reputation for their traditional attitudes to women? Embarking on a debate on the role of women in traditional agricultural societies was a bit beyond my linguistic ability though. Instead I contented myself with checking the fit and looking with renewed respect at the black-clad old ladies on the street outside.

The shop owner wasted no time in finding a second set of overalls for Chris, which we also agreed to buy. Only then did I realise we had hardly any cash with us, and this wasn't the kind of shop that was going to accept a UK credit card.

'Is there a bank in the village, or somewhere we can get some cash?' The shop owner smiled wryly.

'No, sorry, the nearest bank is in town.'

'Town' was another 20 kilometres away and it was already nearly six o'clock, so we'd struggle to get there and back before this shop closed.

'I'm really sorry but we don't have enough cash. We'll have to come back another day.' Now I was feeling bad for having wasted this man's time on a wild boiler suit hunt.

'It's OK, you can take the stuff and then pay me tomorrow. You're staying at Joe's farm, yes?'

Blimey. Either this man was desperate for business or genuinely trusting – by the time you added up the cost of two boiler suits and a pair of boots, it was a reasonable number of Euros to have as an IOU.

'Are you sure that's OK?' I asked.

'Fine, fine. No problem. Do you need a bag for them?'

Flushed with success from our shopping trip we returned home, bouncing a few more parts off the van as we headed down the track to the farm. And then spent the remainder of the evening trying to clear at least some of the layer of grime away from 'our' room. We were beginning to realise just how futile our mad clean up in the swimming pool had been. We were the cleanest thing that had passed this way in the last 20 years and removing any protective layer of dirt we may once have possessed could well have been a mistake.

Try as we might to be positive about the family home, there was no doubt that it was, to use a technical Scottish term, absolutely minging. There was no fridge and few cupboards, so food was left out on the table until it was either eaten, or had rotted away. Meanwhile three kittens would regularly walk across the food on the table, leaving small kitty pawprints in the butter and smeared bits of litter tray elsewhere. A thick layer of dirt was firmly ingrained into everything and the children made no attempt at washing their hands, even after emptying the bucket. I tried not to think about the risks of getting a stomach bug, especially in combination with the bucket situation. It was clear that staying here wasn't going to be an easy option.

But in other ways, once you got over the slight queasiness, it was fascinating to see people trying to live the rural idyll, Good Life style. The house had no drainage, no running drinking water or hot water and the only cold water was the direct divert from the river. The electricity came from solar panels, which meant it had to be used with care – if the kids decided they wanted to watch the TV there wasn't enough power for the old and battered washing machine, and vice versa. After a few days, Chris confessed one of his more worrying daydreams.

'You know, I've always wondered about living like this. In a sort of low footprint, environmentally sound way. I've always kind of thought I'd like to do it for a while.' The chances of making it to another anniversary bottle of wine were suddenly looking a bit slimmer.

'You have?' I replied, struggling to keep the panic out of my voice. 'I thought we were pretty sustainable anyway. I mean we're not exactly high energy consumers and the house is bloody freezing most of the time. Isn't that enough?'

'I know, but we still have mains drainage and hot water, central heating if we choose to use it and all that stuff.' And long may it continue, I thought to myself.

'But you know,' Chris continued, 'I get the feeling that staying here might be enough to put me off the idea'

'Hallelujah!' I quipped.

'No, seriously, it's all just so much harder than you expect. It'd all be fine as long as it was always warm, never rained and you never got ill.'

'And you had the world's most tolerant wife.'

'Anyway,' Chris continued, ignoring my negativity, 'I think if nothing else this'll be a useful testing ground. If we stay here for a while then we'll definitely know if it's something we want to try. You know, kill or cure, so to speak.' Hang on, I thought, how did *we* get into all this? But I decided it was best to keep quiet – I had a sneaking feeling that we'd both know exactly just how low our 'eco-footprint' could go by the end of this stay.

A few weeks earlier, I'd arranged a flight home from Santiago in early December to see my parents and exchange Christmas presents. So we decided we'd try and stick it out at the farm until then and see how we were doing. And despite the lack of luxuries, we quickly got into a routine, starting with an early morning splash with cold water. Occasionally this was tempered with a hint of luke-warm water if we'd remembered to fill the flask with hot water heated in a kettle on the fire the night before. After a brief muesli breakfast, we'd head out into the fields for the morning, usually helping to move the sheep out to their day's pasture first, then settling down to some fencing work once they were installed for the day. Some days we had to clear the route for the fence first, cutting back brambles, acacia and bracken, then digging holes for the concrete posts, before finally rolling out the wire and tightening it to sheep proof tension. Of course it didn't always work, and occasionally we would tighten the wire, step back to admire our handiwork and then watch as one of the concrete posts keeled over slowly, sliding out of the ground like a giant grey slug.

We usually stopped working a bit before lunchtime and headed back to clean off at least some of the mud. Oscar spent the morning entertaining himself with Lua, which meant that by lunch-time he could barely walk and had to spend the afternoon lying in a darkened room, panting gently. Our afternoons varied – when there was decent weather we'd head out for a wander around the chestnut groves, or I'd go for a run on the road nearby (invariably causing a pile-up as car drivers slowed down to stare) or on damp afternoons we'd light the woodburner and settle down with books until supper time.

In the evening we'd head across the road to the main farmhouse and have dinner with the family. This was pretty hard work until the kids went to bed, both of them being inclined towards Little Miss tantrums, making it impossible to have a conversation. But once they'd headed to bed we usually got a chance to get in some serious Spanish practice and Sabela would talk to us about life in Galicia, the Civil War and other bits of Spanish history. Most of my Spanish history comes from Laurie Lee books and Ken Loach films, but I probably learnt more at that dinner table than I could have picked up from a thousand history books.

Sabela was only a few years older than me, but the bitterness and anger she still felt towards Franco and the nationalists was far in excess of anything I've ever witnessed. And once she started, it was like a steam train rolling downhill. There was no way of stemming the tide of anger and vitriol until she'd worn herself out and we could finally get a word in edgeways to ask a question. Many of her family in A'Coruna had either disappeared or emigrated during the Franco years and much of the land around the farm belonged to 'unknown owners' – people who had either fled or disappeared.

I began to realise how little I knew about the recent history of this country that so many Brits visit. I can't recall a single mention of it in history lessons at school. I could probably give you a brief run down on the Roman Empire, but I certainly left school unaware of even the briefest details of recent history in this part of Europe. Why is that? And why were the Spanish themselves so reticent to talk about it all? Where were the monuments to those who'd been involved, when was the Remembrance Day for those who'd lost their lives on either side of the struggle?

Sabela's answer was that the Spanish weren't yet ready to examine their recent past – that to commemorate any part of their recent history would act as a red rag to a bull and reopen old wounds. And the political culture of the late 20th century seemed to agree. In 1977 an amnesty law was passed that effectively ensured that no one was bought to trial for actions taken during the Franco years. And an unspoken 'Pacto del olvidado' or 'pact of forgetting' has encouraged Spaniards to keep silent on their feelings as they try to move on into a brave new Spain. Our discussions with Sabela showed that the scars have yet to heal and have to be treated with care – the sticking plaster of silence may need to be left for now, because removing it might cause the bleeding to start again.

After such philosophical discussions, and once our heads had reached the stage where they could no longer follow the rapidly accelerating flow of Spanish, we'd head back across the road to our room. By stoking up the fire we'd manage to keep the room warm for a few minutes, before drifting off into dreams of new strategies to make the next day's fence just that little bit more solid.

As time passed we also began to realise that Joe and Sabela didn't know a whole lot about farming. Joe had gone to university to study systems engineering, but had left before he finished the course. He'd decided to hit the road for a few months and hooked up with Sabela after only a few weeks in Spain. The two of them had lived the travelling life for a while, touring craft markets and other 'alternative' hangouts, before Sabela's biological clock had taken over and they'd settled down on the farm.

To my surprise, they'd been there for over ten years, but had yet to make a significant impression on either the house or the land. Joe seemed to be a man full of schemes, but few of them had come to fruition and so the house and surrounding land still looked as if it was barely tolerating them as passing visitors.

Sometimes I found their inability to get it together deeply frustrating. There were so many things around the farm that could be done to make their lives easier, but they were incapable of making a concerted effort to get things sorted. With the possible exception of the computer system. In ten years they'd not got round to installing a proper compost toilet, or any form of drainage system, but Joe had managed to install a fully functioning computer network, and a state of the art electrical system to run the computers and DVD player. I guess everyone has different priorities, but each time I faced the horror of the bucket I wondered just what they were thinking.

Chapter 19

Our lowest ebb

After two weeks of this life, the time came for me to head to the sunny delights of Stansted airport, courtesy of the horrors of Ryanair. We planned to spend a few days in Santiago first, taking in the tourist sights, and then Chris would head back to the farm with Oscar. Leaving the farm I felt a surge of relief and once we'd put a few miles between us and them we fell to a full scale bitching session – moaning about the lack of hygiene, discipline for the kids and general inability to do anything pro-active. We discussed the rural idyll and low footprint lifestyle and realised that if we ever did decide to go down that route, we'd be doing it fairly differently from this family. On the other hand, we had to agree it was turning into one hell of an experience. Having reached the age where I'd started to take a shower, flushing toilet and telephone for granted, it was probably quite good to be reminded of what life was like without them.

Arriving in Santiago we headed for the campsite and both rushed to the showers for a much needed clean up. Emerging into the watery twilight I discovered a lone cyclist setting up his tent near our van. I was impressed with his stamina – it might be Spain but it was still December and the weather was both cold and damp. A cycling holiday in this temperature – combined with a tent – seemed almost as masochistic as our current farm life. Wandering over to his tent, I offered a greeting in Spanish.

'Umm...Hola,' he replied, in a very British accent.

'How's the cycling?' I asked in English. 'Have you come far?'

'Well, I've cycled from London, but I've only done about 60 miles today,' he answered, with a self deprecatory laugh.

Bloody hell. Here I was moaning about not being able to have a shower when I wanted and needing to boil the kettle on the woodburner and this guy had cycled from London, reaching Santiago in December.

'Blimey. Where are you heading?'

'Well, I'm hoping to get to Africa. But first of all I have to get to Lisbon by Christmas. I suggested to my Mum we could meet up for Christmas in Oporto, but she got confused and forgot which town I suggested and now she's booked tickets for Lisbon instead, so I need to get there in the next two weeks.'

Poor guy. Lisbon seemed a heck of a long way in this weather, with only two wheels for company. He seemed to be taking it remarkably well though.

'I didn't like to tell her on the phone, so I just said that'd be fine. As long as I keep doing about 60 miles a day I should get there by Christmas Eve I think.'

Feeling sorry for him, I invited him over to the van for supper – at least then he could have a meal in the dry.

Once Oscar had given him the once over, Colin the cyclist folded himself into the van and proceeded to devour about two kilos of pasta. During the meal he told us he was only 20, and had worked in a variety of dead end jobs in order to pay for this trip. He was hoping to spend some time cycling round Africa before settling down in a village somewhere for a few months. I was amazed at his self possession – he seemed completely unfazed by the mammoth task he'd set himself and came across as a genuinely mature and in control person. After spending the previous three weeks with two thirty-somethings who were incapable of even making sure there was milk in the house, it was a dramatic contrast.

We spent the evening engrossed with Colin's life plans and his amazing achievements on the bike. It was probably the perfect antidote to bitching about Joe and Sabela. The next morning we waved him off, onto the noticeably hilly-looking road and headed down to the city to explore.

Santiago itself left me with mixed feelings. Whilst the cathedral

196

was dramatic, the surrounding streets seemed full of tourist tack and windblown litter, with plastic shells (the ubiquitous symbol of pilgrimage on the Camino de Santiago) and shiny walkers' poles a plenty. There were one or two genuine pilgrims entering the city and it was heart warming to see the sudden skip in their step when they caught their first glance of the cathedral spires. But we also saw two young lads running what looked like a suspiciously slick scam on the more vulnerable of the pilgrims. They'd taken to standing outside the Cathedral, telling passing pilgrims how they'd just arrived too, but had run out of cash now. The good hearted souls they approached seemed keen to help what they thought were kindred spirits and handed over their cash willingly. They probably believed they were off to spend it on new boot soles and some blister treatment. But seeing the same lads on the second day made us more suspicious – there's a limit as to how long you can have just arrived in a city and we saw the routine take place with several sets of innocent walkers. Somehow it took the edge off what is a beautiful city, but which seemed rather tarnished by its own success.

After some quick Christmas shopping I headed to the airport and left Chris and Oscar to return to life on the farm. Arriving at my parents' house I discovered that weeks of speaking Spanish had affected my ability to remember where to put the verb in an English sentence, but apart from my mild stammering and distinct scruffiness, I was otherwise unscathed.

I spent a pleasant week relaxing with my folks, enjoying daily showers, a flush toilet, an electric kettle, a table free of cat turds and other luxuries. Chris had a less pleasant week. He continued to help with the fencing and Joe began to get more stressed as the deadline for completing the work approached. Because he was receiving a grant from the Spanish government to pay for the work it had to be completed ready for an inspection by the local office a few days before Christmas. Various friends came round to help and Chris spent more and more hours out with the pliers and hammer.

More worryingly, Oscar began to behave oddly. According to

Chris, whenever I'm away, Oscar becomes a bit grumpy and sulks in a corner. Of course I've never seen this, so it's hard to judge whether it's all in Chris' imagination or whether Oscar, the uncaring dog, does actually notice if I'm not there. I'd expected him to be delighted to return to the farm and Lua's open paws, but instead of continuing the ongoing shagathon, Oscar became more introspective. He started refusing to eat and had to be coaxed into playing with even his most favourite toy, the squeaky squirrel.

The text messages I received from Chris became more and more frustrated, awaiting my return so that Oscar could stop being so out of sorts. By the day I was due to fly back, even my Mum had to agree that it seemed my dog needed me.

The flight back was unpleasant in the way that only budget airlines can manage properly. It was delayed and overcrowded and the couple next to me spent the whole time asleep, sweating quietly. I assumed they were recovering from a heavy night on the drink and wasn't particularly sympathetic, an attitude that would come back to haunt me later.

Arriving in Santiago it took some time to convince the sceptical bus driver that I really did want to go to an obscure Galician town. He clearly didn't believe it was an appropriate destination for a foreign visitor with a backpack and was determined to put me on the bus bound for Barcelona. Just as the bus pulled out of the bus station an unnerving text from Chris arrived:

'Just been 2 vets. Oscar v v ill. From tick. Treated, but not sure if he will recover.'

My stomach lurched. The longest two hours of my life followed, as I spent the rest of the bus journey turning it all over in my head and trying to hold back the tears. Oscar had never asked to be involved in this whole escapade. Everyone had warned us we were taking a risk. We knew about nasty tick-borne diseases but I'd tried to ignore the doom-mongering and pass it off as xenophobia for dogs. Now it was looking horribly like they might be right.

Oscar was obviously properly ill, not just missing me and I had to face the thought that he might not survive. To my mind this meant we would be responsible for his death. We'd chosen to drag him to this god forsaken part of the continent. If it wasn't for our selfishness he'd be safely ensconced by the fire in Tarves, his only real risk that of becoming a fat lap dog, waddling down the road.

The journey seemed to drag on forever and I was terrified Oscar would die before I got back to the farm. In my head, not only would I have indirectly killed him, but I wouldn't even get to say goodbye. I felt sick to the pit of my stomach and chewed my nails to pieces. Finally the bus pulled into town and I saw Chris standing by the road. Normally when one of us is away we take Oscar to meet the returning half of the family. The wag of his tail is usually sufficient to mitigate our gripes and moans about the train being delayed or the drunken hen party screeching across the carriage. But this time Chris was alone and my first question as my foot hit the tarmac was dog related.

'Where's Oscar? Is he OK?' I felt like I was starting to go mad, screaming out a million questions all at once.

'He's got a disease called piriplasmosis. It's carried by ticks,' Chris answered, as calmly as he could. 'If it goes untreated, then it kills the dog, but the vet thinks we've caught it early enough.'

'THINKS!?!' I wanted to scream. 'Thinks' isn't good enough. I needed to *know*.

'He's had one injection and then he needs to take antibiotics for the next two weeks. He hasn't eaten much for the last few days though, so he's quite weak. But she looked at his blood under the microscope and she said he'd still got some white blood cells, so his body should be able to fight it off slowly once the drugs start working. He's okay really.'

'But if he's okay, why isn't he here now?' I managed between stifled sobs.

'I thought it would be better to leave him in the van until you got here. Calm down, I thought I was doing the right thing. He had to have an intra-muscular injection and the vet wanted to muzzle him for it because they're so painful. But he didn't even react to that. He's just really, really weak'

When I got to the van Oscar was lying on the front seat. I opened the door and any lingering hope that it might not be that bad was quashed. Whereas I'm normally greeted by a thudding tail being whacked onto the ground and some enthusiastic sniffing, all I got this time was a single, tiny quiver from the end of his tail. Just one small lift of his tail and not even an opened eye. Of course the pathos of this was enough to open my already wobbly floodgates. I sat on the pavement by the van and sobbed my heart out. I couldn't believe that my own selfishness had done this to the dog I loved so much. Eventually Chris pushed me into the van and Oscar and I travelled back wrapped together on the front seat, his ears getting gradually wetter as I sobbed into them.

On the way I called my parents with the update – which must have been a difficult phone call for them to receive – not only did they also adore Oscar, but they knew that this would be tearing me apart. They headed off to research the disease on the web for me, and we carried Oscar into our room. I briefly went over the road to the main house to tell them I was back and to warn them I wasn't going to be up for supper. As soon as Sabela saw my tear-stained, blotchy face she gave me a big hug, but then rather spoiled the effect.

'What's wrong? It's just a dog.'

And that is probably why I'm not a farmer. Oscar has never been, and never will be, just a dog. Oscar is part of the family. Of course I failed to explain this in any way through my muffled sobs and I headed back across the road, leaving Sabela shaking her head in confusion. We spent the rest of the evening trying to make Oscar as comfy as possible, before going to bed – knowing that sleep was impossible, but hoping it would at least be somewhere warm to lie and wait.

Poor Oscar spent the night panting gently – only this time it wasn't due to some extra curricular activities with Lua, but because his temperature was so high. Unusually for him he needed to go out in the night, and things were obviously pretty bad because he couldn't even lift his leg to pee. Which of course started me sobbing all over again.

In the morning we realised that he'd also peed in the room where he'd been lying, something he hadn't done since he was six weeks old. So having persuaded Joe that it was OK to have him in the house because he was so completely house trained, he'd now been too ill to make it outside and we were faced with trying to clean up without revealing to Joe and Sabela what had happened.

In between the discreet scrubbing of bedding, we had to admit that Oscar didn't seem much better. Joe rang the vet for us and we headed back into town, Oscar struggling to walk the few yards from the van. But just as we seemed to have hit our blackest hour, there was some good news

'His temperature has dropped from yesterday, so the drugs are starting to work. It means he should recover, but it might be a slow process.' The fact that Oscar had just submitted quietly to having his temperature taken was a clear indication that he was still a long way from this normal self. And more worryingly, we couldn't persuade him to eat, as Chris – who was holding it together a lot better than me – tried to communicate in his suddenly faltering Spanish.

'Oscar doesn't eat anything. And the tablets say take after food, but we are able to coerce to eat him not. Now he does not eat five days.'

'I know. It will be difficult and he won't want to eat for a while. I'll give him a vitamin shot to help him keep his strength. But you have to oblige him to eat. He won't get better without food and the tablets.'

'How though? How do we 'oblige' him to eat?' I asked, aware that any social skills I might once have possessed were long gone, and that I was snapping at this woman.

'Try baby food' she suggested, professionally rising above my snippiness. 'He can lick it from your hands. And once you get him to start eating again, you should feed him liver. Just cook it a little bit and feed it to him in cubes. It will help his blood.'

I have to be honest and say that most of this conversation passed me by – I was so worried about Oscar that my ability to comprehend even single words of English had disappeared, so I struggled to follow the fast flowing Spanish. But between us, we managed to understand enough to work out what we needed to do and Chris was dispatched on a liver and baby food search, whilst I took Oscar back to the van.

Returning to the farm, the real struggle began – we couldn't even persuade Oscar to lick the baby food from our fingers, so how we were supposed to get enough down him to act as a cushion for the antibiotics wasn't clear. Just as we were getting to the swearing stage, Joe came in to check on his disaster struck volunteers. After watching us struggle with Oscar for a while, he came up with a minor brainwave.

'What about one of the syringes I use for the sheep? You could use that to squirt the food in? It'll be a bit slow, but at least you'll be getting something inside him.'

'OK, if you've got a spare one, that'd be great.'

Joe disappeared into the tool shed cum vegetable store cum animal drug store downstairs and reappeared with a set of syringes. To my relief he then left the room as we sucked the baby food up the syringe and forced it into Oscar's mouth. Fortunately Oscar was too weak to put up much protest, but it didn't make us feel any better as we took it in turns to hold his head whilst the other one squirted in pureed chicken and rice formula, followed by the recommended dose of antibiotics.

A few hours later the food seemed to be helping and Oscar had stopped panting and was finally starting to sleep properly. By evening time he could even be persuaded to have a tiny corner of one of my Mum's mince pies. After breaking off a corner for him, I ate the rest of the pie myself, feeling distinctly un-festive but in need of a sugar hit.

The following morning, Oscar seemed slightly chirpier and could just about walk around the farmyard. We left him sleeping in our room for the morning, and headed down the hill to catch up on the fencing work. But as the morning wore on, I began to be aware of a distinctly queasy feeling and by lunchtime I had to give in and return to our room. On my way, I stopped off at the van and picked up our waste water bucket, figuring it was best to be prepared.

Chris came back an hour or so later to find a very pale, sweaty wife, leaning over the bucket, throwing up violently. And of course, the sick dog was still lying there, needing to be pipette fed. And we were out of liver, so he needed to head back to town and buy more liver for the dog. Or should he stay in and hold my hair and pat my back whilst I leant over the bucket and retched? A tricky choice for anyone. I suspect juggling these two delights was the darkest hour for Chris and I've no doubt he was also cursing that anniversary bottle of wine and all that had followed. It had finally become his turn to realise that this shouldn't happen to a dog, wife or husband.

I'm pleased to report that when given a choice between dealing with a sick wife or a sick dog, Chris took the course of any self respecting man, and dealt with the dog first. Then, he emptied my bucket, tied my hair out of the way and headed into town to fetch more liver for the weak dog. Just as Oscar had told me in Poland, he will always win, in sickness and in health. Although on this occasion, I was so glad he was alive that I didn't begrudge him his star treatment. But I also had to be impressed with the way Chris had managed to step up and deal with a half dead dog and a vomiting wife. We weren't in the easiest of situations and Chris certainly wasn't having that much fun. But he hadn't moaned or fussed, he'd just got on with the job in hand. I was still harbouring intermittent black thoughts about his failure to control the obses- sion with his thesis, but these last couple of days had given me a good opportunity to remember the reasons why I'd married him. Living together in a campervan, 24 hours a day wasn't that easy and there was no doubt it had put our relationship under some strain. But the flip side of the coin was realising that, in general, one or other of us seemed able to hold it together – no matter what the crisis. And as long as we didn't both go down the tubes, maybe we'd be alright. And maybe that's what being in a relationship is all about – knowing that it will go wrong at times, but that somehow, one or other of you has to pull through and, if necessary, drag the other one with them.

Fortunately my bug only lasted a few hours and after some intense interaction with the base of the bucket I began to feel better. I spent the rest of the night sweating and shivering but by the morning I was feeling more human, although I wasn't up to any mince pies. At this point Chris began to crack under the stress and voiced thoughts he'd normally have the sense to keep to himself.

'You know, I think you probably got that bug because you're so unhygienic with Oscar,' he mused.

'I beg your pardon?' There was an icy chill in my voice that should have bought him to his senses.

'Well, when he was really ill you shared that mince pie with him. You probably got some germs from the bit you ate.'

'I didn't eat the same bits as him! I broke a bit off for Oscar and ate the rest myself. It wasn't like he licked my half or anything. I am not unhygienic with Oscar. And even if I am, I don't care. He's my dog and I love him.'

'Fine. But just be aware that this is the result.'

Fortunately for Chris I was feeling too weary to find something large to connect with his head and I contented myself with a sullen silence instead. But my revenge wasn't far away. At three o'clock the following morning a rather small voice spoke up in the darkness:

'Can you pass me the bucket please? I'm not feeling very well.' The temptation to ask if he'd been sharing any mince pies with the dog was so, so strong. But I was within projectile vomiting distance, so it seemed best to feign sympathy. I suspect my smug thoughts were quite loud enough to carry through the darkness.

These were undoubtedly the worst few days of the whole trip. For probably the best part of a week I honestly regretted having left Scotland. I regretted taking the dog, I regretted staying on a farm with no hygiene or drainage and I regretted sitting next to the sick people on the plane, who I suspected had passed on their germs. For that week, I would have swapped everything to be back in the warmth, comfort and safety of our normal lives.

But slowly Oscar seemed to be coming back from the brink. He returned to the vet for a second intra-muscular injection and this time he made it abundantly clear just how damm painful it was. For the first, and I hope only time in his life, he snapped at the vet as she tried to push the needle in. By the time the injection was finally done we were all shaking. But we also had to continue to feed him liver for two weeks along with his antibiotics, and after the 'it's only a dog' conversation I wasn't feeling particularly inclined to start frying up liver in the main farm kitchen. So we used our small frying pan from the van on the top of the woodburner, which gave our room an interesting aroma of fried liver, stale dog pee and slightly unclean people.

Although Oscar was gradually regaining strength, he was still a long way from being out of the danger zone. We continued with the mixture of baby food and liver, but in an attempt to start reintroducing normal dog food, we tried blending it all together to put in the syringe. I stole the small hand blender from the farm kitchen and mixed together baby food, liver and some dry dog food that we'd soaked in water. This turned out to be more substantial than the blender's capabilities, and it turned into a lumpy, soggy mess that stank to high heaven.

We were both on the edge of returning to the vomit bucket as I tried to feed it to Oscar, and, unsurprisingly, he didn't seem particularly keen on it either.

Admitting that this wasn't a successful dog food recipe, I gave the blender a quick rinse out and handed it back. Given the disgusting state of the kitchen, I didn't make much effort to clean off the dog food and raw liver slime, assuming that these people were so unhygienic they'd never notice. Plus I hadn't seen them using the blender whilst we were there, so I figured by the time they used it next, we'd be long gone.

So of course, it served me right when we went over for supper that night and discovered Sabela using the very same blender in a large pan of what looked suspiciously like it might be our supper.

'Hello, how are you? How was work? What's for dinner?' I asked, tentatively.

'Soup. Pumpkin soup.' Oops. Oh well. Pumpkin with a hint of stale liver and dried dog food probably wasn't so bad. Maybe?

'Just a small bowl for me thanks.'

Did I catch just a glimmer of a smile on Sabela's face?

Chapter 20

While Shepherds watched

Oscar's dramatic illness and slow recovery had scuppered our plans for moving on when I returned from Santiago. The vet insisted that she needed to see him again two weeks after the first treatment, which meant we had to hang around in the area until at least Boxing Day. We'd then have no real chance of finding another farm or more work until after New Year, so it seemed pointless moving on before January. We debated whether or not we could cope with a Christmas spent with two slightly disgusting adults and two tantruming children.

'I'm quite happy to do some more fencing work and stuff over Christmas. It's just the thought of coping with the kids that I can't face.'

'And then there's the pig killing feast they're talking about. We seem to have a choice between getting involved in the pig stabbing or babysitting the kids.'

'Great. There isn't an option for babysitting the pigs and stabbing the kids is there?' I muttered.

'Don't be uncharitable. Alba's not so bad, it's just Paz and her need to be a primadonna that I find hard.'

'Joe was talking about them maybe going away for a day or so though,' I pointed out, hopefully. 'And I think they're going to a wedding on January 2nd, so they might go away then.'

'Maybe we could suggest to them that they go away for a few days, you know, have a bit of a break and stuff and we can look after the farm. That way we get somewhere to stay for Christmas, but without them, and they get a break. Joe said they hadn't stayed away from the farm for over two years.'

'Do you think we'd be safe looking after this lot?' I asked, my eyes bulging at the thought.

'Don't see why not. The sheep just need to be walked out to the field and bought back in the evening. We know we can look after Lua, or at least Oscar'll be happy to look after her once he's a bit stronger and you know what to do with cats. Other than that, there's a few blackcurrant bushes to plant and fencing and stuff.'

'I suppose so. Do you think Joe'll think we're safe though?'

'Yeah, I reckon. I mean it's not like he's a seventh generation farmer is he? He must've started somewhere.'

'OK, well, you can suggest it and see what he says. It might just be a cunning plan.'

Chris ran the plan past Joe and after he'd had a discussion with Sabela – who was the real head of the household – the deal was done. They would go to her family's home in A'Coruna on Christmas Eve and stay there until January 3rd. We would stay and look after the farm and generally keep things ticking over until they got back. And if it all went horribly pear-shaped they would only be two hours drive away, so we could always ring and call Joe back if necessary.

It all seemed like a perfect plan. But just as we were starting to relax and think we might have finally got back under control, Joe dropped a minor bombshell.

'By the way, I meant to mention this earlier. I'm getting some extra sheep on the 20th.' At the moment the flock was a piddly 22 sheep, who'd been hanging out together all summer and had – as much as sheep do – bonded, and tended to act like a flock, all going one way or another. Which didn't always mean they went the way you wanted them to go, but at least you knew that when you lost control of them they'd all hang out together, rather than splintering into competing factions. So once you found one of them, you'd found them all. Introducing new sheep at this stage would be likely to result in two flocks. One would be made up of the old timers, who'd hang out together come what may; but a separate, New Labour type of flock would also form. The New Labour flock would follow a leader from within their own crowd, no matter where the other Old Labour flock went.

Which doubled the amount of time you'd need to spend searching the hillside for them, because you probably wouldn't find the Old and New Labour sheep hanging out together. If you see what I mean.

'OK. How many sheep?'

'Oh, about another 20 or so I think. Thereabouts. They're all quite young though. Well, I think they are.'

'And are they all supposed to fit into the yard at night? It's only just big enough for them at the moment.'

'Yeah ..that's a thought,' Joe scratched his chin. 'Maybe I should extend it a bit?'

Chris looked at me in despair.

'That might be a plan, Joe.'

So, a couple of days before the family left, we put up a new fence outside the sheep's barn (which was another of the derelict houses, in only marginally worse condition than the family residence). Later that evening a lorry drove up, deposited 23 sheep in the yard and then sped off into the darkness, leaving us to collect up the stray sheep that had bolted before the fence was closed. After a lot of chasing round in the dark, and much yelling and shouting in Spanish, we'd tracked down 21 sheep. There were still 2 runaways and Sabela and I headed off in search of them. I'd taken a torch with me, and whilst Sabela carried on ahead, I followed more slowly, peering to either side. After about 200 yards, I caught the reflection of four small eyes, burrowed into the edge of a field.

'I can see them, I can see them.' I yelled, in my best Spanish.

'Behind me, or in front of me?' Sabela yelled back. Or did she say 'in front of me or behind me'? Shit, this was a really bad moment to have a memory lapse on the preposition front, but for the life of me I couldn't remember which was in front and which was behind. And were the sheep in front of her or behind her anyway? Didn't it depend which way she was facing?

The eyes continued to stare back at me. I tried to make reassuring sheep noises whilst mentally running through a catalogue of evening class memories. Where is the bank? Is there a toilet near here? Can I order the calamaries and a glass of red wine? No, no, this was no good. Bollocks. I'd just have to plump for one and hope that on the 50 / 50 chance the gods were with me.

'Delante,' I yelled and heard the sounds of Sabela scurrying on ahead and into the darkness. Bugger.

'Detras,' I yelled instead. 'I think….' I tailed off lamely.

Obediently Sabela turned round, diplomatically cursing in Galician so I had no idea what she was saying about my parentage. As she came level with me, I held the torch up so she could see the reflections. But now, there was only one pair of eyes. One pair had scarpered whilst I was dithering around in lost preposition land.

'I thought you said you could see *them*,' Sabela pointed out accusingly.

'I did, but one's gone.'

Sabela sighed. 'Well, let's get this one back; we'll just have to leave its friend for now.'

We picked up sticks and with some pokes and prods, drove one very scared sheep back to the fold. But after more fruitless searching and recounts, we had to admit we were one short.

In the cold light of morning, there was still no sign of the missing sheep. We spent a few more hours wandering the hillside making pathetic baa-ing noises and yelling 'Here Bessie', but only got strange looks from Oscar in return. Still, a 5% loss rate wasn't too bad, and Joe resigned himself to a flock of only 44 sheep.

Later that afternoon, just as we were about to return to our fencing work, the phone rang. After a fast and increasingly incredulous Spanish conversation Joe put the phone down, looked at us and shrugged his shoulders.

'They've got the sheep. Back there. Where they came from.'

'But I thought you said they were coming from 20 miles away.'

'I did.'

'So it walked back 20 miles just to be where it used to live? Are you sure you didn't buy a dog by mistake?'

'I'm starting to wonder now. Apparently someone found it this morning, shut in a dog kennel about 10 miles from here, so they got the number of the owner from its ear tag and dropped it off at lunchtime. They've still got their old ear tags in, so they took it back to the old owner.'

'What was it doing in a dog kennel?'

'She thinks someone must've seen it by the side of the road, picked it up and taken it home for their Christmas lunch. But before they'd had a chance to start roasting it, someone else found it in the kennel and took it home.' Suddenly I felt like I was in a Wallace and Grommit film. Any minute now Grommit would roar in on a motorbike and return the lost sheep. I wasn't sure if I was disturbed by the idea of the high speed sheep rustling going on round here, or impressed by the fact that it had been returned to its rightful owner. When I'd lost stuff in Scotland it generally wasn't returned with anything like the speed that the lost sheep service operated round here. On the other hand, if people were picking up stray sheep at the side of the road as if they were frozen turkeys in the supermarket, we might have to be a bit more skilful in our shepherding work.

Joe headed off down the road to collect the sheep, now renamed Supersheep and we wandered off to check on the others, shaking our heads in disbelief. An hour later, Supersheep had been safely returned to the small field by the house and was being given a few hours of respite to recover from her ordeal.

As it turned out, this was the worst thing we could've done. Lua, having lost interest in Oscar, decided that this new arrival was her next play thing. Stunningly crap sheepdog that she was, she jumped the fence into the field and set to playing a game of 'let's-see-what-you're-hiding-under-this-wool-shall-we?' By the time Joe noticed, poor Supersheep had been mauled along one side and was pinned

211

to the fence in terror. Cue much shouting at Lua and we began to realise that we were being left with double the number of sheep, one injured animal that seemed to be suffering from wanderlust and a psychotic dog that couldn't decide if it wanted to eat, herd or shag the sheep. The idea of a Yuletide full of peace and goodwill was suddenly looking a lot less likely.

And just when we thought it couldn't get any more chaotic, the weather decided to add its two pennies worth to the party. The night time temperature had been steadily dropping throughout the week, until we reached a sort of critical mass point where the days, whilst sunny, weren't quite long enough to thaw out the previous night's frost. In our normal lives, this would just have meant that we needed to chip our way into the car in the morning, and perhaps put the heating on a bit earlier. But back here in mid 15th century lifestyle, it had a far more significant effect. I turned on the makeshift tap in our room early the next morning and was greeted by a small dribble and then an eerie silence.

'Chris…I think the water's gone off.'

'It's a river. It doesn't go off,' came the muffled response from the sleeping bag.

'Well, there's nothing coming out of the tap.'

'I have a nasty feeling that might be because it's frozen,' said the sleeping bag.

'What, the tap? Is it that cold in here?'

Chris slowly poked his head out of the sleeping bag. 'No, it's probably OK in the tap, but when I took Oscar out the other day I walked along the route of the pipe from the river. It's just lying on the ground and the valley's really steep-sided, so it won't be getting much sun. I think it might've frozen in the pipe up there, so we've just been using up what's left between here and there for the last day or so.'

When questioned about the sudden lack of water, Joe seemed remarkably blasé.

'Yeah, it's done this before. In fact two years ago we had no water for two weeks because it was frozen. It'll start working again once it clouds over a bit and stops being so cold at nights. Of course then it'll start raining instead and it'll be a real quagmire of mud by the house so, you know – you can't win either way.'

'Any thoughts on solutions?' I asked, somewhat haughtily.

Apparently not. Joe was about to go off to spend the week in a house with running hot water and it was clear that, even if he was still here in body, his mind was already far, far away. He made a few half-hearted suggestions about running some extra pipe alongside the existing one and keeping the water running so it couldn't freeze, but his heart wasn't in it.

We spent the following day running up and down the hillside, dragging huge irrigation pipes with us. But we couldn't get enough new pipe to reach all they way back to the house (a distance of about half a mile) and we couldn't get enough pressure if we took water from any closer to the house. By the end of the morning, we still needed to clear one section of frozen pipe or give up on the whole thing.

So we took a petrol driven water-pump up to one of the pieces of pipe and spent an entertaining afternoon trying to pump water through it to force the ice out. We were expecting a kind of ice-pop cannon under the high pressure of the pump, but the other end of the pipe only produced small pipe-sized sticks of ice, which came out so slowly it looked like it was suffering from bad constipation. But after the first few Popsicles had appeared, the flow began to dry up and we knew the rest of the pipe was too badly frozen for success. Even with the pressure of water coming from the pump, we couldn't get up enough force to clear the ice blockage. We had to accept that we were going to have to wait for the weather to cloud over and warm up.

'Still, at least it's beautiful in this weather. The sky's such a bright blue and the sun seems so bright, even if it is only out for a few hours. And it makes all the leaves on the ground nice and scrunchy

213

sounding and crisp.' I said, trying to find a positive angle.

'True. And whilst it stays chilly at least we won't be sweating, which is good because we haven't got any water for washing.'

'We'll just have to fill buckets at the spring at the bottom of the hill and pull them back up with the trailer on the back of the tractor.'

'Yeah. Maybe I'll drive though. I'm not sure I want to see you and the buckets of water fall off.' Chris laughed, referring to an unfortunate incident I'd had earlier in our stay. Joe's tractor was small, little bigger than a ride-on mower, which meant that the seat was exposed to all the elements. Whilst trying to drive it down a particularly bumpy track, I'd underestimated the slippiness of the seat in rainy conditions, especially when wearing waterproof trousers. When the tractor hit a particularly large bump, the seat jolted sideways and I flew up in the air. Landing back on the slippy seat, I'd skidded off the tractor and onto the ground, fortunately only bruising my pride in the process. But the tractor was on auto drive, so it continued merrily down the hill, leaving Chris to run after it and attempt a flying leap back on to grab the brake, whilst I sat on the floor and rubbed my battered backside. After that, Chris had been doing most of the driving.

Inconsiderate jokes about my tractor driving aside, it looked like we were about to be abandoned to a slightly different set of circumstances to the ones I'd had in mind. I'd envisaged us spending relaxing days by the fire, roasting chestnuts and drinking Spanish wine, occasionally heading out for a walk in the sun to check on our merry flock. The reality was looking somewhat bleaker in mid winter.

But the day of abandonment dawned and Joe and Sabela began packing their bags, already relaxing into their brief interlude of freedom. At lunchtime we came back from another unsuccessful attempt to fix the water and waved them off, trying to look as if we were at least vaguely under control. As their car bounced off up the drive, we heaved a sigh of relief. We may have been left with a succession of small disasters, but at least we'd be getting some peace and quiet for a while.

'OK,' Chris said, as the dust from the car began to settle. 'What's first?'

'Well, I know it's boring, but maybe we should try and clean the kitchen. If we do it now, then we'll be able to have Christmas lunch without having to disinfect everything first.'

'I can't say I'm filled with enthusiasm, but I guess you're probably right. Can you get some of those plastic gloves out of Oscar's bag – you know, the ones for the tick treatment.'

'OK, that tick stuff didn't exactly stop him getting bitten did it, so we may as well get some use out of it.'

Gloving up in plastic, purple gloves, we took a deep breath and headed in. But just as domestic bliss began to reign, it was time to start on our first attempt to single handedly get the sheep back from their grazing and into the barn for the night. Despite the desertion of the village for the last four weeks, predictably enough, the few inhabitants who seemed to have restoration projects there had pitched up for Christmas. And with no repeats of Morecambe and Wise on the telly, what better Christmas entertainment could you ask for than two people being completely outsmarted by a bunch of sheep. Especially when they've thrown in two utterly useless sheepdogs for good measure as well.

Any hope we might have had for Oscar to suddenly discover a latent gene for shepherding were fast fading. Every time we got the sheep into anything like a single group he would get wildly over excited and compete with Lua to see which one of them could run through the middle fastest. Thereby scattering all the sheep to the four winds, and leaving us to start the slow process of trying to round them up. Again. We eventually managed to get them into the yard by building a series of barricades to channel them towards the gate, and using walkie-talkies to yell instructions to each other. It was getting dark as the last stragglers finally gave in their game of tag and the gate was closed with slightly more gusto than was necessary.

I'm sorry to have to report that Oscar's sheepdog career only lasted two more days, before he was forcibly retired, and had to be shut in the bedroom every time we tried to do anything sheep-related. Borderless collie he may be. Sheepdog he isn't.

Chapter 21

And lo, a lamb is born.

After all the stresses of the past month, I was looking forward to a relaxing Christmas day. On Christmas Eve we headed into town and filled up with food and wine, then had a general de-griming session in the swimming pool. By evening, we had a cleaner kitchen, plenty of food and a roaring fire. On Christmas morning the weather began to break, which in some ways was disappointing, because I'd been planning a post lunch walk through the frost kissed landscape. But on the other hand, that meant we were looking at maybe getting running water back in the next couple of days, so it was a sacrifice I was happy to make. Everything took longer than we expected, but finally, by mid afternoon, we were ready to sit down to a Christmas meal and a bottle of sparkly stuff. And we even managed to get Joe's computer system going, so we could watch a trashy film on DVD afterwards. Apart from the fact that we looked like Michelin men because of the layers of clothes we were wearing rather than because of the food we'd been eating, it was all very much like a normal Christmas day.

As it got dark we fetched the sheep in for the night, looking for all the world like the shepherds in the school nativity play, minus the tea towels. And as the sun set we began to relax – finally Oscar seemed to be well and truly on the mend, neither of us was puking and we'd mastered the art of farm management. Or so it seemed.

Boxing Day dawned cloudy and damp, and we lay in bed for a while, enjoying the warmth of down sleeping bags for a few more minutes. From our room we could hear the gentle lowing of the sheep (is this starting to sound like a Christmas carol?) so we knew they hadn't been eaten by wolves in the night. We figured they could nibble on hay for a bit longer whilst we stretched out and relaxed.

Suddenly, crystal clear in the surrounding quiet, came an exceptionally high pitched baa. Not your standard, deep, guttural baa, but a new squeaky version. We looked at each other in silence.

'Did that sound like a lamb to you?' Chris asked.

'Nah, it's probably just one of the sheep, maybe one of them's got a cough or something.' I burrowed deep into the warm duvet of denial, as a more persistent squeak came from outside.

'That was definitely a lamb,' Chris said firmly.

'It can't be. We haven't got any lambs,' I responded, equally firmly.

Baa, baa, came the noise from outside.

'For heaven's sake,' I sighed. 'I'll go and have a look, I need a pee anyway.'

I stepped over the sleeping dog and out into the misty, damp world. Traipsing through the damp straw I stumbled, bleary-eyed, to the edge of the sheep pen. There. Only sheep. But as I turned to head back into the bedroom, the squeaky baa rang out again and a tiny, wobbly lamb emerged from beneath the other sheep.

I watched in horror for a few minutes as the sheep ignored the newcomer. The lamb tried them all, but each one made its polite refusals and told it in no uncertain terms that they weren't its mother. Which implied that the actual mother wasn't doing a whole lot. Working in a rural environment had given me enough knowledge to know that if we didn't persuade the mother to take a bit more interest in the near future, young Bleaty here wouldn't last much beyond lunchtime.

I stumbled back to the room and tersely filled Chris in with the details. Lie-in sadly forgotten, we dressed quickly and headed back to the sheep pen. Climbing over the fence, I wandered amongst the sheep and tripped over another lamb in the process.

'There's two of them,' I yelled back to Chris 'but I can't find the mother. Can you pass me the torch?' Taking the torch I pushed through the flock of hungry sheep standing around me and went into the pitch black barn behind their pen. There in the far corner, lying down, was one seriously pissed off sheep. As I approached her she looked up hopefully, as if to say, 'You're a woman, you know what I've just gone through. Give us a hand now will you?'

'It's no good looking at me honey. I've only ever had a dog.'

On closer inspection I discovered she'd got what I guessed was the placenta (and who says you don't learn anything in GCSE Biology) stuck, which was causing her significant distress. One of the lambs was standing nearby, so I picked it up and tried to persuade her to be interested. She, in turn, made it clear that unless I fixed up her back end, she wasn't going to be obliging me with any lamb feeding.

At this point GCSE Biology ran out and I realised I had no idea what to do next. The closest I've come to witnessing a birth is watching ER and I couldn't remember any sheep scenes in that. Chris was none the wiser – he doesn't even watch ER, so had even fewer ideas on how to deal with a home birth.

'Well I don't think we can just leave it with the placenta hanging out. She's obviously bothered by it' I said nervously.

'Yes, but if you pull it out...' Chris started, and I wondered when this had suddenly become my problem. Why would it be *me* pulling it out? I tried to clarify what seemed like a fundamental point, but he talked across me confidently, 'if *you* pull it out, *you* might dislodge some, I don't know.....'

'What?'

'You know. Women's Things.'

I rolled my eyes. 'Helpful. Thanks for that.'

'I don't know. It's not my field. You're the one with the agricultural knowledge.'

'Not in sheep.'

'Your family are Welsh for heaven's sake. Whereas mine are from the inner city. So I, quite clearly, know nothing whatsoever, in any shape or form, about sheep.'

Aha! Finally an idea. My Dad grew up on a farm on the Welsh borders, so he must know about sheep. I could ring him. Forgetting all about the time difference and the fact that it was Boxing Day, I grabbed the mobile and dialled.

'We've had lambs.' I said, skipping any of the usual how are you, Happy Christmas stuff. And some deep, long forgotten farming memory must have stirred inside my Dad. Rather than laughing, or worrying with me, he uttered an impressed sounding, 'Well Done', as if I was about to take them to market and pick up Farmers Weekly on the way home.

Slightly taken aback by this new positive spin on things, I explained the Women's Things problem and my Dad proceeded to give me instructions on how to get the placenta out. I relayed these to Chris, promised to ring my Dad with an update later and rang off. By the time I'd put the mobile down, Chris had come up with a plan.

'OK, I'll hold the head end and you can use some more of the vet's plastic gloves.'

Oh please, I thought. I'm a thirty-something project manager with a mortgage and a car. I had a corner desk. With a window. I shouldn't be crawling round in straw and dung wearing purple pervy gloves and pulling out a placenta. Especially on Boxing Day.

Except I wasn't a thirty-something international bright young thing anymore. I might've had my very own phone extension and business cards beforehand, but that was then, and this was now.

No choice then, but to pull on the gloves, smile wryly at their effect on both Chris and Oscar and head on in. Chris grabbed the head and held tight, I lifted up the tail, stuck in one gloved hand and pulled hard but steadily, like I'd been told.

With a horrible slithering sound and a distressed sounding baa, which was enough to put me off childbirth for life, the offending article came out of the sheep and landed in a pile at my feet. The improvement in Bessie was dramatic. Not that a sheep can ever be described as looking chirpy, but, after spending a few moments checking I'd finished shoving my hand in unspeakable places, she stomped off to the nearest bit of hay and settled in to chew.

'Now hang on, not so quickly Bessie,' Chris told her. 'Just because you've got them out, doesn't mean you're finished.'

The time had come to enact the second set of instructions from my Dad's Lambing for Dummies course. We had to get Bessie to accept the lambs – so far she'd only acknowledged one of them, and even then she wasn't letting it suckle. This part of the plan seemed to involve a lot of rubbing the lambs together and puthering around underneath her. And by now I felt it was more than time that Chris took his share of the parenting duties.

And so he was installed underneath Bessie, hopefully shoving a lamb in the right general area and trying to see if between them they could get the hang of it. The mothering instinct clearly wasn't strong in Bessie, and this process was repeated several times over the next couple of hours. We even called Joe to see if he had any bright ideas, but not that surprisingly, he seemed almost as vague as us. His unhelpful reply was that he usually left the sheep to it and accepted that lots of the lambs would die. Maybe that explained the small size of the flock.

Finally, by lunchtime, mother and daughters (well, we thought daughters anyway, but sheep sexing isn't high up on the Essential Skills section of my CV) seemed to have got the hang of things and we headed into the farmhouse for a well deserved cup of coffee.

'So, any idea if any more of them are going to pop?' I asked 'Did Joe enlighten you as to his breeding program?'

'Well it seems the ram just 'hangs out' with the sheep so he's no idea when any of them are due. He said he didn't think it'd be this early, but if one's gone, the others might go too.'

'Marvellous. Still at least we know what to do now. What do you think we do with the placenta itself?'

'Aren't you supposed to eat it these days? We could boil it up with a little rosemary sauce maybe?'

'I think I may have just gone vegetarian.'

The following day we tried to take the rest of the flock out to the field, leaving Bessie, Bleaty and Bleatier in the pen. Our shepherding skills were improving dramatically and we slammed the field gate shut behind the last sheep, awarding ourselves a perfect ten for today's penning exercise. At which point, Chris noticed an extra sheep coming round the side of the fence.

'Oops. We must have lost one on the way. How did we manage that?'

'I don't know, I didn't see any of them cutting back anywhere.'

Chris frowned. 'Uh oh. That sheep looks familiar. I'm sure that's Bessie.'

'Surely she can't be that crap a mother? She wouldn't have abandoned the lambs, would she?' I asked.

'Well it definitely looks like her. Let's stick her in the field with the others to start with anyway.'

As we shooed the possible Bessie substitute into the field I suddenly realised that Lua had disappeared. My heart sank.

'Hang on. If this *is* Bessie and she's got out, then the lambs might be out too. And Lua's disappeared. What if she can smell them or something. She'll think they're toys and pick them up in her mouth – which'll probably kill them.'

'Oh God, you're probably right. When did she go?' Chris asked, breaking into a sprint.

'I don't know. We need to get back before her though. I'll go up through the vineyard, you go round by the main track.'

We sprinted off, heading in the – unfortunately uphill – direction of the farm as fast as we could manage in boiler suits, padded jackets and safety boots. As I got halfway up the hill, I heard the distinctive bleat of one of the lambs, coming from somewhere up ahead. Two seconds later, I spotted Lua ahead of me, loping up the hill.

'Shit,' I cursed and redoubled my efforts to run up the hill and overtake her. As I came round the corner I saw the lamb less than 50 yards away, wobbling on a small rock step and Lua debating her first strike.

'Lua! Lua! Come here, good dog, buena perra,' I yelled. My legs felt like lead and the cold air was burning in my chest but I managed a final push, sprinted past the confused dog, scooped the lamb up in my arms and then doubled over choking.

A few moments later Chris arrived, grabbed Lua by the collar and took her back to her kennel whilst I limped slowly back to the sheep pen, gasping for air. By the time I made it back Chris had located the second, less adventurous lamb and had replaced the fence barricade that Bessie had knocked over in her eagerness to be part of the flock.

'Ok, if we leave them here we can go back down, get Bessie and stick her back in with them.'

'How?' I puffed. 'We'll never recognise her amongst all the others. They all look the same when you get them together.'

'But we can't leave the two lambs here by themselves, they'll freeze and go hungry.'

'I'm not sure we can stick them in the field either though. They're way too little to manage to get over all those rocks and that field's on such a slope. And it's next to the river. I'm not getting them to survive this far and then having them washed away.'

'I guess you're right. It would be a bit ironic given our waterless state up here as well,' Chris sighed.

'Then they'll just have to all come back in. There's hardly any grass anyway. They can just eat extra hay. It's like at school – you know, if one misbehaves then they can all stay in for detention.' Chris raised his eyebrows at me in amusement, but we duly marched back down the hill, collected up the recently freed sheep and drove them back to their pen.

As we stood watching them munch on their hay, we both agreed on one thing. Next year, we were having mutton for Christmas lunch.

~

The remainder of our time in charge of the farm passed incident free. We had no more unexpected arrivals and were able

223

to hand the herd back to Joe all intact and of course, slightly more numerous than before. The day after the family returned one of the lambs gave up the ghost, which bought home to us the deep frustration that livestock farming must involve. We had a rather solemn moment of digging another hole next to the placenta, and burying our first lamb.

On a more positive note, we even managed to fix the water after dragging the frozen pipes into the sun to defrost and then reconnecting the segments back together. The slightly warmer nights had stopped the new supply refreezing, so we felt rather proud of our achievements when the family returned.

But now it was January and we had to start thinking of our plans for the future. Living on the farm had saved us a load of money, but even with these relatively frugal weeks, we knew the money wouldn't last much longer. The return to reality was starting to beckon. The idea of returning to normality wasn't appealing, but we'd always known that as grown-up gappers, this period would always be just that – a gap, not a whole new life.

We began using our brief time in town to visit the internet café so we could trawl websites to look for jobs in Aberdeenshire. Proper, sensible, grown-up jobs – which seemed almost impossible to imagine. And to my surprise, with practically no effort on my part, a potential job appeared on the screen. I'd known before I left the UK that there were likely to be more jobs coming up in my field in the future, because the European Commission had recently introduced legislation for improving the quality of rivers and lochs across the continent.

I'd already done a couple of presentations for the Scottish government, suggesting ways that they could put this legislation into practice in Scotland. Now a series of jobs implementing some of this stuff were being advertised. The timing was undeniably good – given that the recruitment process in government agencies is notoriously slow, the chances were that if I was successful, I could string the process out for long enough that I wouldn't have to start work until March or April.

The downside was that I'd be working for the government – effectively making me a civil servant. The thought of going from carefree grown-up gapper to grey-suited civil servant in the space of a matter of months, seemed almost too depressing for words. But, as we didn't have 'private incomes', sooner or later we were going to have to head home to keep the bank manager from the door. If we could do it knowing there was at least one pay cheque coming in the near future, it would mean we could run our money down to the very last Euro before we crossed the Channel.

And so, after much soul searching, I made the decision to apply. Of course, that meant filling in the application form at the farm, trying to use the computer when the kids weren't watching telly, or when we didn't need the power for a load of washing. I suspect it wasn't the strongest application I've ever completed, and the final straw came when the server went down in the internet café just as I was about to send it. Fortunately, someone in the local council offices took pity on me (perhaps they could sense that I was a fellow civil servant in the making) and allowed me to use their computer. In the click of a button it was off and the writing was undeniably on the wall.

The idea that our time was starting to run out acted as a spur for several long debates as to what to do next. We explored a variety of possibilities, gradually discounting options when we held them up to the light.

'We could try another farm,' I'd suggested.

'We could,' Chris paused. 'But we don't get to speak that much Spanish here. I know that's partly because Joe speaks English, but when you look at it, most of the work doesn't really involve talking. I mean how much conversation can you have with a sheep or a fencepost?'

'I think that depends on whether or not you're counting swear-words as conversation doesn't it?' I answered, as honestly as I could.

'Well OK, we do seem to do plenty of swearing, but the sheep don't tell us if we should've done it in the conditional or the imperative tense. The trouble is, as long as people are getting the basic gist of what you're saying, they're not that interested in correcting you, or getting the grammar right. They just want to understand enough to make sure you're putting the sheep or the fencepost in the right place.'

'I think that'll be the same in any sort of work we do though. Our language skills aren't good enough to do proper, career type jobs, so any work we do is bound to be manual stuff, which doesn't involve much talking.'

'I think I learnt the most Spanish when we were doing the language course in Girona.' Chris said. 'I suppose we need to figure out what we want to achieve, if you like, in the last couple of months. Do we want to work, so we spread the money out for as long as possible, or do we want to concentrate on the language thing, have more lessons and accept that means we'll use up the cash more quickly?'

This discussion continued for several days, but after much debate we decided that we'd spend the remaining weeks taking more Spanish lessons and get our language skills as good as possible. And if that meant that we went home a couple of weeks earlier, well, so be it.

Once we'd made that decision, we had to figure out where we wanted to spend the time. We were both keen to find somewhere that didn't have a regional language as well. We'd spent time in Girona where they mostly speak Catalan and in Galicia, where they also speak Galician, so now we wanted to find somewhere that spoke Spanish, whole Spanish and nothing but Spanish. What we wanted was a town full of people who were the BBC speakers of Spain. And as it happened, a quick search through our guidebook turned up the perfect candidate. Salamanca.

Received wisdom has it that the people of Salamanca speak the clearest Spanish in the whole of Spain. The town had an Oxbridge style university founded in 1218 and in recent years had been trading on its reputation as a town full of clear-speaking academics, with a flurry of language schools opening. A quick trawl on the web showed hundreds of language schools and, more surprisingly, several campsites that claimed to be open all year round. The decision was made. We were Salamanca bound.

But first we had to say goodbye to the farm and to the family who'd made us their guests – of sorts – for the past few weeks. Of course Oscar was saddest of all – I like to think that, after their early, rather focused meetings, he and Lua had become the doggy equivalent of friends, and had hung out together every day since his illness. If she'd had a passport, I would undoubtedly have kidnapped her and stowed her away. I think Chris knew this was a risk, and he did some careful checks of the van interior before we left.

Even Joe became almost tearful as we left (maybe it was the thought of finishing the fences on his own?) and insisted on filling the Lua-sized gap in the van with a collection of produce from the farm. We must've been the only tourists entering Salamanca with 5 organic pumpkins as passengers (and that didn't even include us). Maybe we'd finally reached the witching hour and our Fuckit Bucket carriage had reverted to its true nature.

Chapter 22

Oscar pulls it off

Other than a few directional difficulties around the town's one way system, our arrival in Salamanca went smoothly. We slipped into a campsite just after dusk, found a parking spot and rushed into the hot, powerful showers. For the first few days we must've seemed like the world's cleanest campers, taking at least two showers a day and spending hours preening in front of the mirror.

On our first day, after obsessive amounts of washing, we headed into Salamanca to get our bearings. And I was awe-struck by what I saw. Salamanca must be one of Spain's most beautiful cities – full of ornate pale sandstone buildings and the most gorgeous Plaza Mayor (Central Square) imaginable. The Plaza is the size of two football pitches and is overlooked on all four sides by high sandstone terraces with balcony windows. The bottom storey is filled with shops and cafés, and on this sunny morning the square was overflowing with people sipping coffee around their shopping bags.

Ornately-carved stone plaques of key figures in Spanish history are stationed at regular intervals around the square. Many of these were names I didn't recognise, but they were interspersed with a handful of familiar faces, including the infamous General Franco. The natives told us that his picture is regularly vandalised and indeed, in the short time we were in Salamanca, we saw it covered in a fresh splattering of red paint and graffiti.

Shopping streets spiral out from the main square and the central area of the city is completely pedestrianised, so you can wander from café to café and from shop to shop in peace. Further to the south are the main university buildings and the cathedral, all jaw-droppingly beautiful with exquisite carvings. And for me, the jewel in the crown of this city's already lengthy list of visual assets is the presence of countless storks, who make their nests on any available roof top. On clear days, the city is a mix of grandiose sandstone buildings, bright blue skies and gently cackling storks. And it didn't even seem to suffer from as much litter as other Spanish towns – or if it did it was more carefully hidden. No wonder the resident students seem so happy, or that so many foreign students choose to come and study here.

By the end of our first week in the city we were completely hooked and had started collecting numbers of possible language schools like sweet wrappers. When we'd decided we were happy to make this place our home for a while, I began phoning around whilst Chris negotiated a long stay deal with the campsite owner. And to top it all, the first café we visited was more than happy to allow Oscar entry. It turned out to be a popular student haunt, so Oscar basked in the adulation of the female students, finally enabling Chris to forgive him for all the worry of his recent illness.

After a couple of false starts, we found a possible tutor and agreed to meet him in the central square to discuss our options. Just as I was finishing the phone call I wondered how to tell him what we looked like. Should I start on a complicated explanation – I'm short and dark, he's medium and pale, I'll be wearing a red rose? But no, of course, for us there was a far simpler way. What was our most distinctive feature? Oscar. All I had to say was to look for the people with the grey spotty dog. He'd find us.

And sure enough he did. Chucho turned out to be friendly and easy-going, and he was more than happy to teach us for a short while each afternoon. More importantly he was also happy for Oscar to come to lessons – in fact, I got the distinct impression that it was the thought of seeing Oscar every day that clinched the deal. Once we'd discussed prices, we made arrangements for our first lesson. Just as he was leaving, Chucho came up with a minor brainwave.

'This town is full of students who want to learn English. You should try and arrange some language exchanges'

'And they are….?' I asked, slightly worried that I might have to try and explain exactly how English grammar is supposed to work.

'You meet someone who wants to learn English and for the first half of the time you talk in English, then you swap to Spanish. Or vice versa. You can correct each other's languages as much or as little as you want. It's a cheap way to get lots of practice. And you will be in demand because there are far more native Spanish speakers here than English.'

'And how do we find out about the people who want to do that?' Chris asked.

'Try the university notice board. Or any of the language schools. They all have boards where people advertise.'

As it turned out, this was one of the best pieces of advice we were given. A quick search in a couple of language schools turned up a list of names and almost within minutes of sending out exploratory emails we had a series of language exchanges – or intercambios as they're known in Spanish – arranged for the following week.

Back at the campsite, we were starting to become regular fixtures. After eyeing us up suspiciously for the first few days, the maintenance man (we called him the 'trabajador' or 'worker', although the 'hablador', or 'talker' might've been more appropriate) had decided that, apart from our mad, scary guard dog, we were alright. Once he knew Oscar was safely contained in the van, he would head over to chat and fill us in on his view of just what was wrong with Spain, Salamanca, the weather, Europe and any other topic that took his fancy. His Spanish took no prisoners and once he got going, words would fly out of his mouth like a dam-burst. Or at least that's how it felt. Usually I'd manage to follow the general gist of the torrent, but every so often I'd get caught in an eddy and have to try and concur in a shrugging, non-committal manner. And if he looked surprised at that for an answer, I'd change tack and try a horrified sounding, 'No' instead. This seemed to be all he needed and he'd head off on another tack, without even pausing to draw breath.

In contrast, the campsite owner seemed to have decided that we were his personal mission to save from a linguistic dead end. Popping in to ask about the electricity connection or to pay our fees turned into a full half hour task, inevitably ending in an explanation of just how we should be using the imperfect tense, or exactly why our choice of the subjunctive in that sentence was, quite clearly, incorrect. Despite that, secretly I rather liked him – if only because he'd told Chris that my Spanish was much better. Juvenile, I know, but when you're faced with being the continual halfwit in any conversation, you have to take any praise you can get, even if it comes at the expense of someone else's self confidence.

The day of our first intercambio dawned bright and clear and we marched solemnly into Salamanca, nervous at the prospect of being let loose on someone else's English at the same time as trying to assimilate their corrections of our Spanish. At the appointed hour, Felipe, from Malaga, swept into view and picking up the grey dog clue, came across to introduce himself. Stuttering slightly, I explained our plan in Spanish.

'Err…hi. We know a café nearby that will let the dog in. Is it OK if we head there?'

'Sure, that's fine,' agreed Felipe and we headed off through the streets of Salamanca, trying to control Oscar's desire to stick his nose in Felipe's crotch whilst we made small talk in Spanish. By the time we arrived at the café, I was more than in need of a drink.

We settled into what were fast becoming our customary seats and both smiled at Felipe in silence. Hoping that he would know the protocol here, we waited a few seconds and the silence stretched into the uncomfortable. Fortunately Felipe soon cottoned onto the fact that he was facing a pair of intercambio virgins and took control of the situation.

'OK, so shall we start in Spanish and then speak English later?' he asked, confidently.

'Si,' Chris concurred. Then silence. In my head, I floundered around for a nice easy introductory topic of conversation which I thought I could comfortably manage in Spanish. It felt like speed dating, only with the added complication of doing it all in a different language.

Slowly, almost painfully, we embarked on a laborious question and answer session, covering all the usual suspects – Where are you from, what do you do, what are your hobbies and other 'first day at new school' questions. It took me a while to tune into Felipe's accent – because he was from the south of Spain he had a habit of swallowing his s'es, turning previously simple words like 'Gracias' into the harder to recognise 'Graciiaa'.

After battling our way through the Spanish half of the exchange, we then moved into English. Any lingering hopes that Felipe's English might be as bad as my Spanish were soon quashed – it transpired that he'd spent the best part of a year working in England, so – aside from his strong accent – he was almost word perfect. More surprisingly, we discovered that most of his English working life had been spent in a café in Bedford, not that far from where I grew up. Tactfully he refrained from offering comment on the delights of 'Bedfordshire – a progressive county' (as the county boundary sign will have it), obviously not sure whether I felt any lasting loyalty to my early roots.

I was quick to set him at his ease and offered him free rein on the moaning front. As it turned out, he didn't seem to have been that bothered by the things that I found hard to take – the flat landscape, the busy roads and grimy town centres. But, more depressingly, he admitted to finding the racism of the area tougher to accept. This surprised me – as one of the most multicultural areas of the UK, I would've thought people would be accepting and welcoming. But instead he told us how he found most girls didn't trust him: because he was dark skinned, he believed they'd expected him to behave in a certain manner, one which he felt was far removed from his true character.

As our hour due to a close, I realised I was completely shattered

– not only had the Spanish half been hard work, but in some ways the English half had demanded even more concentration. Finding and framing questions in a clear, unambiguous manner, whilst avoiding any complicated words or slang, had strained my communication skills to the limit.

But equally, we both felt a strange sense of satisfaction as we meandered back to the campsite. Somehow, we'd both managed to hold our own and keep the conversation going, even though neither of us was quite as bi-lingual as Felipe. And hopefully now we'd survived one intercambio, the others would be a bit less intimidating.

As it turned out, our next foray into linguistic exchange was less successful. A few days later we met up with Raquel and Maria, two female engineering students who were also learning English. They were clearly nervous of the whole experience and spent most of the time giggling and lapsing back into Spanish. In some ways, I, rather perversely, found this a bit of confidence boost – suddenly we were the ones having to supply the extra words and resort to Spanish explanations where necessary. But even when we came to the Spanish half of the exchange, it quickly transpired that we didn't have a whole lot in common. Raquel and Maria had gone from school to university and had yet to discover the delights of the world of work. Their main focus was on learning enough English to get through an exam and tick a box on their CVs, so before long we deteriorated into what was little more than vocabulary listmaking.

Undeterred, we made two further intercambio arrangements – both of which turned out better than we could ever have hoped. Our first victim was called Juan, a Nicaraguan PhD student who was just completing his thesis on the complexities of financial compensation for emotional distress. He was keen to practice his English, but just as keen to learn about other places and to talk about his homeland.

Within a few minutes I realised that what I knew about Nicaragua would probably fit onto a small postage stamp and I bombarded him with questions on history, politics, culture and even – I'm embarrassed to admit – location. The time flew by as Juan explained the changes he'd witnessed and his past as a supporter of the Sandanistas. Although he was only a couple of years older than me, he seemed to have lived through a lot and to have been deeply involved in the complex and often troubled politics of his country. It felt like we could talk for hours and never exhaust all the questions we wanted to discuss. Fortunately it seemed he felt the same way and we arranged to meet up again in a few days, settling into what we now thought of as 'our' café and chatting the coffees away.

On our next intercambio, Juan quickly cottoned on to Oscar's potential. Leaving him and Chris talking whilst I went to the toilet, I returned to discover the two of them deep in discussion:

'I have noticed,' Juan was saying, 'how every woman who walks past Oscar stops and wants to talk to him. The men don't stop, but he seems to be irresistible to women. He is a, how do they say in America, a chick wire?'

'Ummm, do you think so? I hadn't really noticed,' Chris stuttered, sensing my return to the table.

'I think the word you want is 'babe magnet', Juan. And don't fib Chris – I've seen you, smiling at every woman who's patting him and trying to look coy. I'm not stupid, you know. I do realise that's why you always want to hold his lead in towns.'

'Referee!' Chris exclaimed. 'That's not fair. I only take him because you get hassled when he pulls.' A short pause followed before Chris hastily corrected himself. 'I mean when he pulls on the lead, not when he pulls...a...you know what I mean.'

Juan realised we were heading towards a domestic and quickly intervened. 'I think it's great. I think maybe I should get a dog. Or could I just borrow Oscar for a night do you think? I could, how did you say it, pull all the babes I wanted.'

We laughed, but the seed of an idea began to germinate in my head.

'Well, it's Chris' birthday soon and it'd be nice to go out for a meal and a few drinks. But it takes us an hour to walk into town from the campsite, so we couldn't leave Oscar in the van for the evening, it'd be too long. And if we drive the van into town we can't drink. So, what about if you looked after Oscar for the evening – then we can go out and you can take him for a walk in the Plaza and pick up all the women you want?'

'Excellent' Juan concurred. 'I would be very happy to do that. What do you think Oscar? Can you borrow me your lady luck?'

Hearing his name, Oscar lifted his head and looked at Juan. And I swear I saw him wink.

So Juan became our official dog sitter whilst we were in Salamanca. We were hoping to stretch our money to last until the first week of March, which meant we'd be there for both our birthdays and Valentine's day, so we seemed to have a good solution all round. Oscar became Chick Puller in Chief and took to his new role like a duck to water, batting his eyelids and waiting for his tummy to be tickled before graciously taking a back seat and passing the ensnared female over to Juan.

~

After a few days of lessons and intercambios, we were beginning to feel like we were getting the hang of the language student life. Other than our worryingly frequent trips to the cash machine, all seemed to be going well. And, whilst I didn't quite feel like a native, I was starting to feel slightly more like I knew what was going on around me.

Even better, after a couple of weeks in the city, we quite unexpectedly hit an all-time high in our relations with the natives. On a quiet Sunday morning, we'd arranged an intercambio with a new victim and duly pitched up at the café, ready to inflict our linguistic horrors. Learning from the experience of the young and giggly girls, our latest casualty was a slightly older victim – a 30 year old psychologist who I hoped could help with our Spanish and maybe give me a bit of a head examination at the same time. Ana turned out to be disarmingly friendly, honest and open and in no time at all we were chatting away as well as our respective linguistic skills would allow.

Our allotted two hours flew by and just as we began to make packing up noises, Ana asked what we were doing for the rest of the day. Fortunately (and not that surprisingly) we had no plans other than to wander back to the campsite in the pouring rain, so we were both delighted when she suggested we could head back to her flat for lunch. Our first genuine Spanish social engagement – now we were practically locals. A quick phone call followed to check that her flat mates were OK with a visit from a dog as well and we all headed off in the rain to the southern side of the city.

Despite her dire warnings of her flat being in a 'dangerous' part of the city, it seemed no worse than the outskirts of Aberdeen. When we arrived in the flat, which she shared with two others, we offered to help with the lunch preparations, whilst trying to stop Oscar from shaking his damp coat all over the room. Ana had warned us it would only be a basic meal with whatever was in the house so I'd been expecting just a sandwich or some soup. When she suggested Spanish omelette, I was ready for a quick fry-up of some eggs with the odd bit of potato on the side. What I hadn't realise was that in Spanish terms, quick refers to anything that takes less than two hours.

We started peeling the potatoes at about two o'clock, and finally sat down to eat at four, complete with bottle of wine, side salad, bread and a gorgeous thick slab of tortilla (the fried potato and egg of a genuine Spanish omelette). I wondered what you got in a slow meal. Fifteen courses and a butler, I guess.

Conversation flowed as well as could be expected, alternating between English and Spanish when we forgot crucial words. Later in the day, Ana took me aside:

'You know, I was a bit worried about meeting you two. You sounded very strange.'

Somewhat taken aback, I asked why, trying not to sound defen-
sive:

'Why? Was the Spanish in the email not very good?'

'No, it wasn't that. It was the bit about being two people in a
van with a dog, living on a campsite. You sounded like, how do you
call them, people from the sixties, 'ipsters?'

'Hippies,' I corrected, trying not to laugh.

'Yes, 'ippies. But you are too old for that. The email said you
were both in your thirties, and I think maybe you need to be
younger than that to be living like a 'ippie.'

Marvellous. The impression we were giving was of two aging
hippies, clinging to their youth by dragging around a slightly
grumpy dog and a van. Not exactly the glamorous and mature free
spirits that was the image I had in my mind.

'Oh. OK. And do we still seem like that? I'm not wearing
anything purple you know!' I pointed out, trying to rescue my
battered self image.

Ana laughed. 'No, no, you seem very normal. But you don't
sound normal when you are written on paper – do you know what
I mean?'

Begrudgingly, I had to agree with her. We probably did sound
slightly scary and I could see why she might have felt a bit nervous
about meeting us. On the other hand, I was relieved to discover
that we didn't seem to have borne out our written impressions. Of
course, if I'd known that was what she was expecting, I would've
insisted on turning up in full tie-dye regalia, complete with a flower
behind Oscar's ear. Probably just as well we'd played it straight
though – I wasn't quite at the stage of managing much irony in my
Spanish yet.

The rest of our lunch passed off in relaxed style, and after
discovering that Ana was from Galicia, we entertained her with
stories from our Galician farm experience. As it began to get dark
we finally left the flat and started on our long walk back to the
campsite, both feeling remarkably smug.

'Wow,' I said, 'that was a serious amount of Spanish conversation.'

'Yeah, and it didn't feel awkward at all.' Chris agreed.

'And Ana seems so nice. She was very open, I thought.'

'Yeah, especially about us! It hadn't occurred to me that's how we sounded, but I suppose she's right.'

'Well I guess we'll know for next time – maybe we ought to try and sound a bit more normal on any other emails.'

Gradually our days spent in Salamanca began to stretch into weeks, then a month. We continued with our daily lessons with Chucho and regular intercambios, meeting up with Ana and Juan whenever we could. The bars near the campsite provided us with ample evening entertainment, combined with Chucho's mammoth piles of homework. And the procession of campers passing through the campsite provided its own entertainment as well, as we watched a string of British campervans call in for a brief overnight stop before whisking themselves away as quickly as possible in a mad dash to reach the southern sun. Over the weeks we spent there only a handful of vans stopped for more than 12 hours, with everyone else declining the delights of Salamanca and rushing to the beach instead. Most of the campers on the way south thought we were completely mad to be staying more than a day and felt it was their duty to remind us that if we had any true respect for the British flag, we'd get off our backsides and down to a Mediterranean deckchair as soon as possible. It seemed such a shame that they were all missing the delights of the centre of Salamanca in their rush to reach warmer climes.

There were a few exceptions to the southbound rule, including an American couple who began every conversation with the memorable line:

'Hi, we're American, but we're sorry about Bush.'

After an opening gambit like that, I quickly warmed to them and it was soon clear that they, like so many others, wanted to kneel down and worship Oscar. We passed a happy evening in conversation with them and were disappointed when they decided to hit the road a few days later. But as a parting gift to us, they insisted on giving us their small electric heater, which they figured they could do without for the remaining few days of their trip. With night-time temperatures well below freezing in the van, I was delighted with this gift and racked my brains for a suitable exchange. Suddenly, it hit me. What was the one real bargaining tool we had in the van? Other than Oscar, that is? Safely hidden at the bottom of the book bag we had – courtesy of my parents visit to Germany – the last Harry Potter, only published a few months earlier. We'd both read it in a matter of days, but hadn't quite been able to just abandon it and now it seemed we'd finally found a deserving home. Coupled with our last organic pumpkin, it was almost a worthy exchange. And I could tell Paul and Sue, despite their best attempts to be cool, were secretly quite chuffed, at least with the book. From then on, the Harry Potter heater took the chill off the van in a matter of seconds and filled us with the warm glow of satisfaction from an exchange well made.

~

All seemed idyllic in our Salamancan universe until a cold harsh reminder of the real world rang my mobile phone at the end of January. The Human Resources department from the Scottish Environment Protection Agency asked me to attend for an interview – unfortunately, in Scotland. I debated a video conference interview, but could only get vague commitments at the Spanish end and I wasn't filled with confidence at the thought of giving my first presentation in over a year to a camera. Environmentally unsound though it was, I decided to go for the safer option of a flight from Madrid to London and a train up to Scotland, calling in to visit my folks on the way. Laboriously, I set up the arrangements, booked my flights, train and accommodation and began reading some appropriately dull websites.

A few days later, I began to see one of the reasons why the

missing generation was missing. Setting up and preparing for an interview in a different country, whilst living in a campervan, wasn't easy. Within days of me completing my complicated transport arrangements, the HR department had randomly decided to shift the interview date by a couple of weeks. This would have been irritating if I'd been travelling from Aberdeen, but was immensely annoying when trying to travel from the other end of Europe. But my pleas for sanity fell on deaf ears – it was clear they had very little experience of anyone travelling to an interview from outside the country – rather putting the dampers on the European Commission's view of an open job market. Whilst that may be the case in theory, I was fast demonstrating that the practicalities were a long way from ideal.

After rearranging my travel plans, I then faced the prospect of preparing both myself and a short presentation. Again, in theory, this was fine because we had a laptop with us, which we could run from the solar panels on the roof of the van. Or we could, if there was any sun. Salamanca decided to pick the week before the interview to demonstrate its foggy side, with pea soupers descending on the city every day. Under these murky conditions, the solar panels produced little more than half an hour of laptop power and after a while I took to using the electricity socket in the small washing-up room next to the toilets. This had the added bonus that it was heated, so as long as I could ignore the strange looks from passing campers, I seemed to have an excellent office set-up.

A final hurdle was presented on the sartorial elegance front. Unsurprisingly, I hadn't packed any interview clothes in the van and the clothes I had bought with me had now been worn, more or less continuously, for eight months. I wasn't sure that faded, threadbare hiking trousers and a sweaty t-shirt was quite the style I was looking for, so an emergency phone call to Rich at our house in Tarves ensued. To his credit, Rich seemed unfazed at the idea of rifling through my clothes and managed to locate a trouser suit and post it down to my parents' house in record time. That still left me with the problem of shoes (hiking boots or sandals not being quite the order of the day) but I was hoping to pick something up on the way.

Suitably unprepared, I set off for Madrid and negotiated my way through the metro system and onto a plane. I arrived at my parents' house unscathed and passed another couple of days abusing their hospitality. Even the marathon train journey up to Stirling passed quietly and by the time I reached the interview, I was starting to think I'd got it all under control.

Just outside head office, I swapped my comfy trainers for the pair of incredibly uncomfortable, one size too small shoes I'd found in my childhood wardrobe at my parents. Whilst they were obviously from a time before my feet had completed their growth spurt, they were reasonably clean, discreet black lace ups, which I figured would be sufficient for the day. Quick shoe switch completed, I headed into the office and politely announced my arrival.

With scant regard for my little toe, the receptionist directed me to a separate building, a few hundred metres away. I cursed under my breath and wondered whether the skin on my feet would hold out that distance. But looking at my watch I knew I was too low on time to indulge in another shoe swap, so I resolved to take the blisters and headed off up the pavement. As I marched along, I gradually became aware of the sensation that my feet were getting lower and lower with each step. Alarmed, I looked down at my shoes, and discovered that the soles had fallen into bits and were rapidly disintegrating onto the pavement.

Cursing even more, I hobbled into the building and limped to the reception desk. After signing in, I turned round and uttered a small gasp of disbelief. Not only were the shoes breaking up, they were doing it in spectacularly dramatic style, leaving big black marks on the ground with every step I took. You could easily trace the path of my steps as I'd walked into the building and up to the desk and now I was about to add a second line of prints.

Rushing into the toilets, I experimented with styles of walking to see if there was any way of avoiding the black mark trail. It seemed that if I crept along on my tip toes, the trail was marginally less obvious. So I minced back to the waiting area, and once I was finally called through, I minced into the interview room, probably looking like someone suffering from a bad bout of constipation.

We proceeded to go through the usual round of question and answer and as the interview drew to a close, I glanced down at the floor to check the shoe status. Whilst I thought I'd been holding my heels off the floor, I'd obviously lost concentration and the ground around me was a mass of thick, rubbery black marks. I debated making a run for it and leaving them to wonder what on earth was wrong with my legs, but eventually decided honesty was the best policy.

'So, any more questions you want to ask us?'

'Well, not really, but …I think I should tell you…' I started. Then I paused as all three interviewers looked at me with more interest than they'd managed in the proceeding hour. 'So, I didn't have any smart clothes whilst we were travelling and….'

'Oh no, don't worry, you look just fine. I think you're very smartly dressed,' one of the male interviewers responded, rather patronisingly. Listen mate, I thought, I'm not worried about how I look, I'm just worried about whether I've ruined your carpet.

'No, no, it's not that……it's just these shoes are a bit old and I think they might have fallen apart a little bit. There's a slight mark on the carpet.'

'Not to worry,' the HR woman chirped 'I'm sure it can't be……' she trailed off as she came round to my side of the desk. 'Ohh….well, yes……..'

'Anyway.' The third interviewer was clearly trying to suppress his giggles. 'Thanks so much for coming along, we'll let you know in due course. Can you find your own way out?'

I shuffled off and raced to the loos, past the tell-tale tracks, ripped the shoes off and plonked them straight in the bin. A few minutes later I collapsed onto the train and began making a signifi-cant effort on the refreshment trolley. Arriving back at my parents' house, I filled them in on the details of my bad shoe day. My mum nodded sympathetically,

'Yeah, I had some shoes that were the same make and they fell apart on me too. But when I rang them to complain, they said they were meant to be biodegradable. So if those ones were that old, they were probably well into the degrading stage.'

Great. Thanks. Somewhat ironically, the process of applying for a job with an environmental organisation had just convinced me that I didn't care that much about the environment. Or at least, not when it came to biodegradable shoes.

The return journey to Spain passed off smoothly, although I did end up needing an overnight stay in Madrid. I'd booked to stay in a backpackers' hostel near the centre of town and arrived late in the evening, to discover the weekly Tequila party in full swing. Shattered from post-interview stress and travelling, I was in no mood for being surrounded by very drunk 19 year olds and I beat a hasty retreat to my bed. In the morning I was again surrounded, but this time by bright as a button teenagers who obviously had no experience of the hangover from hell that greets the Missing Generation if they have more than two glasses of wine. Their time will come.

To my surprise, and perhaps because they felt sorry for someone who couldn't even afford a new pair of shoes, a couple of weeks later I was offered the job. I spent the weekend discussing it with Chris and Oscar, but, deep down, I think we all knew that we needed to start bringing some money back into the household accounts. With a slightly leaden heart, I rang on the Monday morning to accept the job and negotiate the latest possible start date.

Now that we had some guaranteed income (assuming I didn't get fired for at least the first month) and a definite date of return, Chris needed to figure out what he was going to do with his life. He tried some tentative suggestions of being a gentleman who lunches, but a few sharp slaps soon dismissed that option. When the final results from his MSc appeared, he had, to his delight, achieved the elusive pass with distinction, giving him a much-needed confidence boost after his depressing final months at work. So after a few days of trawling the 'situations vacant' on the web, Chris decided there was no one worthy of his talents (or mad enough to employ him). Instead he was going to head down the self-employed route as a full-time (or so he hoped) environmental consultant.

Whether or not he would have had the courage to do this without the trip is unclear. When we began to face the idea of our return to the world of work, we were both looking at a blank sheet of paper. Technically we were both unemployed, so potentially we could go anywhere or do anything – if we could persuade someone to pay us to do it. In reality, the lure of some secure money in an area I knew was too strong a temptation for me, but at least Chris was able to use the break as an opportunity to sail into pastures new. With new found enthusiasm he began emailing old contacts, designing a website and checking the new business start up pages on the web.

By mid February we had a definite date of return to the UK and a half-hatched plan of action when we got there. We worked out how much cash was left, how many more Spanish lessons we could afford and how many crates of wine we could fit in the van and still be able to close the door. For our final few weeks in Salamanca we took every opportunity to practise our Spanish, emailing and texting anyone and everyone who might be interested in talking to some native English speakers.

Sitting by the cathedral one lunchtime, a text message arrived from Ana suggesting a possible time for a chat. Unsure as to whether an alternative time would be suitable, I began composing a message in return. Laboriously I spelt out all the relevant words and then read them through to Chris for a final check. As I pressed send, Chris looked at me in amazement.

'Do you realise you've just sent a text message in the conditional tense,' he said. 'We didn't even know what that was before we got to Spain and now you're using it in a text message!'

I thought for a few seconds before breaking into a smile. 'You're right. Blimey. Texting in the conditional. I never thought we'd get there.'

Chapter 23

The final fling

As the time for our departure from Salamanca grew near, we began to debate how to leave the city in style. We both felt that we'd made some real friends here – people like Chucho, Ana and Juan as well as various more casual acquaintances. Neither of us wanted to just drive off into the sunset without saying goodbye properly and so we hatched a plan for a leaving party. We'd had a party when we left Aberdeenshire, so it seemed only right that we should have one before we left Spain. But whilst our hearts were more than willing, the logistics of having a party when you live in a campervan aren't that easy.

'So if we add up all the people, it's probably about 12 in total' I said, looking round the van.

'There's no way we can fit 12 people in here. Even with the roof up. And, we ought to invite The Boys as well – if they want to be back in Germany for Easter, they might not be far away by the beginning of March. That might make it 14. And it's hardly barbeque weather.'

'I guess we could all go to a bar or something. But then it's not really a goodbye from us. I sort of feel we should do something that's a thank you to these folks – they've all been so nice to us.' And I did feel they'd been kind. From Ana letting us use her washing machine; to Chucho giving us regular discounts to buy dog treats; to Juan babysitting Oscar (albeit with vested interests). Somehow I wanted to do something that was definitely from us.

A few days later, whilst walking back to the van, Chris was struck by a brainwave.

'What about the campsite bar? It's not being used and there'd be plenty of space in there. We could make some food in the van and take it over, with some wine and stuff.'

'Do you think the owner would let us?' I asked, more doubtfully.

'Yeah, I reckon, he's always said if there's anything he can do to help us. I think he quite likes us. He says our struggle with the language is noble. Well, something like that.'

I raised a dubious eyebrow at Chris. 'OK, well, you can ask him. He seems to prefer talking to you anyway.' Nervously, Chris headed into the campsite office, and returned forty minutes later, looking tired, but flushed with success.

'The man from Del Monte, he say, yes,' he reported back.

'Excellent. Now we just have to pick a date and invite everyone. Blimey. Do you think we're up to having a dinner party in Spanish?'

'It'll be fine,' Chris said. 'We'll just cook something that takes a long time to chew and then there won't be much scope for talking!'

For the next few days we busied ourselves with plans, caught up with The Boys by email and invited as much of Salamanca as we felt we reasonably could. Soon the plans were set. We would spend our last weekend in Salamanca at the beginning of March. The Saturday would be our campsite party and the Sunday was my birthday, so we'd spend it trawling the tapas bars of Salamanca with The Boys, before hitting the road on the Monday. The only flaw in the plan was that Oscar couldn't come into the campsite bar, so we figured we'd have to do regular trips back to the van so that his adoring fan club could say goodbye, whilst Juan would step into the dog-sitting breach on the Sunday.

There was still a week to go before our final fling though, so we spent our penultimate weekend on the Portuguese border, checking out the supposedly dramatic river valley that runs along the boundary. And dramatic it may well be, but in the horizontal snow it was hard to see much beyond your hand. After a few hours of walking stoically in the slush, we headed back to the van – both in agreement that we would be able to do that soon enough on our return to Scotland. Instead we figured we'd make the most of what Spain had to offer and dived into the nearest bar, alternating wine and coffee whilst we waited for the thaw. But it did mean that Oscar just about made it into Portugal, giving him the grand total of 13 countries on this tour. Which is kind of impressive for a small grey dog.

Our final week of Spanish lessons passed without incident – Chucho seemed determined to force as much as possible into our heads and by the end of the week my brain felt fit to burst. Bravely we invited him round for dinner one evening and then, less bravely, we forced him to speak English for a while. And although he gave the impression of being a slightly scruffy country lad, Chucho turned out to speak English with the poshest accent I've heard this side of Eton. But no matter how many questions I asked, he wasn't going to reveal his background. Perhaps he was a missing member of the royal family masquerading as a Spanish teacher. Or perhaps he was educated at Eton. We'll never know, but I felt all the scruffiness of the van a little more keenly when I realised we'd inadvertently invited Prince William round for supper.

By our final lesson, my brain was well and truly saturated, but only as we were leaving did Chucho reveal what he was really thinking.

'I don't know which I will miss most, you two or Oscar.'

'I know,' I answered quickly. 'Oscar'.

Chucho looked at me for a minute and then nodded 'Yes, I think you are right. I will miss Oscar a great deal.'

Yet again Oscar cast me his all-knowing sidelong glance. Then he skipped out of the room and down the stairs, happy in the knowledge that, as always, he was firmly in charge.

Later that evening, The Boys pitched up at the campsite and we passed the evening catching up on each others' travels and filling them in on the full scale horror of living conditions on the farm. We also touched on our growing fear of the impending return to work. Neither Kris nor Wolfgang was clear what they wanted to do when they returned to Germany. In theory, they were planning to return home for various social engagements at Easter and then hit the road again for a couple more months, until they were complete-ly penniless. It seemed Kris was quite relaxed with this plan, but Wolfgang was starting to feel the pinch of being a dropout.   He was impressed with the plans we had set in motion, and was nagging at Kris that they should be doing the same. The worry of whether or not they would be able to find jobs at all was coming to the forefront and the effects of being cooped up in a small space together were taking their toll as well. We light-heartedly compared our argument counts, but we were all starting to realise that the time was drawing near when we needed to return to the rest of the Missing Generation. In many ways that need was financially moti-vated, but it was also born of necessity in other ways. When you reach a certain age, it seems there is only so much time you can spend without at least a few home comforts. More and more, our conversations began to come round to luxuries like washing machines, heating and a change of clothes and we were all noticing the confines of a van just a bit too much.

The morning of our party dawned cold and damp. By lunch-time the rain was bucketing down and we were reduced to scurrying back and forth from van to bar, trying not to let dishes and nibbles disintegrate into soggy heaps. To show how well acclimatised we were to the Spanish lifestyle, we'd set a 2pm start, assuming that lunch would then be eaten at 3 or 4 o'clock. But by 2.30, there were still only four of us and the bar was absolutely freezing.

I fetched our Harry Potter heater and tried not to fret too much. Maybe we hadn't made any friends after all. Maybe no one would turn up. Perhaps they were all laughing at these poor Brits who thought they had friends, but really knew nothing about Spain or its people. Just as I began to sink into despondency, a text arrived from Ana and her flatmates. Apparently they'd set out to walk but had been turned back by the ankle deep mud on the edge of the city. They'd be along as soon as possible, once they'd all changed their shoes.

Suddenly, everyone arrived at once. A rapid-fire round of

Spanish introductions took place, everyone kissed everyone else and we all wondered what language to speak. The Boys both spoke German, obviously, and also good English, but Wolfgang spoke no Spanish. Everyone else spoke Spanish, but not German, whilst Ana's flatmates spoke no English either. Gradually the conversation descended into a linguistic melting pot, with translations being shouted out at regular intervals for anyone failing to keep up with the current language. I have a vague recollection of being asked about Scottish independence and trying to respond in a variety of languages, but I'm not all that certain what I actually said. Or meant. Chris and the van cooker saved the day with a magnificent chickpea and chorizo stew, whilst I contributed to the culinary delight by opening the bags of cakes from the bakery. And, of course, to finish off, nobody wanted coffee because they all wanted to try proper British tea. The pressure was on as I tried to make a decent cup of tea on a camping stove and then rush across a muddy campsite with our miniscule teapot, but eventually honour was satisfied.

All too soon it began to get dark outside, and our guests started to think of heading home. A series of emotional goodbyes ensued, although it was obvious that the most tear-stained farewells were reserved for Oscar. Who deigned to bless his admirers with some casual wags of his tail, whilst searching their pockets for appropriate leaving presents. Finally everyone drove off into the sunset and left the five of us waving goodbye – four grown-up gappers and a slightly confused dog, all aware that the final credits weren't far from rolling.

Dejectedly we wandered back to our vans and spent the evening clearing away the debris and contemplating the rapidly approaching future.

~

The following day dawned bright and clear and added yet another candle to my soon-to-be-in-need-of-a-fire-extinguisher birthday cake. Being the youngest of the four meant I got little sympathy. But as I undertook the customary annual peer into the mirror to assess my wrinkles, the harsh fluorescent light of the campsite toilets helped me feel just slightly past my sell by date.

Undaunted by the onset of a face like a raisin, we headed into town to hit the tapas bars and have a quick look round the sights – for us, our last look and for The Boys, their first. We all agreed to head our separate ways for the morning and meet up again in the central plaza at lunchtime. Standing alone in the square, waiting for the others, I contemplated the stunning beauty of the city and tried not to dwell on how much I would miss it all. I was interrupted from my reverie by the approach of The Boys, complete with lit candles and birthday presents. Stopping in front of me, they sang a loud rendition of Happy Birthday and the combination of the English words, their barely reined in flamboyance and the glowing candles was sufficient to bring most of the Plaza to a halt. Somewhat embarrassed, I blew the candles out and exchanged hugs all round, hoping to stop them before they launched into an encore.

Fortunately the pull of a bar was sufficient to contain any lingering musical ambitions and once Chris had caught up with us, we headed off to taste the best Salamanca could offer. Predictably enough, the afternoon soon degenerated into a mix of wine, tapas and a discussion of the merits of the buttocks of the Spanish males surrounding us. Which probably wasn't great for Chris. But to me it seemed as good a way as any to pass a thirty-something birthday and as I wobbled back to the campsite in the semi darkness I was more than content with my lot. A final evening in the vans followed, comparing travelling notes for the last time and wondering just how we would cope with the return to reality. Would we have itchy feet for evermore, or would this 'get it out of our systems' as aged relatives kept telling us? How would Oscar adjust to life as a sedentary dog and just what were Kris and Wolfgang going to do with their lives? We came up with more questions than answers, but, for a final time on the trip, we found comfort in the fact that there were four of us going through these feelings. We weren't alone and as I prepared to face the return to the daily grind, at least I could think of Kris and Wolfgang doing something similar in Germany.

~

The following morning we were due to leave the city and begin our slow journey north, so Oscar and I headed out for a last run around the tracks of Salamanca. My theory was that some exercise would be good for both of us before we were forced to spend the rest of the day confined in the van. But it seemed Oscar had other ideas. Just as we approached the main road, 2 miles in, he sat down and refused to budge. No amount of shouting, cajoling or pleading would move him and I had to resort to putting him on the lead and dragging him along behind me. This was a curious repeat of behaviour which I'd seen only a few times – normally Oscar is a great runner and will bound along beside or ahead of me, occasionally looking back to check whether or not I can make it up the hill at his speed.

During our stay in Banyoles, near Girona, I'd taken him for regular runs around the nearby lake and a few weeks into our stay he'd suddenly sat down and refused to go any further. Concerned that there was something wrong I'd rushed him back to the campsite, but as soon as we turned and headed for home he seemed to be absolutely fine. A few days later we'd left Banyoles and I hadn't thought any more about his strange behaviour. During our time on the farm he'd been too ill to run, and when he wasn't ill he was getting more than enough exercise with Lua, so I had taken to running alone.

When we reached Salamanca we'd resumed our joint exercise programme and he'd seemed perfectly OK bounding around with me, despite the slightly boring tracks that stretched for mile upon muddy mile through flat farmland. But in the last couple of weeks of our stay he'd begun to spend more time sitting down unexpectedly, especially when I looked back to check on him, or when we approached a busy road. This had become more pronounced, until our final day, when he had a full scale tantrum and I shouted myself hoarse trying to get him to move.

By the time I returned to the campsite Oscar was over his outburst and happily running beside me, but the evidence of our falling-out could be heard in my voice – I sounded like I'd swallowed a handful of gravel and couldn't manage much more than a whisper. I gave Chris a hoarse summary of Oscar's latest diva performance, but neither of us was any the wiser as to what might have caused it or how to deal with it. Physically Oscar seemed fine, with no sign of a limp or sore muscles, so there was little we could do other than wait and see what stunt he would pull next.

I'd scarcely recovered from the 'primadogga' tantrum when it was time to say a sombre goodbye to The Boys. They were off to continue their journey north towards Germany, but were planning to travel via a few scenic stops in central Spain. As ever they were organised and ready to go long before we'd even finished breakfast and so, with heartfelt embraces all round, we waved them off and returned to packing the van for the long road home.

An hour later we were ready to roll and after a final farewell at the campsite office, we headed into town for a last stop at 'our' café. After more emotional goodbyes, we popped into the internet café for a quick email check. Over the weeks we'd been in Salamanca we'd come to know the staff of the internet café pretty well and in turn, they'd come to know Oscar. Each time we went in, we'd checked politely to make sure Oscar could join us and each time they waved him in, watching in amusement as he worked the room in his inimitable doggy style. He'd begin by making a beeline for any young female students, then he'd perform his routine security checks on all the surfers, before finally flopping down to sleep with his head resting on somebody's leg. As we left the café for the last time, Chris explained our forthcoming absence. With his newly developed fluency, he chatted away to the owner about our plans for the journey home, then as we left, he thanked her again for letting the dog in. She looked at him sternly.

'He's not a dog,' came the shocked response. 'He's Oscar.'

And despite my anger at Oscar's tantrum earlier in the day, I had to laugh. Whatever his foibles, there was no denying one thing. Oscar is a dog with a big personality. Whether he's having a tantrum or wrapping a Spanish internet café owner around his little paw, Oscar will never, ever merge into the background.

With Oscar's Salamancan fame confirmed, it was time to hit the road with the sign that said 'North this way'. In no time at all we were heading towards the North Coast and France and the miles were flashing past. But hang on, I thought. Not so fast. We had one final stop before we could contemplate leaving Spain. The Rioja. We may have failed to get work there, but that wasn't going to stop us returning and filling the van to the gunnels with cheap wine. Just because we were going back to reality didn't mean we couldn't take a little bit of our fantasy world with us – if only to numb the pain of the first few weeks back at work.

The following afternoon we rolled back into the Rioja region and headed to the campsite we'd previously visited. We didn't expect the owner to recognise us but to Chris' surprise, when he entered the office, he was greeted like a long lost friend.

'Ahh..it is the travellers from Scotland. How are you? Did you find any work?'

Chris opened his mouth to respond, but was cut off in mid sentence. 'Because now I have work for you. It is only cleaning, but if you still need a job, you can work here.'

Slowly Chris worked his way through an explanation of where we'd been, what we'd done and why we couldn't take him up on his offer of a job. But somehow it seemed to complete the circle – we'd finally been offered work in Spain. After knocking on so many doors, one had finally opened, albeit far too late. So it could be done. Which meant, to my mind, there was still hope: I might be heading back to life as a civil servant, but that didn't mean I'd always be one.

Both feeling slightly smug, we headed into the village to check out the bars and see what we could find on the wine front. First we had to call in on the 'women's café' so Chris could get in touch with his feminine side and consume as much chocolate and sugar as he could manage. Now all he needed was to bring every conversation round to leg waxing or period pain and his inauguration would be complete.

Fortunately, a brief surge in his testosterone levels enabled him to drag me into a real man's bar, with not a hint of chocolate in sight. It seemed a quiet afternoon, so flushed with bravery from our job offer, we parked ourselves at the bar and asked the owner if he was linked with any of the nearby vineyards. And in doing so, inadvertently opened the floodgates of a man who was clearly a budding wine critic. Bottle upon bottle of local wine came out, all of which we had to sample (well, it would've been rude to refuse) and discuss at length, before being asked to give him a potted history of Scotland's distilleries. Two hours later we staggered back out, having purchased a variety of wines and had the conversation of our lives. Maybe the guy was being nice to us because he sensed the opportunity to make money, but the majority of the conversation had flowed easily (admittedly more easily with alcoholic lubrication) and we'd managed to contribute, discuss and generally hang out. Without either of us grinding to a humiliating stop, or committing any social faux pas or even causing the guy to huff with impatience as he waited for us to flounder around trying to find the right verb ending. Somehow it seemed the perfect ending to our time in Spain as we loaded up the van, feeling the sun warming our backs as we forced bottle upon bottle into the not-quite-available space.

Chapter 24

Romeo meets Juliet

From the Rioja we planned to take a straight line almost due north, passing around the left hand side of the Pyrenees and heading into France. But first we had to climb out of the Rioja and down to the Spanish coast, crossing the mountains of the Sierra de Cantabria on the way. Whilst the van had moved on from the worst of its black smoke belching days, it was still only marginally faster than a bike on an uphill climb, so we crawled upwards at a snail's pace. Arriving at the mountain pass, we left the van in a sweaty heap in a lay-by, puffing and struggling to recover its cool. It was beginning to feel like a fading runner in the final stages of a marathon. Any minute now it would start needing regular shots of Lucozade and would get overtaken by a younger runner dressed as Scooby Doo.

Whilst Oscar stayed in and mopped the van's fevered brow, Chris and I admired the view. Stretching out behind us were the vineyards of the Rioja, now all neatly pruned back in rows that snaked across the pale earth. Ahead of us were the lush pastures of the Basque region, each field densely coloured with an intense green, dotted with the occasional black and white cow. This natural geographical divide felt more like a boundary than any of the 'real' borders we'd crossed. We were moving away from the arid interior of Spain with its echoes of Mediterranean culture and into the fertile and damp Atlantic fringes that seemed so much more like home.

But we weren't quite done with the exotic. Freewheeling down the far side of the mountains we screeched into the port of Bilbao, the van storming downhill with the wind behind it. There were no more big mountains to cross and the smallest glimmer of hope that the van might actually make it home began to shine in my mind. In recognition of its new found status we scoured the town for the exotic photo shoot we knew it deserved. And there it was. On a busy street by the river, Chris forced the van into a tiny space and we stood back to admire the view. Foreground – the rusting metal and minor dents of Bagpuss. Background – the shining steel and curving lines of the Guggenheim museum. For a van from a small rural Aberdeenshire village this was seriously classy. The evening sun streamed across the street and lit up both sets of gracefully curving lines in a perfect scene. Now all we needed was a portrait of Oscar next to Jeff Klein's two storey high floral puppy which waits patiently outside the Guggenheim and our postcard collection would be complete. We could really say we'd 'done' Europe.

The following day it was full steam ahead through France with the optimistic aim of hitting the Normandy coastline two days later. This meant a faster rate of progress than we were comfortable with, and we passed long hours at the wheel slowly working through the miles. Unfortunately, the reason for all that greenery soon became clear. Boy can it rain there. By the end of the afternoon, the driving had become almost impossible and we pulled into a motorway service station to pass a slightly damp night in the hope of better weather the next day. We tucked the van into the car park as discreetly as possible and passed a long night listening to the rain batter on the roof and the traffic charging past on the motorway outside. As the night wore on, the traffic on the road eased, but the noise was replaced by lorry drivers revving their engines and honking their horns by the van. As overnight stops go, it was undoubtedly down in the bottom five of the trip.

But because our home changed every night, I discovered again how you can go from the very worst of overnight stops to the very best in only 24 hours. By the next evening, the rain had stopped, the sun was shining and we were parked up at the end of a Normandy road, only disturbed by the gentle quaking of ducks as they paddled past on the slow flowing river just yards from the front bumper. Quaint stone houses peeped over hedges, whilst willow trees, bristling with bright new leaves, dangled their long branches in the water.

It clearly called for a campervan cuppa and we settled ourselves into the van, complete with tea and books, hoping for a calming resting place after what had been a long day of driving on French motorways. But only a couple of minutes passed before a slightly rotund man cycled slowly into the parking area, stopped his bike and appeared to be about to head for us.

'Uh oh,' I said 'here goes.'

But instead he stayed by his bike, took a good look up and down the river, sneaked a quick glance into the campervan and debated if we were a threat to the good name of the neighbourhood. After a minute's contemplation he turned his bike around and headed solemnly back down the road. So far, we seemed to be in the clear.

The night passed quietly with no further bicycle visits and in the morning we lay in bed, contemplating our luck at finding such a great parking spot for our penultimate night in Continental Europe. At which point, we heard the sounds of a vehicle arriving nearby. I sat up and peered out around the edge of the curtain – straight into the eyes of a policeman, sitting in his Citroen and staring at the van.

'Bugger. Police,' I cursed.

'Bollocks,' Chris concurred and hastily began dressing. But no sooner had he dragged on some clothes, and I'd pulled a jumper over my slightly inappropriate striped pyjamas, than the police car had revved its engine, performed a sharp turn and headed back down the road.

'Oh. Okay,' I said, almost a little disappointed. 'I guess we didn't look that dodgy after all.'

'Maybe they just thought it was time we got up,' Chris suggested.

'It's a bit odd though, isn't it? I mean, I can't imagine they do a routine 8.30am call on a riverside car park every day, can you? Someone must've called them, but they obviously decided we weren't doing anything illegal. Which is nice of them, I guess. I mean, they could've come and told us to move on or something.'

'Maybe they'll come back and check we've gone later on today. Perhaps you're allowed one night.'

'It's nice though. It's a really posh area, so they could have been a bit haughty about it. It seems quite civilised to just come and check us out, then leave us to sleep in peace.'

Taking the policeman's hint, we packed up and headed on, free-wheeling down our last Continental hill and into the port of Cherbourg, starting point for the voyage home. But in order to get Oscar back into the UK we still had to comply with complicated bureaucracy to keep his passport in order. Dogs entering the UK must be wormed between 24 and 120 hours before they enter the country. That's a fairly small window of opportunity, especially when it wasn't entirely clear which side of the 4-hour ferry journey was counted as UK entry. A stressful trip to the vet ensued, with Oscar clearly still scarred from the Spanish vet trauma. As he scrabbled to escape the surgery I wondered what Heather, our own vet, would think when she saw him. So far, her only reports on his ten month odyssey would've been from his admirer in Poland. If he behaved like this and hyper-ventilated when I took him back to the Methlick surgery, she'd be convinced he'd been maltreated. When actually we'd done all we could to save his life. Leaving Chris to settle up with the French vet, I took Oscar back to the safety of the van. Still slightly traumatised, he hopped back onto his special dog seat and I sat down next to him.

'Well, Hound from Hell. What are we going to do with you?'

Oscar flopped onto his side, shuffled his head into a comfy place on my lap and stared up at me with his multi-coloured eyes. I don't know, he seemed to be saying, but you better figure it out soon. Because I'll be telling Heather all about this.

A few moments later Chris returned to the van, looking flustered.

'Have you got any cash on you?'

I rummaged in my purse. 'Twenty Euros is the best I can offer.

Why?'

'Because that one worming pill is going to cost us 80 Euros.'

'80 Euros! You're kidding. That's just taking the piss.'

'I know. 80 Euros, every dog going to the UK needs it and, oh look, they're the nearest vet to the port. Nice work if you can get it.' Chris shrugged. 'They'll just have to wait while I go to the cash machine. Or maybe they'll take a card. You know, pet passport, priceless. For everything else, there's Mastercard.'

After begrudgingly paying the French vet £60 for two seconds work, we meandered into the French countryside and strolled along scenic cobbled streets to pass the time before we could set sail. The sun was shining and the place was full of cheerful French people, heading about their business whilst exchanging polite Bonjours as they passed us. But just as we drew level with the last house in the village a hairy black flash shot onto the road and, before I'd even registered that it was a dog, rushed straight to Oscar and pinned him to the ground, snarling and growling. Poor Oscar flailed his legs around in a desperate attempt to escape, but the huge black bear of a dog snapped its teeth closer and closer to his throat. For a millisecond I was paralysed by shock, then fearing the worst I instinctively began yelling and screaming at the dog and stuck my hands into the fray, trying to pull Oscar away from this Hound of the Baskervilles. Chris demonstrated a great deal more presence of mind, and rather than risk losing a hand, stuck his well protected boot into the melée, attempting to kick the other dog off. After what felt like an eternity, our continued shouts and screams finally roused the owner, who wandered out from the house in a lackadaisical manner.

'Get it off, get your dog off,' I screamed at her, not registering that shouting in English wouldn't help.

She shrugged. 'It's not my dog.'

Fortunately for her, by the time I'd translated the French, the real owner had appeared around the corner.

'Get your bloody dog away. Now!' I yelled at this latest arrival on the scene and finally got a more helpful response.

'Juliet! Juliet! Vas!' he grunted and the black dog paused briefly in its molestation of Oscar. Juliet? How much does your dog not look like a Juliet, I wanted to yell. Why don't you call it something a bit more appropriate? Like Rocky? Or Psychopath?

Finally the owner stuck his hand into the writhing mass of dog, grabbed a collar and pulled the dog away. Oscar leapt up and limped to the other side of the road, looking around shakily. I rushed to check him for bleeding but he seemed remarkably unscathed, other than palpitations and sweaty paws. I tried to reassure him whilst Chris remonstrated with the owner, who offered a typically French 'Boeuf!', shrugged his shoulders and wandered back to the house.

Chris and I collapsed onto the roadside with Oscar, doing our best to pet him whilst waiting for our own racing pulses to subside.

'Shit!' I exclaimed shakily. 'I can't believe this is our last day away from the UK and Oscar gets attacked. After ten months, some bloody French bear has to roll him round in the dirt. And the owner obviously didn't give a toss. What a bastard!'

'So much for a relaxing walk to recover from the vet's. Poor dog. What a traumatic day. I'm surprised he hasn't gone grey!' Chris tried a weak joke, but Oscar and I weren't going to be pacified that easily. Looking around him warily, Oscar ventured back into the road, checked up and down carefully, then proceeded to shake himself vigorously. According to dog psychology, shaking is a dog's signal to show it's won the fight and is top of the pack. Only Oscar could get himself rolled round in the dirt, then wait for the coast to clear before unanimously declaring himself the victor.

'Yeah right' I laughed at him. 'Wait till Juliet comes back. Let's see who has the victory speech then. Come on Romeo, its time to run before your delusions of grandeur come crashing down around your paws.'

And with that we hightailed it out of the village as fast as our eight legs could carry us.

~

After such an eventful day, it was almost a relief to drive onto the ferry the following evening. After securing van and dog we headed up on deck and watched as the continent slipped into the distance. We were, undeniably, homeward bound.

But we still had to face the final hurdle of getting Oscar through Customs. Based on our Norwegian experience, all those months before, I was braced for hours of wrangling. So it came as something of a disappointment when we were whisked through in a matter of minutes. A strikingly handsome vet slipped out of the Portsmouth darkness, quickly checked Oscar's details and then waved us through, despite my attempts to string the whole thing out for long enough to get his phone number.

And there we were. Back on British soil after ten months of travelling. Apart from the somewhat battered condition of the van and the overpowering smell of damp dog and leaking wine that now pervaded everything, it was almost as if we'd never been away. Now all we had to do was drag the creaking Fuckit Bucket the length of Britain and we'd be home.

Before we headed north, we met up with Steve, one of Chris' old college friends, who, despite a horrific year with leukaemia, seemed to be on the mend. Steve and his partner had been planning to settle in the south of Spain and had got as far as buying a plot of land before the disease took over. Although the treatment was working, things didn't look too certain now – the doctors would only talk of remission, not cure. Talking to them made me realise how lucky we'd been – not only had we had the opportunity to spend nearly a year away from work, but we were all still in good health. My thyroid condition seemed to be under control and I had more energy than I'd had since I was a teenager. And even Oscar – who'd tried hard to contract life threatening illnesses – had to admit he wasn't in bad shape for an extensively travelled dog.

In the excitement of being away I had forgotten just how

fortunate we were to have even the basics of life and seeing Steve with his freshly re-growing hair was a sharp reminder. Sometimes it seems all too easy to forget to be happy in the good times. I'd spent a lot of time at the beginning of the trip worrying about what might go wrong. And taking an ailing campervan, an adult relationship and a dog with you means there is plenty that could go wrong. It took me several months to realise that worrying about it wouldn't help and it also meant I ran the risk of wasting an amazing opportunity to enjoy having a good time.

By the time we reached Germany, I can clearly remember brushing my teeth at one particular campsite, feeling really at peace with the world. All seemed, quite frankly, bloody marvellous with my life and I felt a spring in my step as I skipped, Heidi-like, back to the van. We'd made it through Eastern Europe with only a broken turbo; Chris and I were still happily married; Oscar was bouncing around like a puppy and I was fit and healthy after the thyroid struggles. We were due to meet Kris and Wolfgang for coffee later in the day and my parents would be joining us the following week, so we wouldn't be stuck for conversation in the near future. Life seemed stunningly perfect and I exuded smugness over my fellow campers.

About thirty minutes later, I was alone in the woods walking Oscar when I was struck by the last remnants of the Slovakian tummy bug. Thirty one minutes later I was frantically scrabbling around in the soil, digging a hole for that least pleasant of outdoor ablutions and feeling remarkably few similarities to Heidi. As I slowly recovered my composure, I mused on the salutary lesson I'd just been taught. Enjoy the good times when you can, because the shit may be just about to hit the fan.

Looking at Steve, I remembered all the reasons why we'd gone away in the first place. Because you don't know what's coming next. And you don't know when it'll be your turn for the shit. So we have to take our chances and enjoy life while we can. Because none of us know when our own version of the Slovakian tummy bug will catch us unawares, or what size hole we might need to dig.

Later that day, we headed into the New Forest, and began a fruitless search for a campsite. As it got dark, it was clearly time to call into action Plan B, which had worked so successfully in the Lago de Sanabria park.

Spotting a likely looking pub, Chris headed in, then reappeared slightly too quickly for my liking.

'What did they say?' I asked, nervously.

'They said yes it's fine, yes we can park here for the night, yes we can go in for food and finally, yes, Oscar can go in too.'

'Excellent! Well done! Any idea where we are though?'

'Absolutely none whatsoever, but hey, there's beer and a bed, so who cares.'

In a matter of seconds, with now military precision, we'd prepared the van, headed into the pub and installed ourselves by the bar for the night. A succession of locals then proceeded to park themselves next to us, admire Oscar and insist on buying us drinks. By the end of the night we felt like we'd lived in the village most of our lives, even though we still didn't know what it was called. In the morning I woke to the clink of empty bottles and looked at my equally dazed husband.

'Do you remember a man coming in and talking about his sausage making machine?' I asked him.

'I think so…..maybe,' he responded, after a few seconds thought. 'Why?'

'I just wanted to check I hadn't dreamt it. That's OK then.'

~

For the next week and a half we meandered north, calling in on old friends who we rarely saw when we were in Scotland and giving out bottles of wine like an alcoholic ice-cream van. Until eventually we arrived on the edge of Aberdeenshire, starting point of this most magnificent of journeys.

As we drove towards our village, I found it hard to comprehend

265

the enormity of what we'd just done. We'd covered more than 13,000 miles, been away for a little over ten months and here we were, finally driving back to our house. The van that had seemed such an utter heap of crap the previous summer was now pulling us up the final slog, still more or less intact, containing most of what we'd packed so long ago. And even more unbelievably it still had us in it – all three of us had made it round. We'd discovered that you can drop out for a while and you won't necessarily end up penniless. And that the pet passport system really does work – the European borders are open to the canine race, even if not everyone is quite ready for the arrival of the slightly hairier than average tourist.

And what about Europe itself? Was it as integrated as the Commission had tried to tell me? Probably not, I reflected as we trundled towards home. Yes, the borders were open and we could, in theory, work where we wanted. And some of the fundamentals of the human race couldn't be changed by any nationality or border – like slightly lecherous older men after a few shandies and the unbreakable bond between women and chocolate. But each country also seemed to have retained its individuality – whether that was the Spaniard's idea of fast food or the Finn's nonchalance towards the elements. We may have passed countless Tescos and Lidls on the way round, but it seems there are certain characteristics that you just can't homogenise.

I continued to muse on these thoughts as we silently drove the final few miles to our village. And what did it mean for Scotland I wondered, as I gazed out at the rain speckled landscape. How had Scotland fared in our search for the perfect European country? How much did our homeland feature in the make up of the European Utopia? In truth, relatively little. It doesn't have the best recreational resources or the best cafés or the best wines or the best shops or any of those things. But what it did have was an awful lot of nearly the bests. And whilst that might sound like damning with faint praise, in my view it's much more of a positive.

All of the countries that had contributed something to our fictional European paradise also had some pretty big negatives – for Norway's amazing recreational facilities, you had to factor in the astronomical prices and winter darkness; for every one of Spain's vineyards there was also an overflowing rubbish dump located on the edge of town. Nowhere was perfect. But for me, Scotland has a unique combination of 'pretty goods', without so many of the 'very bads' mixed in. It isn't necessarily the European Utopia – certainly not with the current drizzle – but it's more than good enough for me.

As we approached the bottom of Tarves hill I felt tears of emotion start to overwhelm me. I couldn't believe that we'd finally done it. We'd been, we'd seen, we'd conquered (well, Oscar had). And now we were back. After all the 'might happen' scenarios that I'd worried about. The majority of which, if we were honest, had happened. The van *had* broken down. The dog *had* tried to die. But we'd still done it.

And there it was, just exactly where we'd left it. Our house. Chris pulled onto the drive, switched off the engine and looked at me.

'Well.' he said, in a feat of understatement.

'Round of applause for the Fuckit Bucket,' I yelled and we both cheered. Soon, the noise was enough to wake a sleeping dog, who looked around in confusion for a few minutes. Then he skipped off down the road to give his 'My grown-up gap year' slideshow to the assembled dog population (the black Labrador next door tells me this consists of 48 shots of lampposts and a further 19 pictures of Lua's bottom).

While Oscar bored the fur off his doggy pals, I sat in the van, mulling over our completed feat. After 13,000 miles and £10,000 it seemed I'd learnt two things now. Life changing decisions are probably best taken sober, but they're a hell of a lot more fun when taken after a bottle of wine. And you shouldn't believe everything a Latvian mechanic tells you.

Chapter 25

New roots, or new routes?

The first few weeks after our return had a strange feel to them. There were undoubtedly some huge bonuses to being back. We could both stand up at the same time without banging into each other. In fact, we spent most of those first few weeks in separate rooms, waving our arms around wildly, just because we could. Our house, although small, seemed huge in comparison to the van. And it was full of luxuries. When it rained we could look out the window, shrug, then turn on the TV. Or ring a friend, or perhaps read a book without first wiping the mould off the corners. Courgettes no longer had to be stretched out for three meals because, most surprising of all, there was money coming into our bank account, not just going out. And some things had changed for the better whilst we were away. Pubs had gone smoke free, which was a sharp contrast to the smoke filled dens of Spain. Our village shop had turned all continental and was now stocking three varieties of olives (believe me, for a small Aberdeenshire village, that *is* cosmopolitan!).

But there were also downsides. We had to go to work. I had to commute to Aberdeen and battle large organisational bureaucracy. Although it was a new job, and there was a lot to learn, I still had to turn up each day, whether I wanted to or not. We couldn't buy wine for 2 Euros a bottle. And the road was no longer wide or open. I had the security of knowing where I'd be sleeping that night, but it wouldn't be overlooking a mountain lined fjord.

But if we found there were a lot of adjustments to make, what of Oscar, travelling dog extraordinaire? He returned to village-wide acclaim and was the talk of the town for several weeks. He did run in and tell Heather all about his maltreatment, but she's learnt to take him with a pinch of salt and now, when he needs a jab, she comes out to the van, rather than expecting him to brave the surgery. Occasionally, when he feels his life has become too routine, he'll take another hissy fit, like the tantrums he had in Banyoles and Salamanca. Which is his way of telling me that he's bored of this walk and it's time to find a new route for him. General mundanity does not suit Oscar. The same walk several times in a day is simply not acceptable to a dog that's visited 13 countries in 10 months.

As Oscar slowly adjusted to the life of a slightly more sedentary dog, it occurred to me that his desire for ever changing scenery and new people could be put to good use. Oscar has always been the kind of dog who is hugely enthusiastic to see you, and appears to be about to love you to death, then suddenly loses interest and meanders off to find his next victim. Every morning, the first sound I hear is the thump of Oscar's tail on the bedroom floor as he realises my eyes are opening. And every morning I think he's turned into a devoted, loyal and loving dog. But each time, before I've even swung my legs out of bed, he's ambled round to the other side to look for Chris. Or trotted to the back door in case there's anyone more interesting in the garden. Which was why I decided that, post trip, we had to find another way to keep him entertained. What he needed wasn't just a constant supply of new lampposts and different walks, but a supply of new people too, and preferably ones who wouldn't be offended when he ditched them in a matter of minutes.

And so began Oscar's new career as a therapy pet. Pets as Therapy is a national organisation that brings together dogs like Oscar with people in hospitals and nursing homes who are unable to have a pet of their own. Through a network of volunteers, they check that the dogs have a suitable temperament before providing them with insurance and a special identity tag. Not long after our return I took Oscar for his induction test, where he pulled the wool over the assessor's eyes in his own inimitable style. In a matter of minutes she was fully convinced of his loving, affectionate nature. 'A joy to meet' she naively wrote on his report card, whilst Oscar sat smugly at my feet, head resting lovingly on my leg.

Appropriately certificated, he's now free to inflict himself wherever people are in need of a pet. In practice this mostly means a nursing home in Aberdeen where the patients, all Alzheimer sufferers, seem to relish his visits. As Oscar sallies up to them, a moment of recognition flickers across their faces and they coo over him, before feeding him unsuitable biscuits. To Oscar's credit, he doesn't bat an eyelid, regardless of what madness they might utter. Even a recent offer of some false teeth as a treat was something he was clearly considering seriously. Then when he's had his fill of tummy tickling, he leaps up, shakes off a few hairs as a reminder of his visit and heads onto the next patient. A few weeks later, its time to do it all again, and he goes through the whole enthusiastic 'meet and greet' routine once more. Sometimes I suspect he brings more benefits to visitors than patients. Sitting with a dying relative is heart-breaking, so when a grey dog sidles up to the nearest visitor and thumps his tail on their leg, it often brings out their first smile in hours. For a dog with a ten second attention span it's ideal. And having seen him interact with people across the whole of Europe I know I can trust him completely. He's never embarrassed, uncomfortable or judgemental. He's just Oscar. Happy to see you. Regardless of who you are, where you're from or your mental state. For at least five minutes.

But it wasn't just Oscar who needed a new challenge. A few weeks after our return I was struck by a need to see 'closure' on my Spanish learning and entered the Spanish Government's exam for non-native speakers. Against his better judgement, Chris agreed to join me and we began preparing for a full day of written and verbal examinations. Every time I felt I couldn't be bothered, the ghost of Chucho, our Salamancan teacher, seemed to appear at my shoulder, looking on in disappointment. And I'd head back to the books and struggle on. Eventually, we dragged our distinctly nervous selves down to the Spanish embassy in Edinburgh for judgement day. Chatting politely to the examiners was nowhere near as much fun as our cafe inter-cambios – the coffee was much worse and we couldn't use Oscar as a conversational backstop when we dried up. But amazingly we both passed the diploma and can now, in theory, prove we have sufficient linguistic ability to work for a variety of Spanish companies or even the Spanish government. If we go back, we may not have to resort to dealing with fencing or shepherding. And maybe this time I would learn to play the harmonica.

But despite Oscar's therapy career and our supposed linguistic confidence, within a few months of returning, we were beginning to feel decidedly normal. Whilst we might be a bit on the old side for international bright young things, we had at least become quite 'socially acceptable'. There were lots of positives to being home and we were no longer the grungy smelly drop outs hanging around on a Latvian garage forecourt, facing failure. But deep down, I think we both knew the word dropout was printed through the middle of us, like a stick of rock. And sooner or later, it was always going to break out again.

After a respectable period enjoying the luxuries of a house, a distinct yearning to be squeezed back into an over-sized cupboard began to clutch at me. We pulled the contents of the van out onto the drive and gave it the most thorough cleaning of its life. A ten month collection of fluff, dog hair and unidentifiable objects blocked our vacuum cleaner, although at least there were no black thongs under the bed. When it was no longer a health and safety hazard, we put everything back in, apart from the dog hair. The van was once more ready to hit the road. Of course now we had proper jobs, so we couldn't just drive off into the sunset for months on end. But we could hit the road for a long weekend.

Every couple of weeks we'd try and take a Friday afternoon off and, black smoke still belching, we'd bump back down Tarves hill and scout out a new part of Scotland. And for a few days we could re-live the whole 'Vannie' experience again. We'd get to see new sights, find different places and have some time away from the hectic bustle of our work commitments.

But the Fuckit Bucket was determined we should get to experience absolutely everything again. Not just the good bits, but the bad bits as well. It broke down at every opportunity. And I'd sit in another lay-by, brewing another cup of tea and waiting to see if Chris could manage a temporary fix or if it was time for yet another chat with the breakdown man. Every time we broke down, a little bit of our already limited trust in the van was eroded. It may have dragged us all the way around Europe, but now it seemed incapable of even making it to Aberdeen. Depression began to seep around us and weekends away started to seem more hassle than they were worth.

Then, on one particularly traumatic weekend, the van's health took a real nose-dive. It sounded like there was a deranged monster trying to knock its way through the floor and I was genuinely concerned that the whole engine would shake itself free. Like the responsible adults we are, we took it home, parked it on the drive and did our best to ignore it, carefully averting our eyes each time we walked past. But all too soon, the horror of the MOT test approached. Or more to the point, it didn't. Our local mechanic took one look and told us that there was no chance of success – the engine had 'blown a piston' and was in terminal decline. Oh, and the turbo was broken as well. Again.

Every time the van had failed on us so far, we'd managed to find a way of fixing it. But this time we had to question if we could do it again. After much soul and bank account searching, a new plan was hatched. We'd replace the whole engine. Surely then it had to work. If we bought a reconditioned engine and turbo there'd be nothing left of the original, always-troublesome engine. It'd be a new lease of life for the van and we could continue to travel the highways and byways of Scotland. We filled the mechanic in on the plan when we met him in the pub one evening.

'Sure' he said, 'why not. It'll work and the rest of the van is okay. But it won't be cheap. In fact, are you sure you can even afford to be in here? You better split a pint between you if you're going to do this.'

It wasn't the vote of confidence we were looking for, but, determined somehow to avoid Bagpuss going to the great scrap heap in the sky, from where its innards had already been rescued once, we pressed on anyway. A new engine arrived and after nearly four weeks in the garage, a re-invigorated van was back on our drive. Time to hit the road again.

And for a few weeks, all seemed well. Or, at least, well-ish. The engine was better. Not perfect, but definitely better. It still smelt a bit odd and seemed to smoke more than was necessary, but in theory, it ought to have been fine. But, in some almost indefinable way, the relationship between us had changed. We'd spent too long worrying about the van. It had become like an unreliable and slightly mad uncle, prone to temper tantrums when least expected. Even though everything was alright today, it felt as if we were treading on eggshells, waiting for the next big blowout. Would this be the day it broke down again, or would we manage to squeak by for another few hours?

Weekends away were no longer the relaxing tonic to work that we needed. We just couldn't quite trust the van anymore. It was like an unfaithful partner. You never knew what it was thinking. And so the weekends away began to diminish further. Work became busier and neither of us had the inclination to add an on-edge weekend to an already stressful schedule. Within 2 years of returning, we had become quite, quite normal. And the travelling dropout stamp that we'd believed was branded through us seemed to have faded to illegibility. Before long, the Ikea catalogue was going to be the highlight of our lives.

But you couldn't rub out the effects of our European odyssey quite that easily. We both knew we weren't really happy with this turn of events. And something deep inside both of us fought to the surface. Try as we might, we just weren't quite ready to settle down into a 'routine'. Something was going to have to give.

The life of a civil servant was the first strand to break. Chris' consultancy business had been a roaring success and he'd reached the stage where he wasn't able to take up all the work that was offered. Meanwhile, I couldn't claim to be enjoying the life of a faceless pen-pusher. And here, perhaps, was a way to escape. We could turn the business into a partnership, extend the range of skills it could offer and see where we went from there. But that would mean we would both be self-employed, with no long term security and we'd have to work together. Was that too much of a risk to take?

And of course, the world changed in 2008. Jobs became scarce and words like recession, depression and deficit became common parlance. If people had been surprised when we ditched jobs in 2005, they were horrified when I considered repeating the experience in 2008. But the trip has undoubtedly changed our attitudes to work and money. Because we'd stepped out from the world of reliable pay cheques once before, the idea of being self-employed seemed a lot less scary. We know that, if necessary, we *can* make that courgette last for three meals, so it's easier to watch the fluctuations in our bank account with a slightly more relaxed mind. And I think we've both learnt that if we can survive together in a single 'room' for the best part of a year, the occasional bicker over who's doing the filing this week won't necessarily result in a trip to the divorce lawyer. There's no doubt that the world is a different place now, and that heading off on the open road, or going self-employed is more of an undertaking than it once was. But that doesn't mean it's impossible.

Interestingly, Kris and Wolfgang went through a similar experience. When they returned to Germany, they set up a successful travel agency together, so every so often we chat on the phone about the frustrations and delights of being your own boss. So far, all four of us seem to be surviving the ups and downs of an uneven cash flow and the occasional moment of business related pillow talk. I wonder if we would all have been brave enough to do this without the trip? Somehow, I doubt it. All four of us, and maybe even Oscar, have come to accept that we may not fit into a conventional mould.

And whilst the change to being a partnership of entrepreneurs resolved some of our post-trip depression, we still had to tackle the problem of the van. Was it time to give up on our travelling dreams? If we couldn't trust the van anymore, what was left? A small suitcase and the occasional week away in the sun? Were we ready for that? It was looking that way. Soon we'd be putting Oscar in kennels and staying in nice hotels without him. One of us needed to make a final push against the flow, before we were swept away and into the main stream.

Then, not that long ago, another wedding anniversary came around. We went out for what's now become our traditional picnic and I was soon reclining on a blanket, munching my way through biscuits and cheese. Chris caught my eye.

'Tamsin…..I think we need to talk.' Uh oh. This didn't sound good. 'I've, well, I've been doing a bit of surfing on the web recently.'

'OK' I interrupted sharply, 'if you've been downloading the porn I don't want to know. And if you've met someone, just remember the dog stays with me.' Chris shook his head sadly.

'I'm not even going to try and analyse why after so many years of marriage, you still think so little of me. It's not that.' He took a deep breath. 'I think it's time we got a new van, that's all. I think Bagpuss needs to be replaced.' The words tumbled out and I raised my eyebrows. 'We just don't trust it anymore. We should sell it to someone who's got the patience to deal with it and get ourselves a new van. And I think I've found one on the internet. It's just right. Exactly what we need. It's still a van though, not a campervan, so we'd have to do all the conversion stuff again. But we've done it once, so it'll be a lot quicker this time.' My eyebrows went higher as he paused momentarily for breath. 'Really, it won't take long at all. And then we can go for another trip without worrying about breaking down all the time.'

I sighed and closed my eyes.

But you know what happens next, don't you?

Enter stage left, the sparkly stuff; exit stage right, the common sense. Chris spent the next half hour doing his best sales pitch and by the end of the second glass, I was won over.

'Yep you're right. Time for a new van. Bagpuss needs to find someone who can love him properly. And we can get a Bag-kitten.' I chuckled at my own witticism as only the drunk can.

But the head of the household still had to agree. By this stage Oscar was sleeping on his back on the blanket, all four legs dangling in mid air, ready to defend us at a moment's notice.

'What do you reckon, Oscar? Could you face a few more borders?' Oscar opened one upside-down eye and looked at me suspiciously. 'Oh come on, you know you loved it before. We could go and see Kris and Wolfgang again, they adored you.' The other eye opened. 'And,' I said, revealing my trump card, 'we could maybe call in and see Lua.' Oscar's tail began to thump on the ground in a resounding series of wags.

'Well' said Chris. 'I believe that may just be motion carried.'

And by the end of the night, a man on Ebay was significantly richer and two penniless grown-up gappers were poring over the European road atlas, plotting a route to Russia.

And a borderless collie was packed and ready to go.

Acknowledgements

Many thanks to all those who helped bring this book to fruition. Most especially, thanks to Judy Moir for her editing skills, to Katrina Brown for providing an early sounding board, to Chris for his digital wizardry and to my Mum for her meticulous proof-reading.

Printed in July 2019
by Rotomail Italia S.p.A., Vignate (MI) - Italy